+the concept art of **Min-Woo Hyung**

justice N mercy
正義と慈悲

Justice N Mercy
art by Min-Woo Hyung

English Translation - Youngju Ryu
German Translation - Steffi Schnuerer
Japanese Translation - Yuko Fukami
Associate Editor - Peter Ahlstrom
Production Artist - James Dashiell
Graphic Designer - Anne Marie Horne and Namhee Park
and JinKyung Chung
Cover Design - Kyle Plummer

Editorial Director & Editor - Jeremy Ross
Digital Imaging Manager - Chris Buford
Production Managers - Jennifer Miller and Mutsumi Miyazaki
Managing Editor - Jill Freshney
VP of Production - Ron Klamert
Publisher and E.I.C. - Mike Kiley
President and C.O.O. - John Parker
C.E.O. - Stuart Levy

A **TOKYOPOP**® Art Book

TOKYOPOP Inc.
5900 Wilshire Blvd. Suite 2000
Los Angeles, CA 90036

E-mail: info@TOKYOPOP.com
Come visit us online at www.TOKYOPOP.com

ISBN: 1-59532-980-3

First TOKYOPOP printing: October 2005
10 9 8 7 6 5 4 3 2 1
Printed in Korea

justice N mercy
正義と慈悲

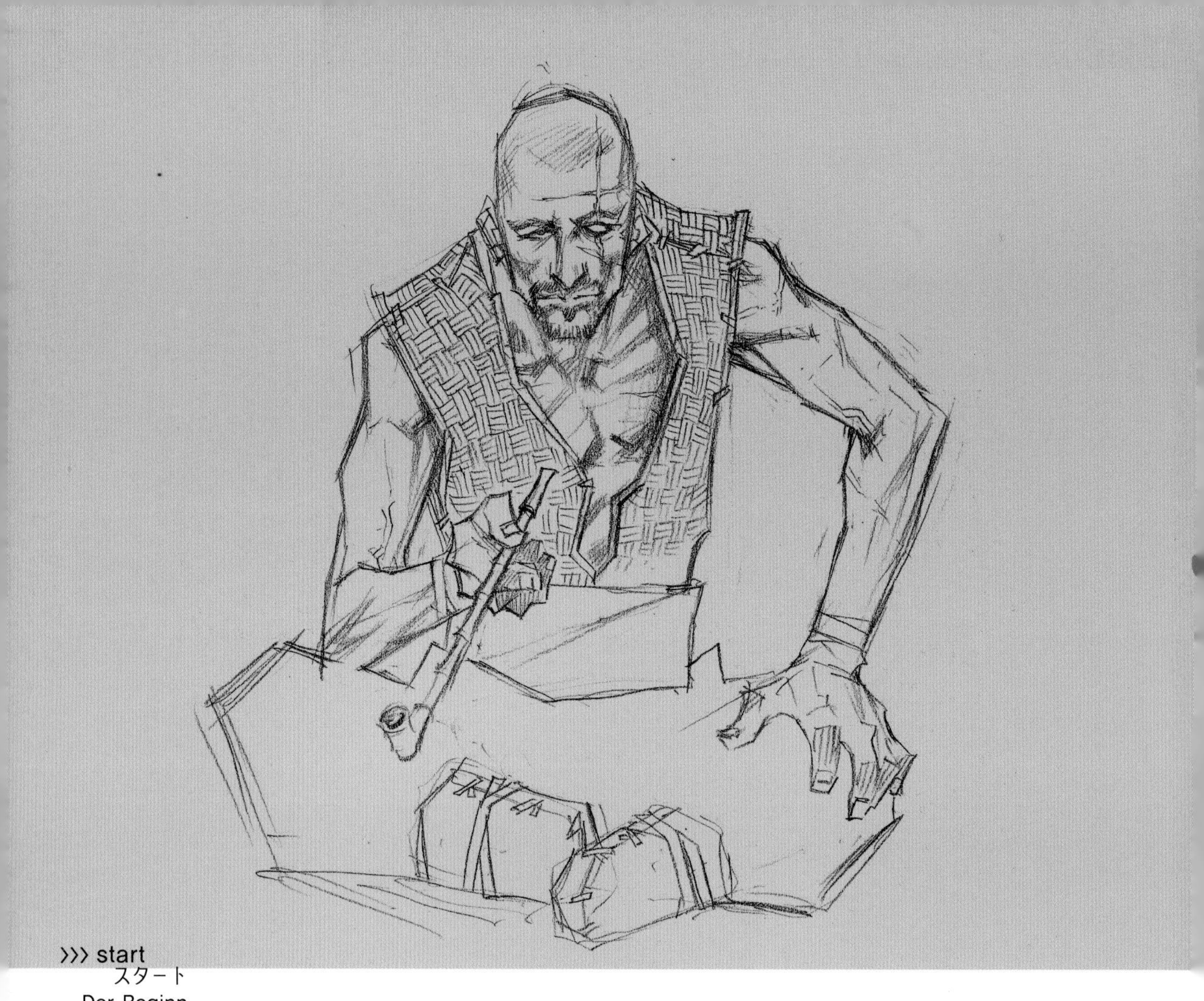

>>> start
スタート
Der Beginn

Sword...
An unrequited love; a dream
that will last a lifetime.

刀…
報われない愛、一生かけてみる夢。

Schwert...
Eine unerwiderte Liebe; ein Traum, der ein
Leben lang andauern wird.

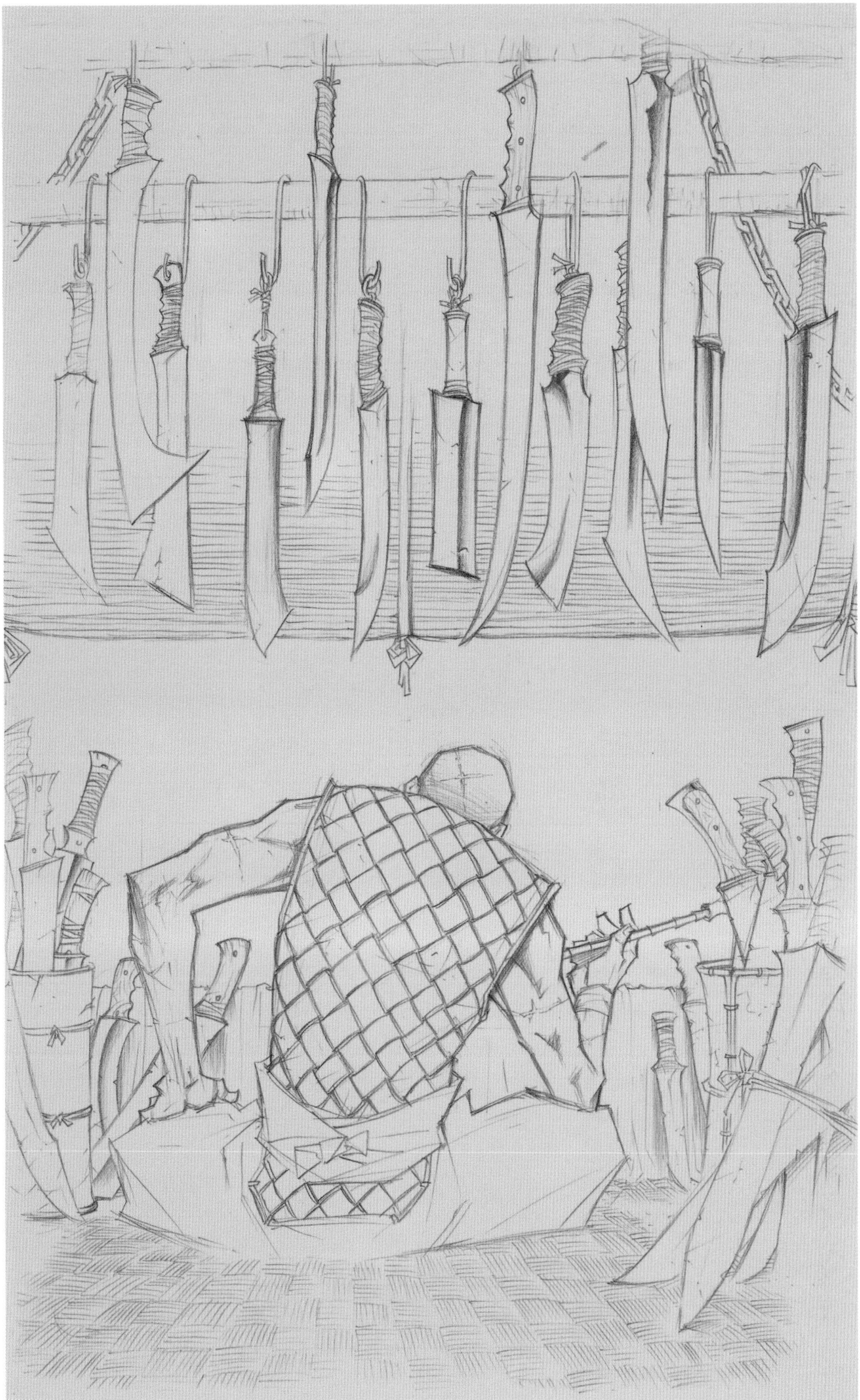

›› Introduction to the TOKYOPOP edition

›› はじめに TOKYOPOP版

›› Vorwort zur TOKYOPOP- Ausgabe

†TOKYOPOP is delighted to bring this striking art book from Korea to the world. Min-Woo is a prime representative of the extraordinarily imaginative artwork that is coming out of the hotbed of talent that is Korea today. At long last, Korean graphic novels, feature films and animation are earning the critical and fan acclaim they deserve — as well as changing the face of comics around the world.

Ever since TOKYOPOP licensed Min-Woo's *Priest* graphic novel series from Nam Ho Kim at Daiwon for U.S. publication, we have all been huge fans of Min-Woo's work. *Priest* is a dark and rich story that has caught the attention of countless tastemakers in America, from Hollywood execs and writers to designers and fine artistsnot to mention a legion of fans. As Mike Carrey said in his introduction to *Priest* Volume 6: ". . . it's currently evolving into one of the most enthrallingly unpredictable stories in the entire medium."

These pages will appeal to fans of Min-Woo's black-and-white sequential art and they will cement Min-Woo's reputation as a character designer and colorist. If youre not already a fan, then be prepared to become one once you behold Min-Woo's amazing work.

Min-Woo is more than an incredibly talented artist—he is also a cool guy and a good friend. Our time spent in Seoul hanging out with him, his family and friends has always been fun. And we can attest from firsthand experience that what he says in his interview is true: most of Min-Woo's friends are simply crazy. . . and we at TOKYOPOP hope to always qualify as among them.

Special thanks go to Eddie Yu and his colleagues at Studio Ice for helping to make this edition possible.

Jeremy Ross
Editorial Director, TOKYOPOP

†韓国よりすばらしい画集を皆様にお届けいたします。並外れた想像力に富むミンウーさんは、芸術活動にとって好環境である現在の韓国の代表的な存在と言えるでしょう。韓国の漫画や映画、アニメなどは、長年の業績をやっと認められ、現在ファンや批評家から高い評価を得ています。そして、世界中の漫画に影響を与え始めているのです。

TOKYOPOPがミンウーさんの長編漫画シリーズ "Priest" をダイウォン（Daiwon）のキム・ナムホーさんとライセンス契約を行い、アメリカで発行して以来、我々はミンウーさんの作品の大ファンとなりました。"Priest" は、暗く豊潤な物語で、大勢のファンはもちろん、ハリウッドの重役やライター、デザイナーや芸術家などアメリカの流行の仕掛け人と呼ばれるような多くの人たちより注目を受けています。"Priest" 6巻の序文にマイク・カイリー氏が述べた通り、「Priest は、漫画という媒体の中で最も心を奪われ、意外性のある物語となりつつある」のです。

今回の画集は、ミンウーさんのモノクローム・シークエンシャル・アート（1色漫画）のファンを魅力するだけでなく、キャラクターデザイナー及びカラリストとして、彼の地位を確立するものになるでしょう。ミンウーさんの見事な作品は、見る人を全て彼のファンにしてしまう魅力的なものです。

ミンウーさんは才能あふれる芸術家である他、我々にとっては、かっこいいクールガイであり、良き友達でもあります。ソウルで彼や彼の友人、家族と過ごしたひとときは、いつまでも楽しい思い出となっています。彼がインタビューで言った、彼の友達はみんな常軌を逸している、という言葉が真実である事も保証します。そして TOKYOPOPは、いつまでもその常軌を逸した仲間の一員でいる事を願っています。

エディー・ユー氏とStudio ICEの皆さんにはTOKYOPOP版発行に際してご協力いただきました。ここでお礼を述べたいと思います。

TOKYOPOP 編集ディレクター
ジェレミー・ロス

†TOKYOPOP ist hocherfreut, der Welt dieses eindrucksvolle Art Book aus Korea präsentieren zu dürfen. Min-Woo ist einer der herausragenden Stellvertreter des außergewöhnlich phantasievollen Artworks aus den Talenteschmieden des heutigen Koreas. Endlich ernten koreanische Comics, Spielfilme und Animationen den Beifall von Presse und Fans, den sie verdienen. Außerdem verändern sie das Gesicht von Comics rund um den Erdball.

Seit Min-Woo's Serie *Priest* für TOKYOPOP durch Nam Ho Kim von Daiwon zur Veröffentlichung in den USA lizenziert wurde, sind wir alle große Fans von Min-Woo's Arbeit geworden. *Priest* ist eine dunkle und reichhaltige Geschichte, die die Aufmerksamkeit von unzähligen Trendsettern in Amerika geweckt hat, von führenden Köpfen aus Hollywood über Autoren bis hin zu Designern und bildenden Künstlern—ganz zu schweigen von der Armee von Fans. Mike Carrey sagt in seiner Einleitung zu *Priest*, Band 6: »Diese Arbeit entwickelt sich zurzeit zu einer der packendsten, unberechenbarsten Geschichten des gesamten Mediums.«

Diese Seiten werden Fans von Min-Woo's sequentieller Schwarz-Weiß-Kunst begeistern, und sie werden Min-Woo's guten Ruf als Charakter-Designer und Kolorist festigen. Wer noch kein Fan ist, sollte darauf vorbereitet sein, durch den Anblick von Min-Woo's verblüffenden Arbeiten einer zu werden.

Min-Woo ist mehr als ein unglaublich talentierter Künstler—er ist auch ein cooler Typ und ein guter Freund. Die Zeit, die wir in Seoul mit ihm, seiner Familie und seinen Freunden verbrachten, hat immer Spaß gemacht. Und wir können aus erster Hand bestätigen, dass das, was er in seinem Interview sagt, wahr ist: die meisten von Min-Woo's Freunden sind einfach nur verrückt . . . und TOKYOPOP hofft, sich immer dazuzählen zu dürfen.

Besonderer Dank gilt Eddie Yu und seinen Kollegen von Studio Ice für ihre Unterstützung, diese Ausgabe möglich zu machen.

Jeremy Ross
Redaktionsleiter, TOKYOPOP

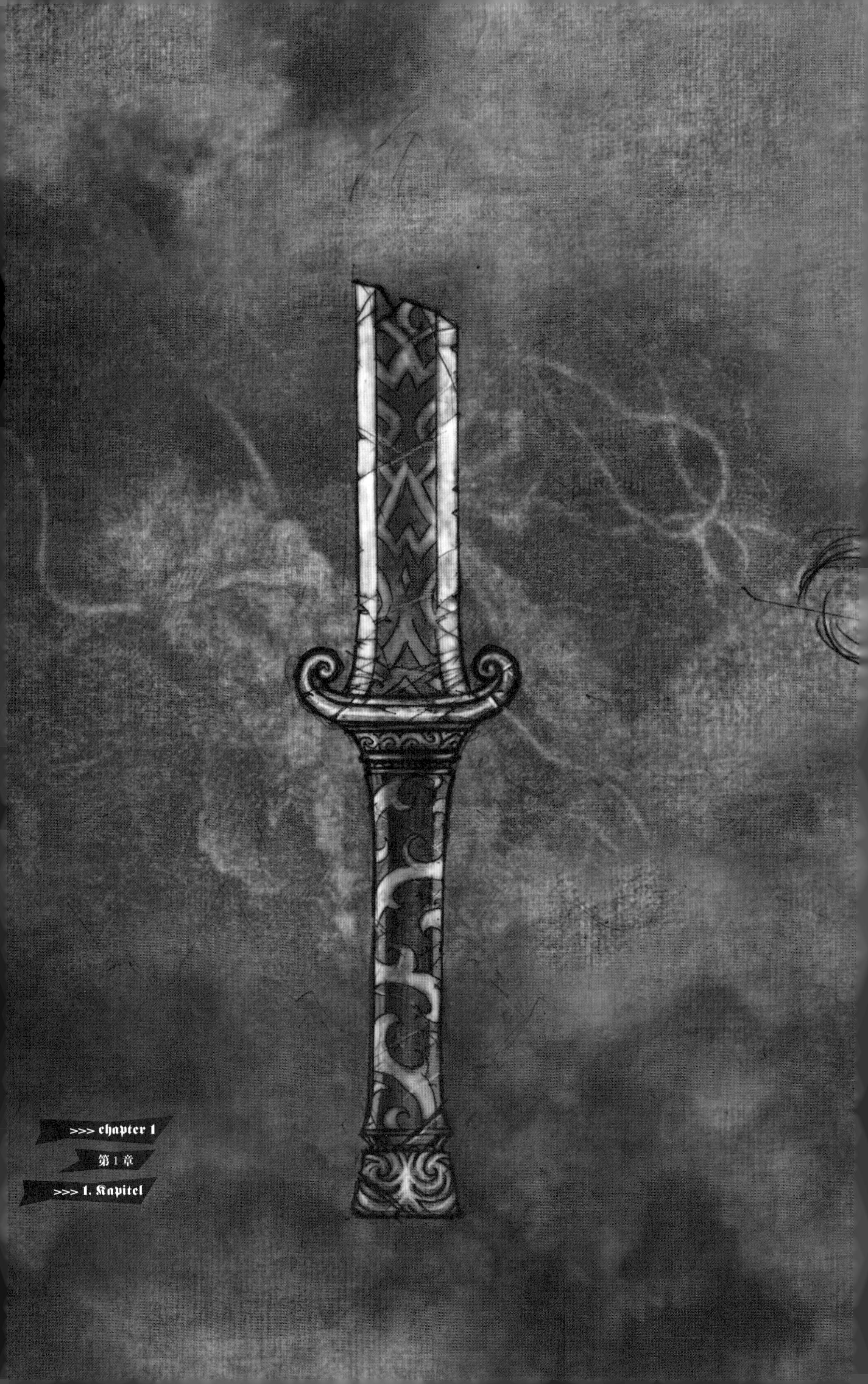
>>> chapter 1
第1章
>>> 1. Kapitel

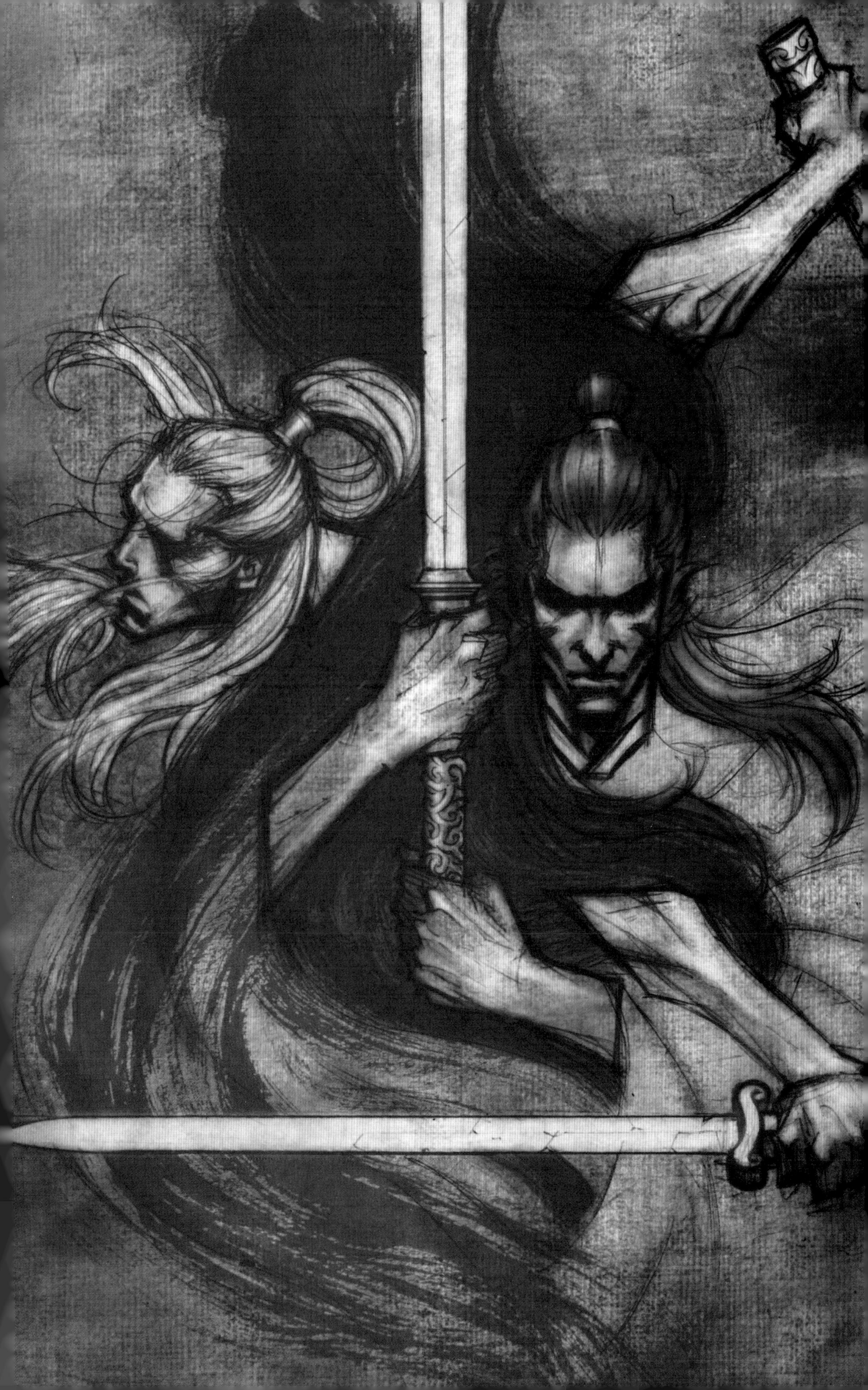

†When I was first approached with the idea of putting an art book together, I rejected it. My opinion was that art books were for people who do a lot of color work or have a large body of drawings that should be presented in some orderly fashion. Neither applied to me—I didn't work much with color, and I didn't have that many sketches either, so the thought of putting an art book together embarrassed me. As time went on, however, I realized that a part of me was really excited by the idea. It saddened me somehow to think that in the eight years since I turned professional, all I've been doing is struggling to meet deadlines for regular serials (and always missing them anyway!). And there were a lot of pieces that I felt very attached to, several cover layouts and other illustrations that I put aside along the way. I remembered how excited I was working on them, like a little kid in a candy store. It seemed a shame that they wouldn't see the light of day.

And so . . . here they are! My hope in publishing this book is that by presenting these illustrations I've been carrying around with me in boxes and by giving them a permanent home, I'll finally be able to shake off the nagging feeling that I've left something undone.

Thus this selfish desire won out over what I believe to be the basic principle behind art books. The pieces herein reveal both the continuity and change in my work over the years. Will the fans find these disparate, even trivial drawings interesting? It's a thought I have no little anxiety over.

I can only hope that this won't end up like a depressing birthday party celebrated all alone . . .

Min-Woo Hyung

†画集を作ってみないか、と最初に声をかけられた時、僕はその提案を受け入れなかった。僕にとって画集とは、色を使った絵をたくさん描いている人や、既に多くの作品を描いている人たちが、それを整理して発表するためのものだという先入観があったからだ。僕は、そのどちらにも当てはまらない。色を使った作品もあまり描いていなかったし、スケッチがたくさんある訳でもない。画集を出すなんて大層な事が出来るはずが無い、と思った。しかし、時間が経つにつれて、自分の一部は画集というアイディアに対して大変エキサイトしている事に気がついた。また、プロになって8年の間、レギュラーの連載の締め切りに追われる生活しか送っていない自分が悲しく思えた。（どっちみちいつも締め切りには遅れるのだが！）表紙のレイアウトや、その他のイラストなど、そっととっておいたお気に入りの作品がたくさんある事も思い出した。それらの作品を描いた時に感じた、駄菓子屋さんを目の前にした子供のような興奮も思い出した。それらの作品が日の目を見ないで、ずっと寝かされているのももったいないような気がしてきた。

と、言う訳で出来た本なのだ！　この本を出す事で、今まで大切にとってあったイラストなどに公開の場を与えられ、今までずっと感じていた、「何かやり忘れている」感が取り払えるのではないか、と期待している。

つまり、この本は僕の個人的な願望が、僕が信じていた信念より強かった、という理由で出来た本とも言える。この本に収められた作品は、継続と変化を見せてくれるだろう。ファンの皆さんは、バラバラで取るに足りない絵をどうとらえてくれるか？　小さな不安、とはとても言えない不安を感じている。

「一人で送る寂しい誕生日パーティー」にならないよう願うのみである。

ヒョン　ミンウー

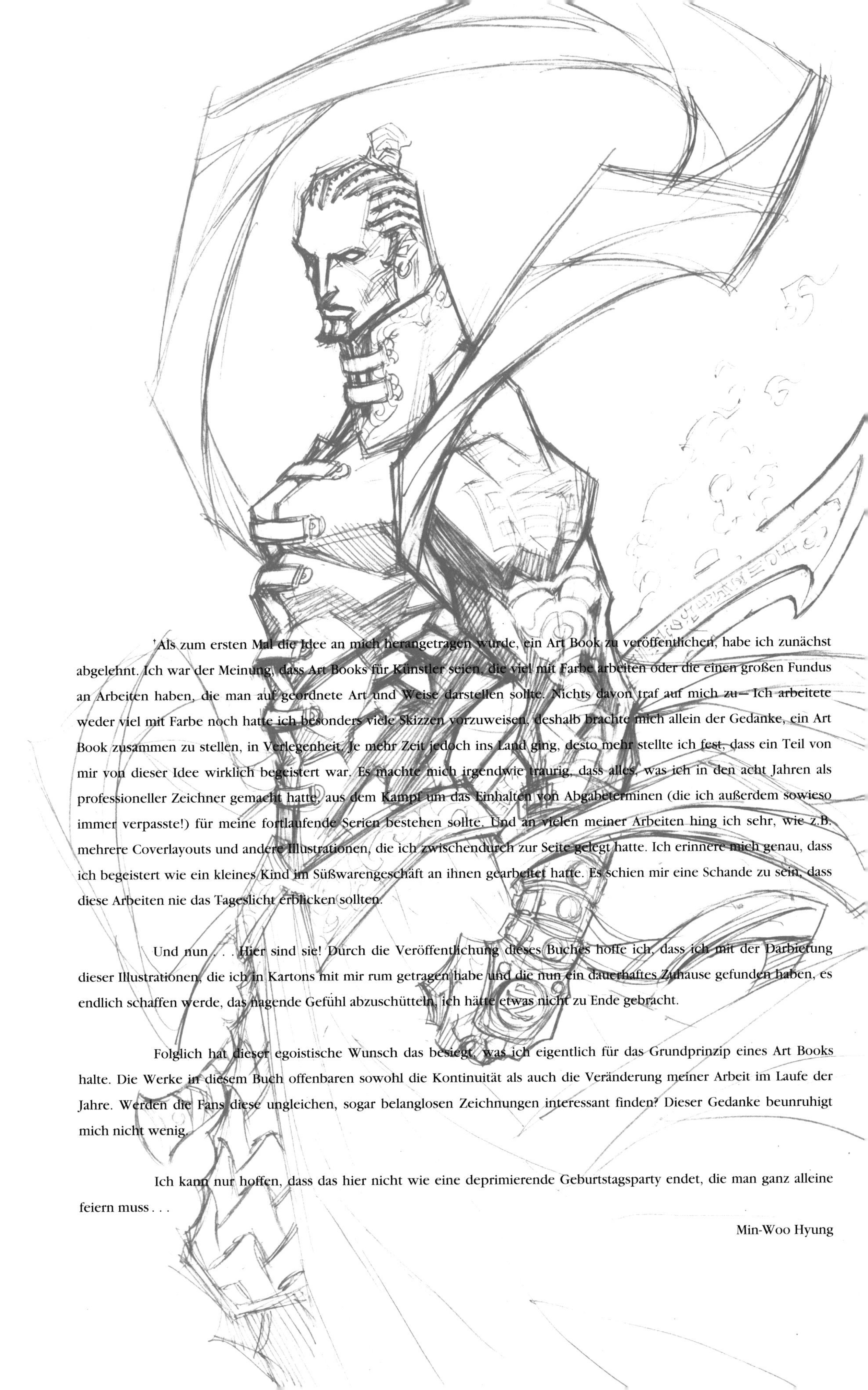

Als zum ersten Mal die Idee an mich herangetragen wurde, ein Art Book zu veröffentlichen, habe ich zunächst abgelehnt. Ich war der Meinung, dass Art Books für Künstler seien, die viel mit Farbe arbeiten oder die einen großen Fundus an Arbeiten haben, die man auf geordnete Art und Weise darstellen sollte. Nichts davon traf auf mich zu— Ich arbeitete weder viel mit Farbe noch hatte ich besonders viele Skizzen vorzuweisen, deshalb brachte mich allein der Gedanke, ein Art Book zusammen zu stellen, in Verlegenheit. Je mehr Zeit jedoch ins Land ging, desto mehr stellte ich fest, dass ein Teil von mir von dieser Idee wirklich begeistert war. Es machte mich irgendwie traurig, dass alles, was ich in den acht Jahren als professioneller Zeichner gemacht hatte, aus dem Kampf um das Einhalten von Abgabeterminen (die ich außerdem sowieso immer verpasste!) für meine fortlaufende Serien bestehen sollte. Und an vielen meiner Arbeiten hing ich sehr, wie z.B. mehrere Coverlayouts und andere Illustrationen, die ich zwischendurch zur Seite gelegt hatte. Ich erinnere mich genau, dass ich begeistert wie ein kleines Kind im Süßwarengeschäft an ihnen gearbeitet hatte. Es schien mir eine Schande zu sein, dass diese Arbeiten nie das Tageslicht erblicken sollten.

Und nun . . . Hier sind sie! Durch die Veröffentlichung dieses Buches hoffe ich, dass ich mit der Darbietung dieser Illustrationen, die ich in Kartons mit mir rum getragen habe und die nun ein dauerhaftes Zuhause gefunden haben, es endlich schaffen werde, das nagende Gefühl abzuschütteln, ich hätte etwas nicht zu Ende gebracht.

Folglich hat dieser egoistische Wunsch das besiegt, was ich eigentlich für das Grundprinzip eines Art Books halte. Die Werke in diesem Buch offenbaren sowohl die Kontinuität als auch die Veränderung meiner Arbeit im Laufe der Jahre. Werden die Fans diese ungleichen, sogar belanglosen Zeichnungen interessant finden? Dieser Gedanke beunruhigt mich nicht wenig.

Ich kann nur hoffen, dass das hier nicht wie eine deprimierende Geburtstagsparty endet, die man ganz alleine feiern muss . . .

Min-Woo Hyung

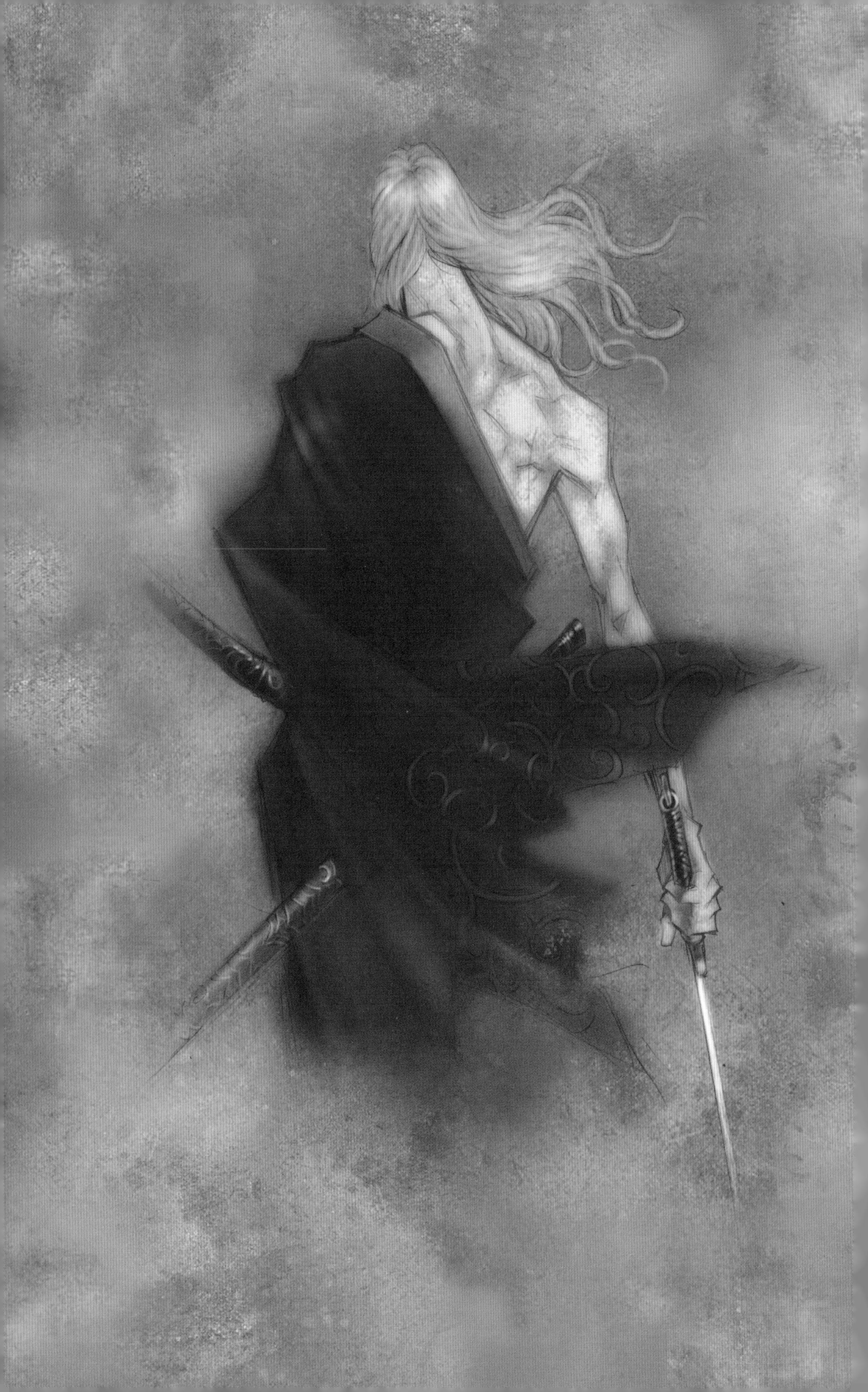

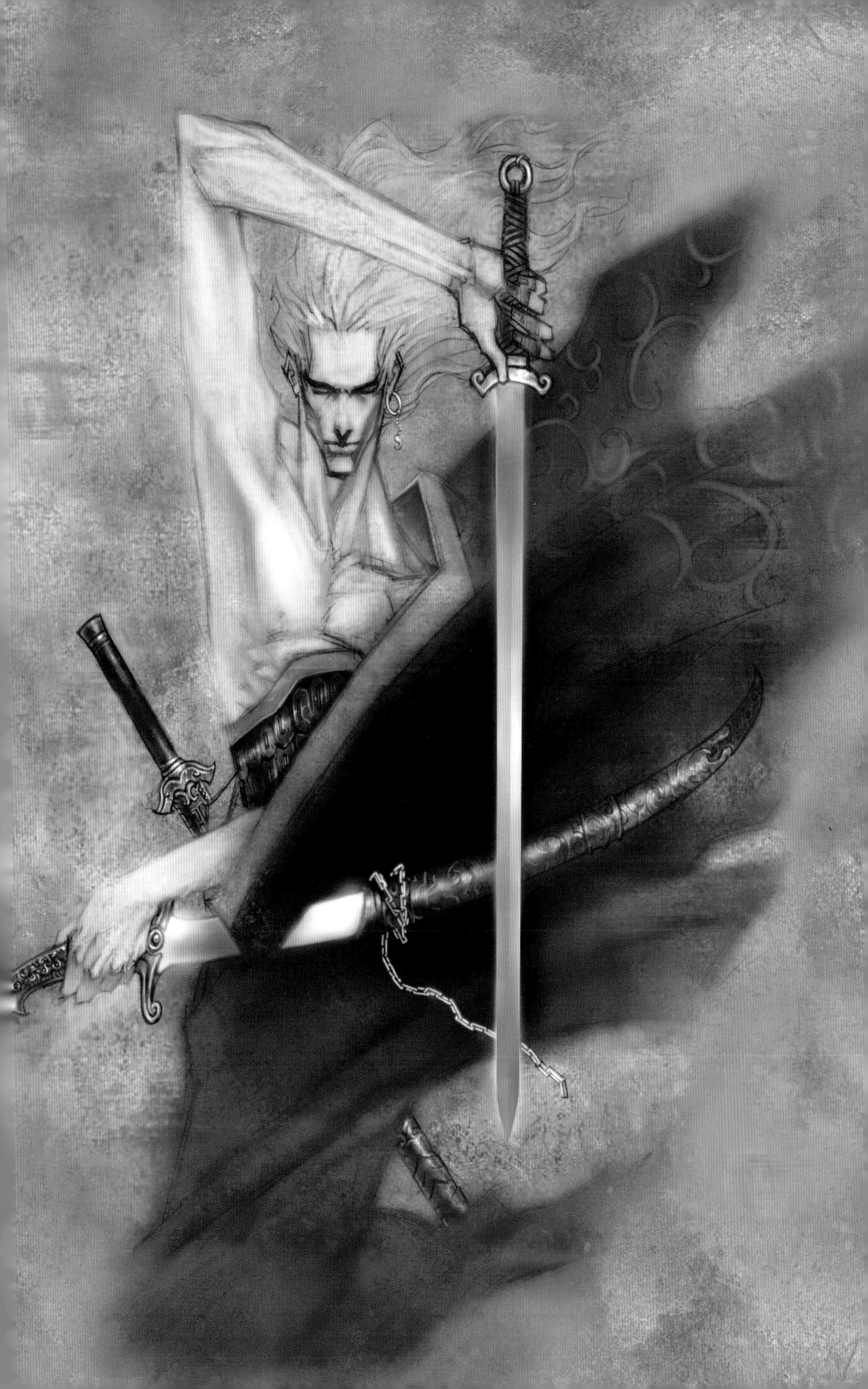

In July 2003, Min-Woo and I attended Comic-Con in San Diego. Our trip to the States included a signing at TOKYOPOP, the publisher of Min-Woo's critically-acclaimed *Priest* series in the U.S. We also had meetings with movie studios and top agencies who showed a lot of interest in turning Min-Woo's series into a movie. We are partnering with TOKYOPOP to get the movie made, and there is active interest in Hollywood.

On this trip, I got to see the passionate side of Min-Woo as he explained the vision behind his work to agents and movie producers. His English is not fluent, of course, but his knowledge of Hollywood movies is incredible, and the producers were visibly surprised by his insights regarding both the overall vision of the project and particulars concerning personnel. Watching Min-Woo give a detailed and sophisticated answer to the question of which director might best suit his work, I realized once again how solid Min-Woo's foundations are.

Min-Woo's work has a quality that would appeal greatly to moviegoers. During our visit to the U.S., we spent a day in Hollywood and it just so happened that a premiere of *Lara Croft Tomb Raider: The Cradle of Life* was being held at Grauman's Chinese Theater. We saw limos drop off the director, star Angelina Jolie, other actors, and related crew members at the premiere. Afterward, the party atmosphere continued in a post-premiere event across the street. This experience convinced me beyond any doubt that we'll one day be having a premiere of our own at the Chinese Theater.

We returned from the States with burning hearts and the desire to start a serialization targeting the States market specifically. But first, we decided to put various concept pieces together in preparation for this project and publish them in Korea. This volume is the result. The book focuses on character pieces and contains only a small portion of what is already available in print. Our hope is that this book will be a valuable resource to all who love Min-Woo's work.

Many people offered their generous help to make this volume a reality. Gwanshik Shin was always there when we needed him, Dongseop Kim did the photography, Tattoo artist Yushi generously offered the use of his studio for the photography sessions, and Jinkyeong Jeong did the design for the volume. We owe our gratitude to them and to many others. It is our hope that this volume will serve as a cornerstone and help boost Min-Woo's popularity in the U.S.

2003年7月に、私はミンウー氏と、サンディエゴのComic-Conに参加しました。この時のアメリカ訪問で、ミンウー氏は、絶賛されたPriestシリーズのアメリカでの発行者となったTOKYOPOPと契約を交わしました。彼のシリーズの映画化に興味を示した多くの映画会社や有名なエージェントとミーティングを行いました。たちはTOKYOPOPをパートナーとして、映画化の実現に向けて努力しており、ハリウッドは今も大いなる興味を示しています。

この旅行中、エージェントや映画のプロデューサーに作品の背景にある彼のビジョンを情熱的に話すミンウー氏に、今まで見られなかった彼の一面を見たような気がします。彼の英語はあまりうまいとは言えませんが、彼の映画の知識は大変なもので、プロジェクトの全体的なビジョンや人材に関するこだわりなど、その見識はプロジューサーをびっくりさせるほどのものでした。監督の人選についての質問に、ミンウー氏が詳しく、知的に答えるところを目撃して、彼の基礎知識がいかにしっかりしたものか思い知らされたようでした。

ミンウー氏の作品は、映画ファンを魅了する特質を多く備えていると思います。アメリカ訪問中のある日、「トゥームレイダー2」がグローマンズ・チャイニーズ・シアターで封切りされているところに居合わせました。監督やアンジェリーナー・ジョリー、その他の俳優や関連スタッフが次々とリムジンに乗って現れるところや、その後もプレミア上映後のイベントの華やかなパーティーの雰囲気が道路を越えて続いているのを目撃して、これだ！私たちはいつかきっと、同じようにチャイニーズシアターで封切りをするんだ！と確信しました。

アメリカから帰国した私たちは、アメリカ市場をターゲットとしたシリーズを開始する意欲に燃えていました。しかしその前にプロジェクトの準備として、様々なコンセプト作品をいくつかまとめて韓国で出版する事にしたのです。この画集はその結果です。収められた作品は、キャラクター作品が主で、また既に印刷されている作品のごく一部にすぎませんが、ミンウー氏の作品を愛する人々にとって大切な財産となる事を祈っています。

この画集の製作に関して、多くの人々にご協力いただきました。シン・グワンシク氏(Shin, Gwanshik)は、私たちの限りない支えとなってくれました。キム・ドンソップ氏(Kim, Dongseop)は写真撮影、入れ墨師のユウシ氏（Yushi）は撮影用にスタジオを提供してくださいました。本のデザインはジョン・ジンキョン氏(Jeong, Jinkyeong)です。彼等やその他大勢の応援してくださった皆さんにお礼を申し上げます。この一冊がミンウー氏のアメリカでの人気を形作る足場となる事を望んでいます。

Im Juli 2003 besuchten Min-Woo und ich die Comic-Con in San Diego. Unser Trip in die Staaten beinhaltete eine Signierstunde bei TOKYOPOP, die Min-Woo's von der Kritik gefeierte Serie *Priest* in den USA verlegten. Außerdem hatten wir eine Reihe von Treffen mit Filmstudios und erstklassigen Agenturen, die alle großes Interesse daran zeigten, Min-Woo's Serie zu verfilmen. Zusammen mit TOKYOPOP versuchen wir gerade, das zu realisieren und es gibt reges Interesse aus Hollywood.

Auf dieser Reise entdeckte ich die leidenschaftliche Seite von Min-Woo, als er die Vision hinter seiner Arbeit den Agenten und Filmemachern erklärte. Sein Englisch ist natürlich nicht fließend, aber sein Wissen über Hollywood-Filme ist unglaublich. Die Produzenten waren offensichtlich von seinem Tiefblick, der von der allumfassenden Vision des Projektes bis hin zu spezifischen Rollenbesetzungen reichte, überrascht. Während ich Min-Woo dabei beobachtete, wie er eine detaillierte und ausgeklügelte Antwort darauf gab, welcher Regisseur seiner Arbeit am besten entspräche, stellte ich wieder einmal fest, dass Min-Woo auf felsenfesten Füßen steht.

Min-Woo's Arbeit besitzt eine Qualität, die Kinogänger besonders reizen müsste. Während unseres Besuchs in den Staaten verbrachten wir einen Tag in Hollywood, und zufällig war zur gleichen Zeit die Premiere von *Lara Croft Tomb Raider: Die Wiege des Lebens* in Grauman's Chinese Theater. Wir sahen, wie die Limousinen den Regisseur, Hauptdarstellerin Angelina Jolie, andere Schauspieler und Crewmitglieder bei der Premiere absetzten. Danach ging die Party bei einer Premierenfeier auf der anderen Straßenseite weiter. Dieses Erlebnis überzeugte mich jenseits aller Zweifel davon, dass es eines Tages wir sein werden, die eine eigene Premiere im Chinese Theater feiern.

Wir kehrten mit brennenden Herzen und dem Wunsch, eine Serie zu schaffen, die speziell auf die Bedürfnisse des US-Marktes zugeschnitten sein sollte, aus den Staaten zurück. Zunächst aber entschieden wir uns in Vorbereitung auf dieses Projekt, verschiedene Teilkonzepte zusammen zu stellen und sie in Korea zu veröffentlichen. Diese Ausgabe ist das Ergebnis.

Viele Menschen haben großzügig ihre Hilfe angeboten, um dieses Buch Wirklichkeit werden zu lassen. Gwanshik Shin war immer für uns da, wenn wir ihn brauchten. Dongseop Kim hat die Fotos gemacht, der Tattoo-Künstler Yushi hat uns dankenswerterweise sein Studio für die Fotosessions zur Verfügung gestellt und Jinkyeong Jeong hat diese Ausgabe designt. Unser Dank gilt ihnen und vielen anderen. Wir hoffen, dass diese Ausgabe ein Meilenstein wird und dabei hilft, Min-Woo's Popularität in den USA zu steigern.

Eddie Yu エディ・ユー
Editor-in-Chief, 編集長 Studio ICE

Contents | 目次 | Inhalt

justice N mercy: the concept art
正義と慈悲：コンセプト・アート
justice N mercy: Die Kunst des Entwurfs

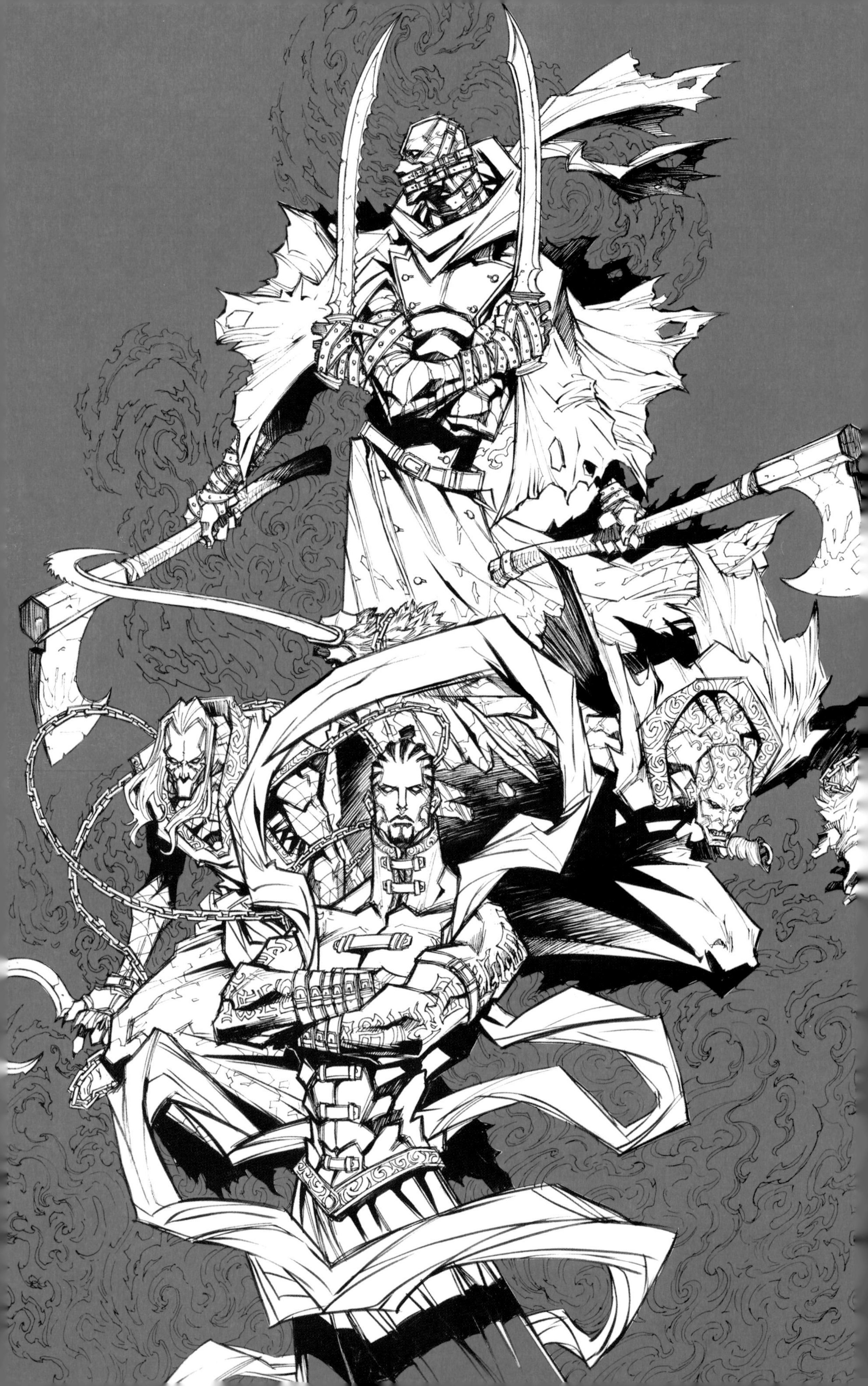

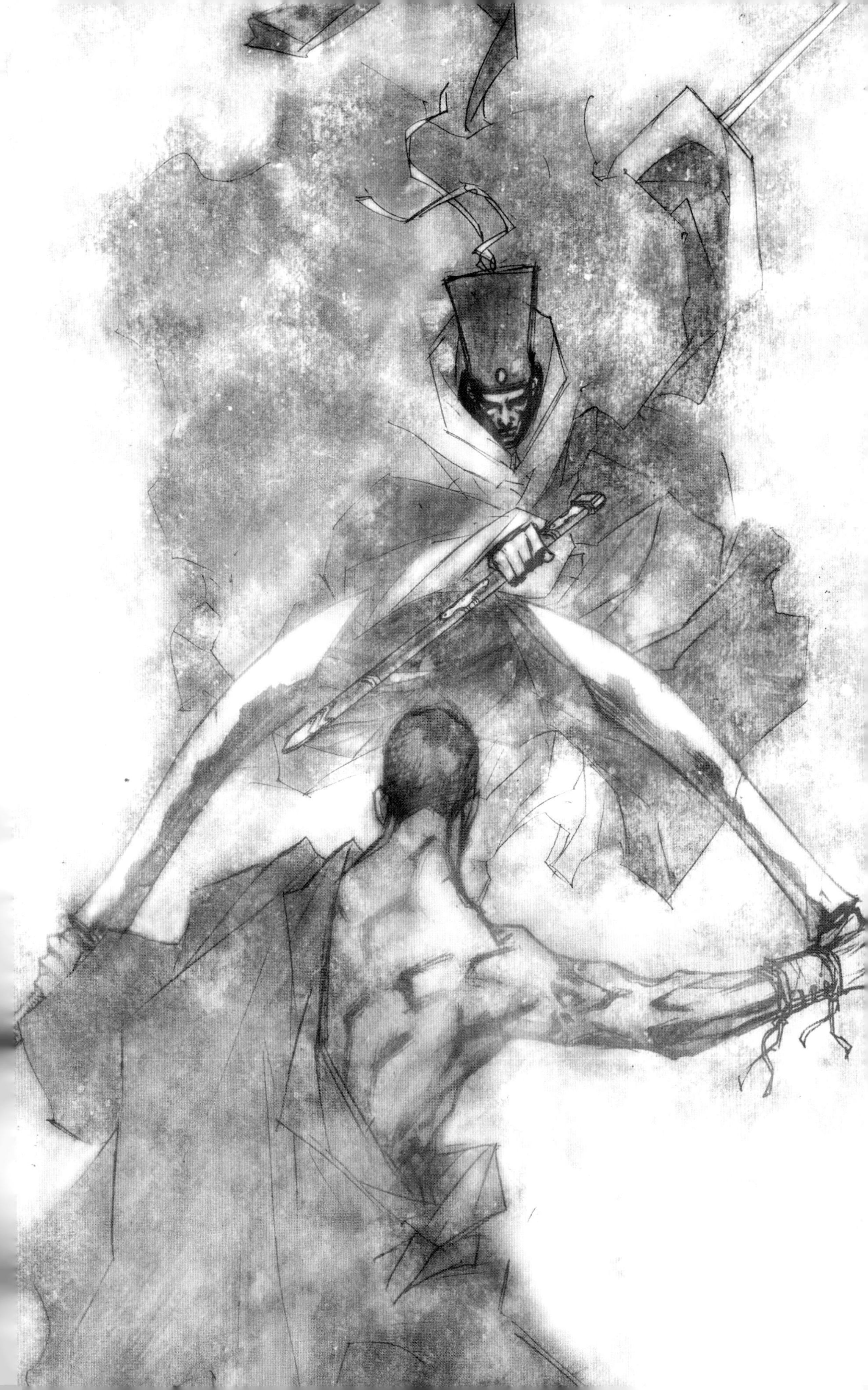

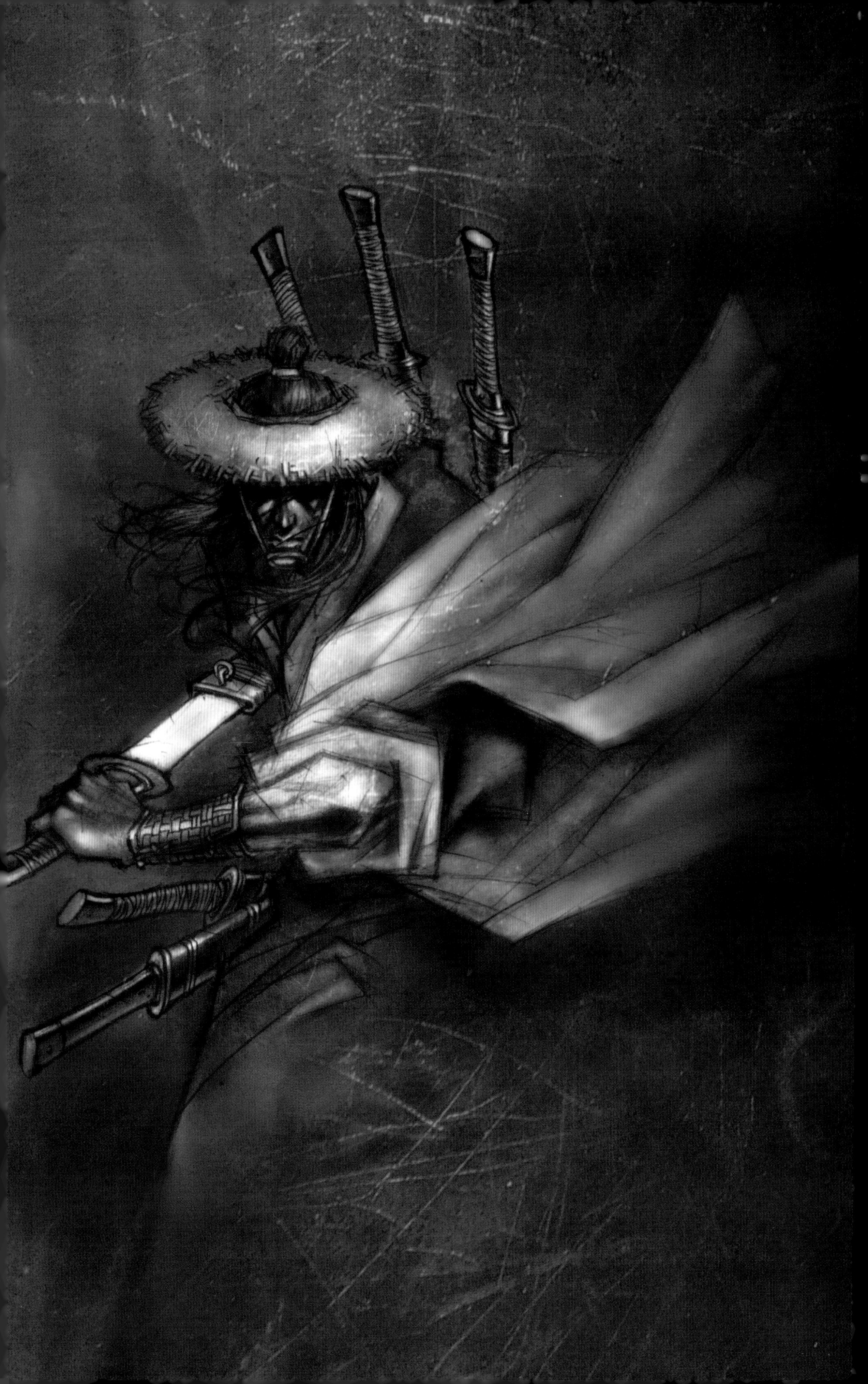

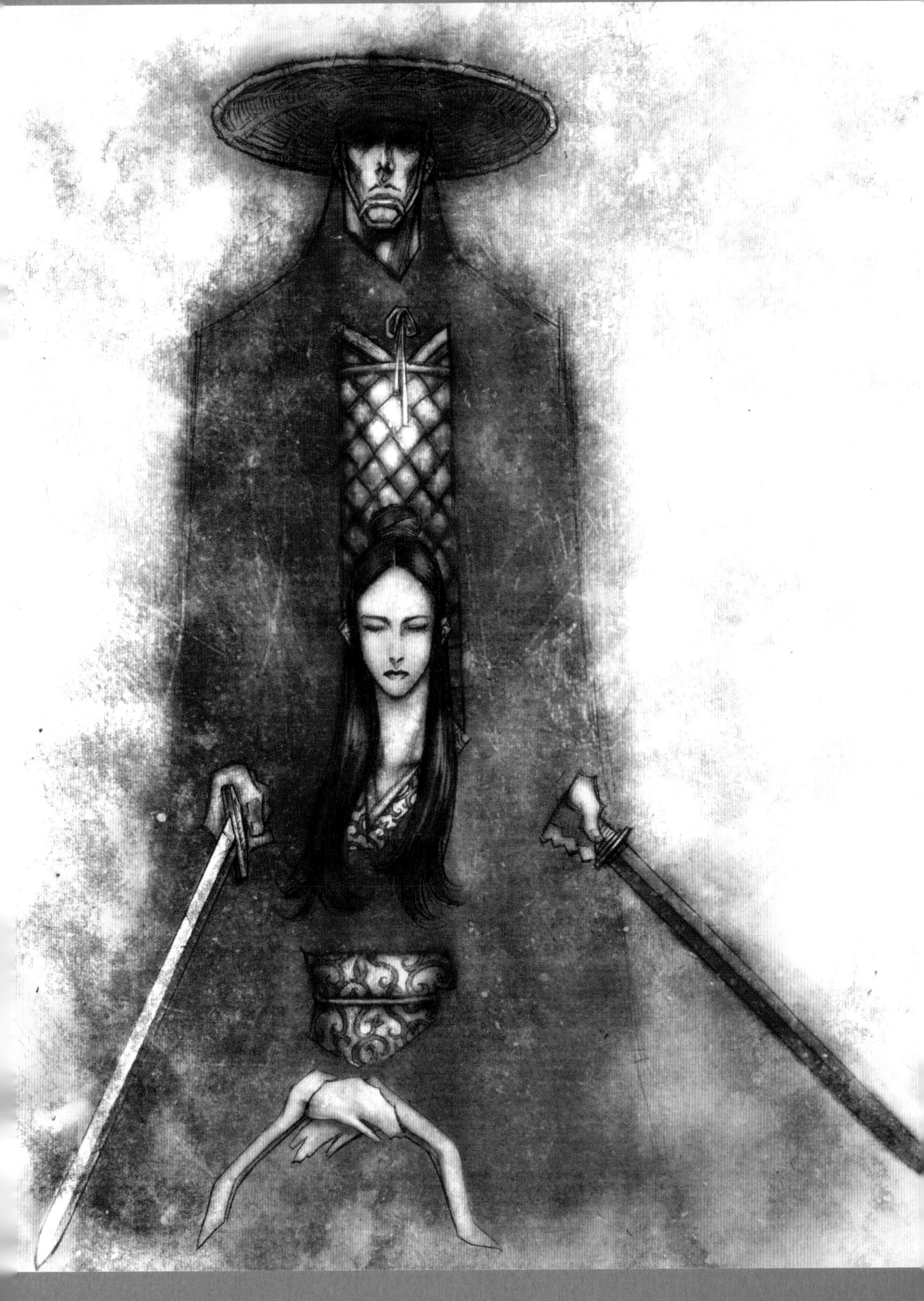

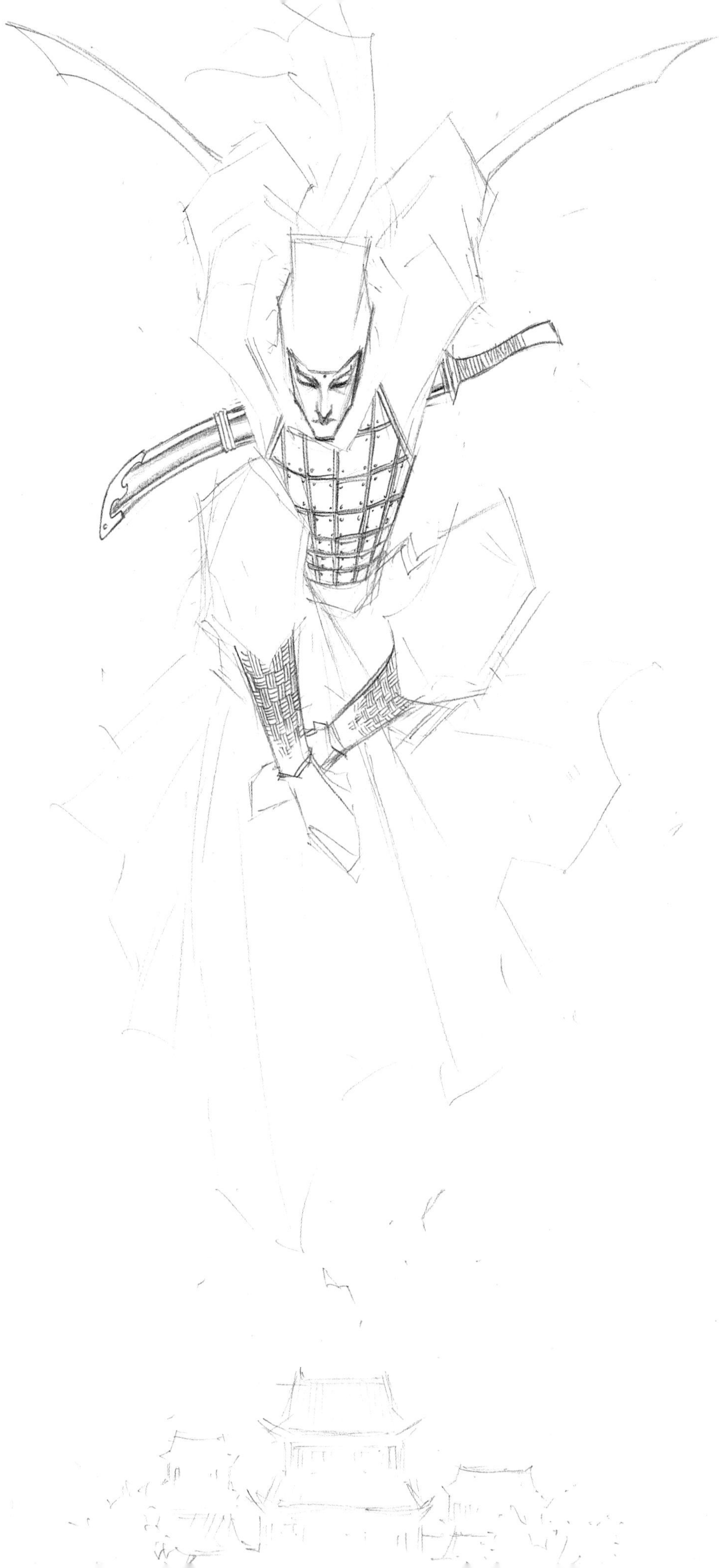

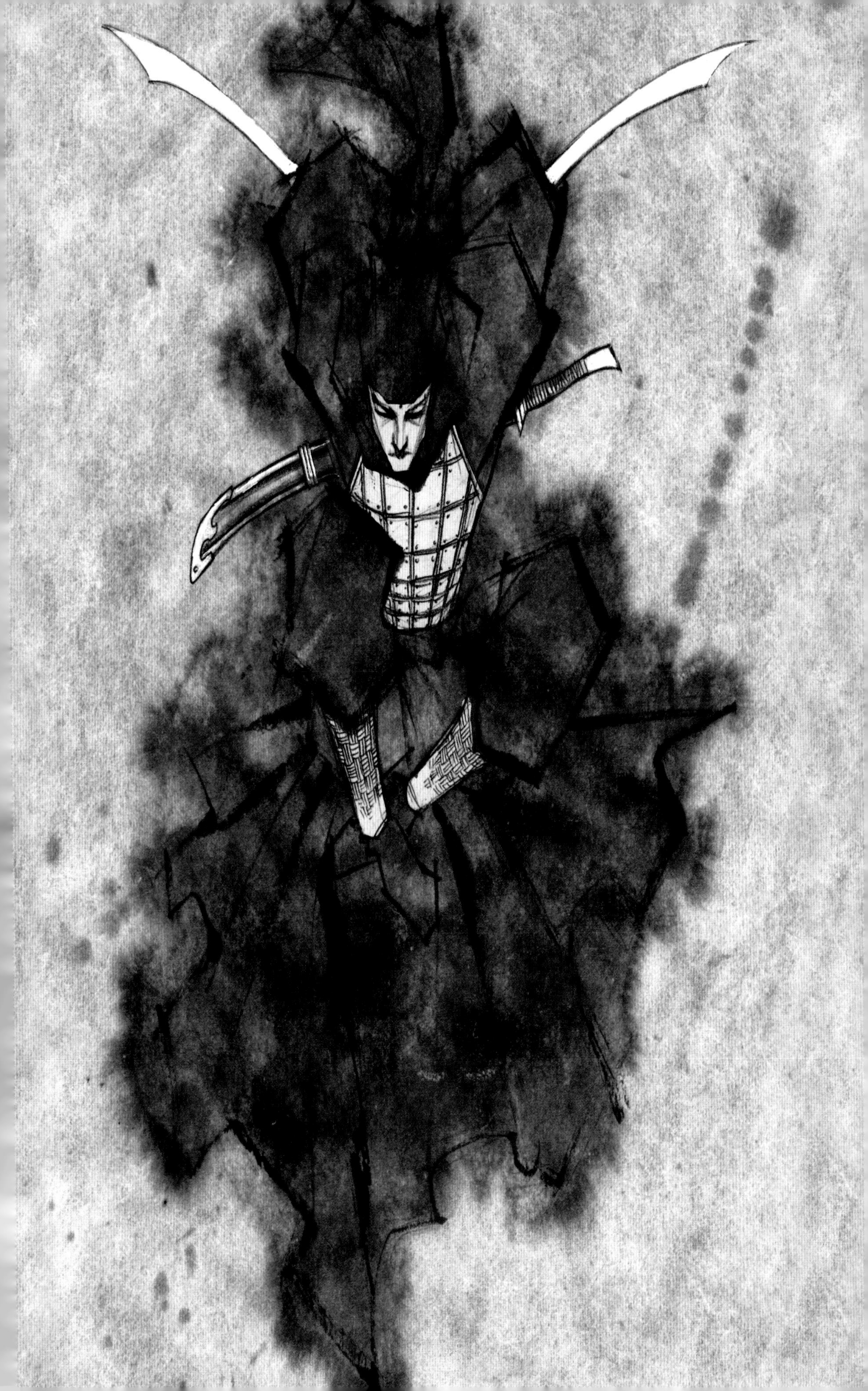

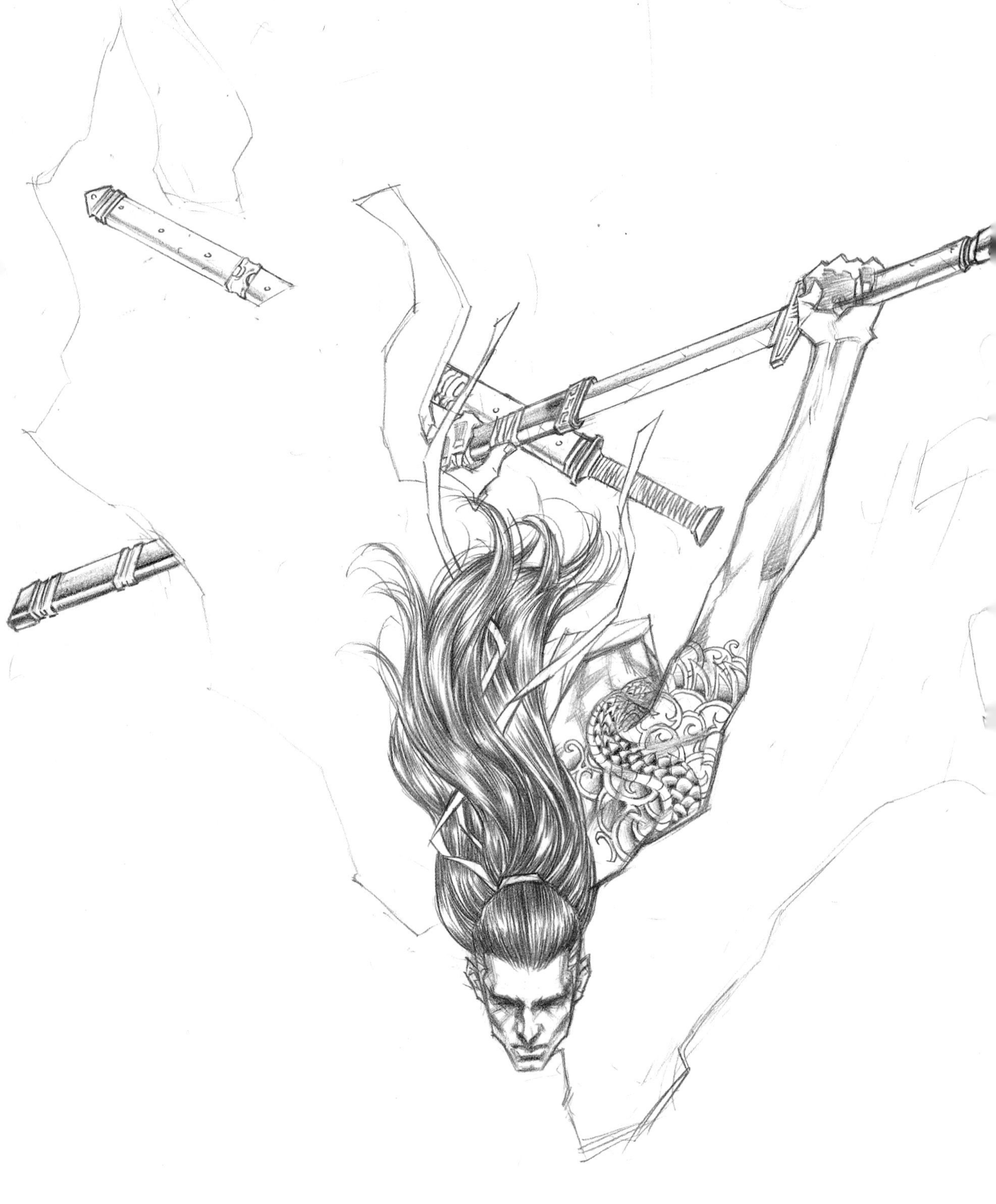

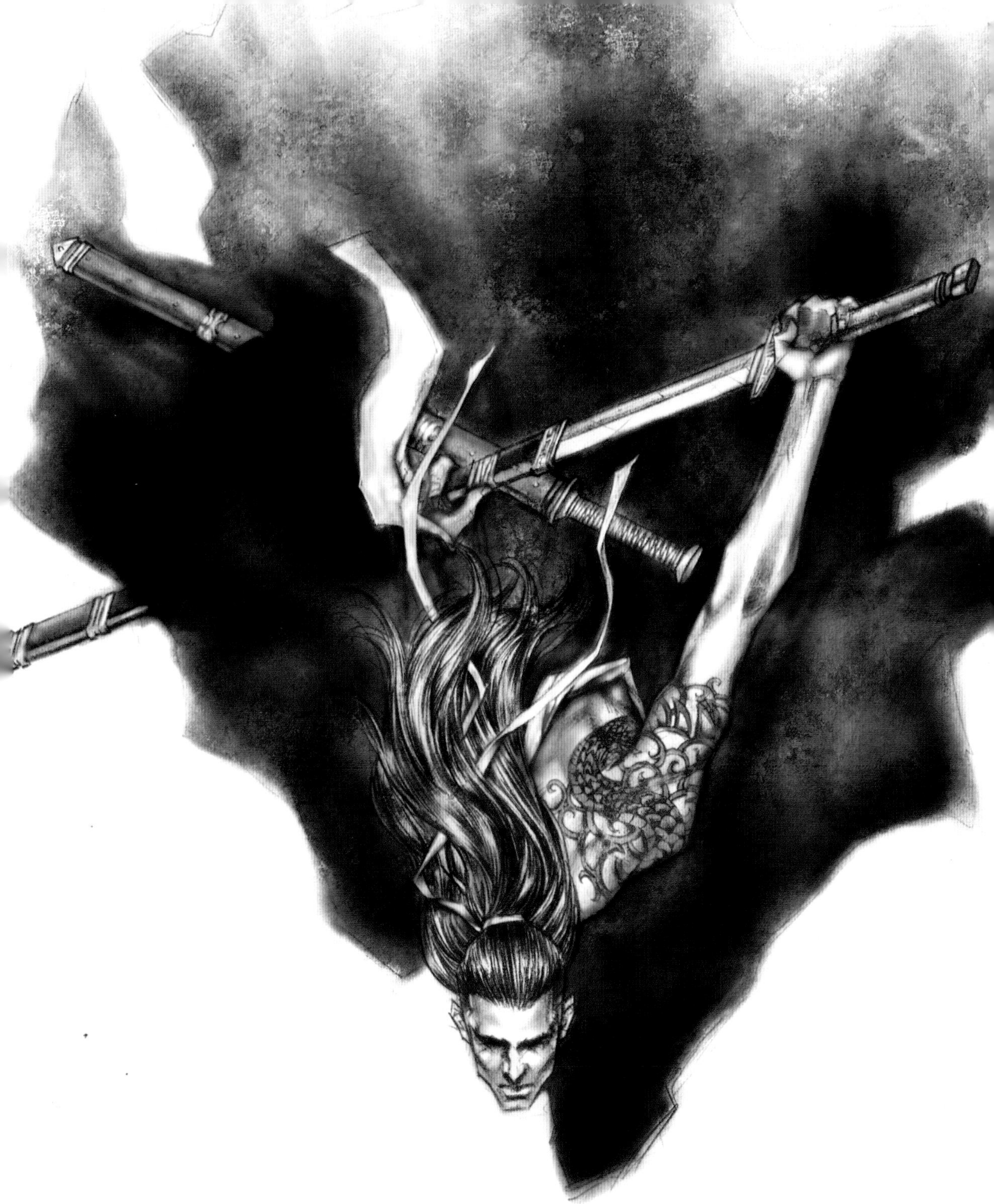

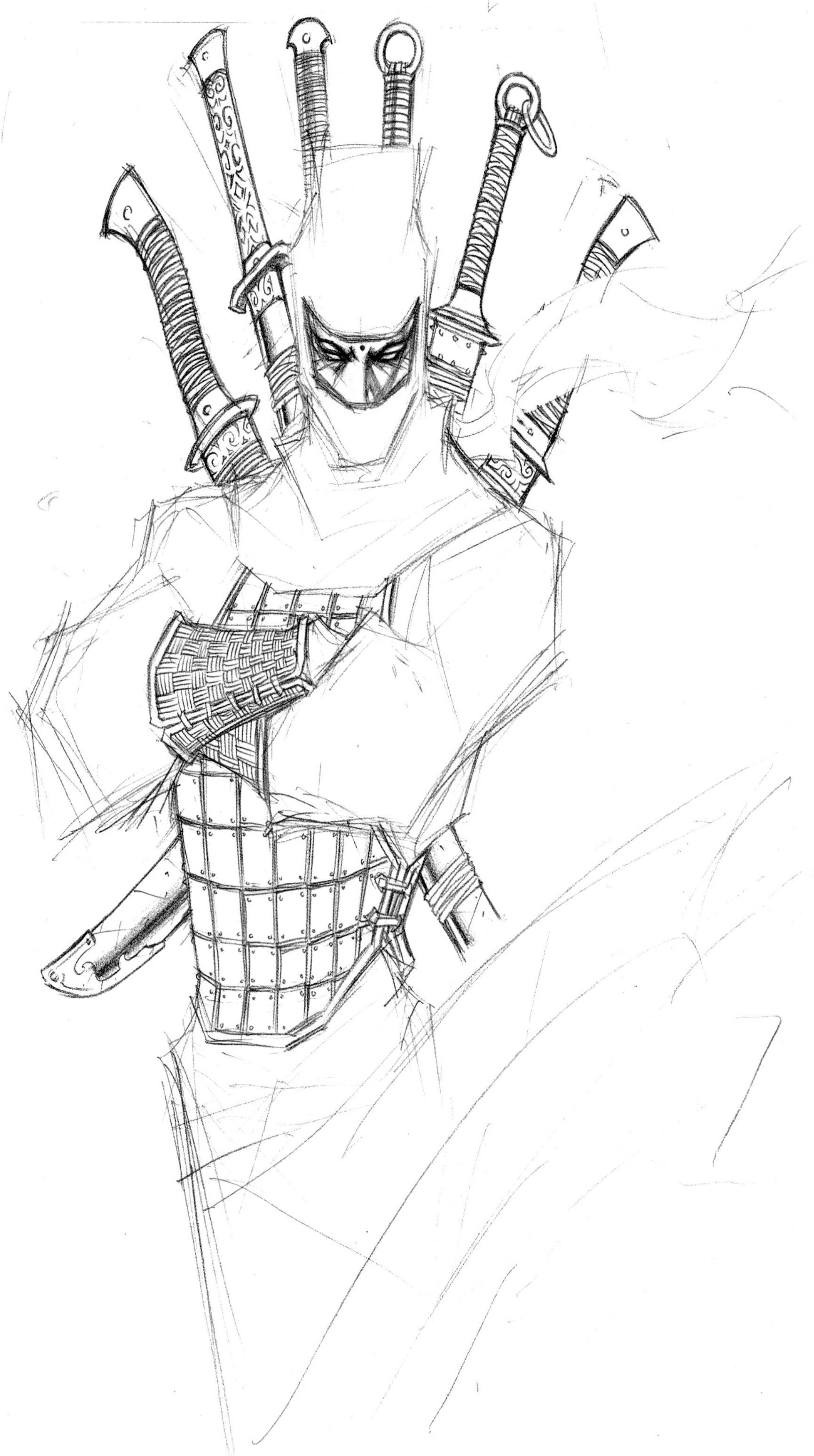

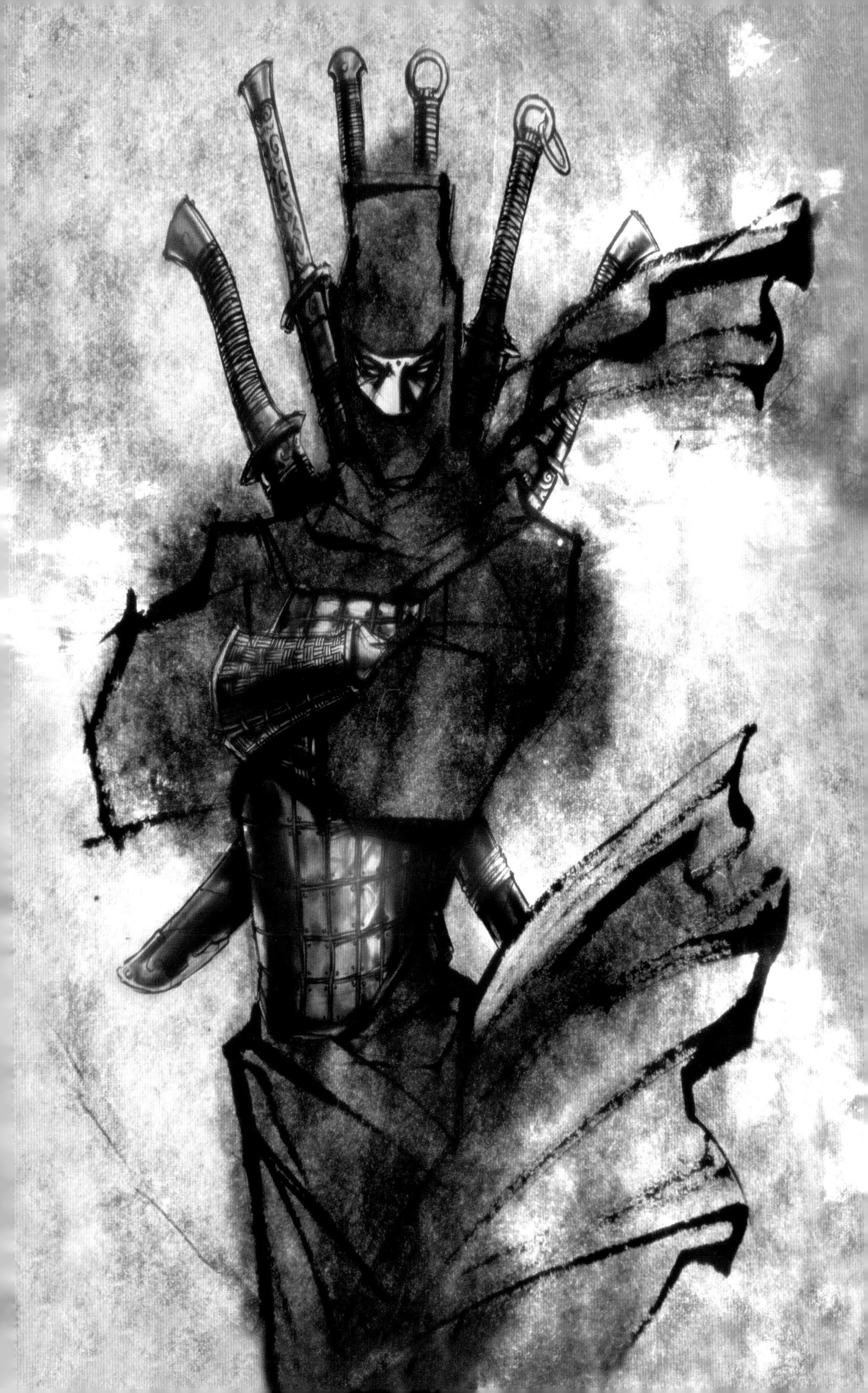

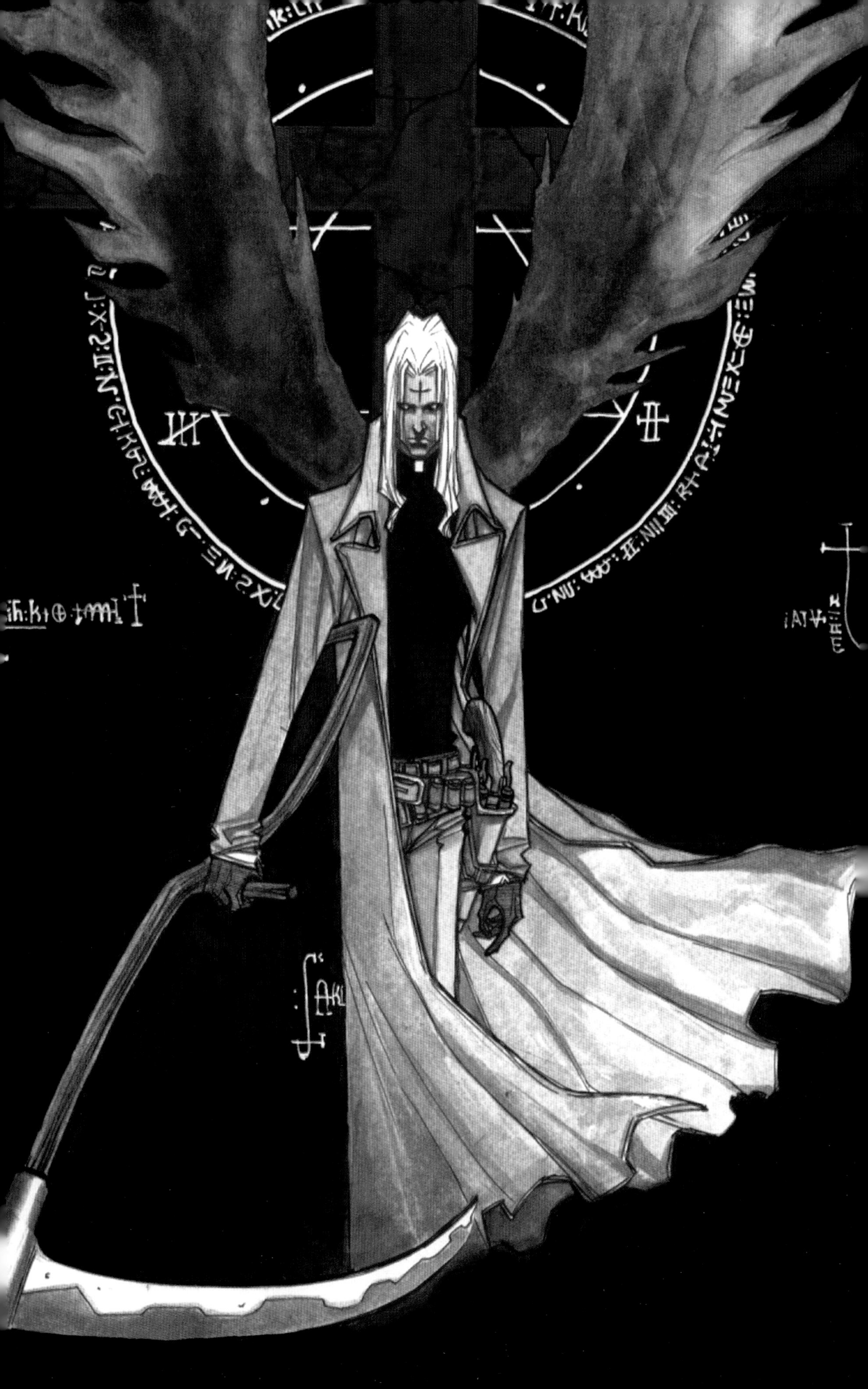

Even at this moment,
my heart is filled with reverence for you.
I will not waver on my decision.

Great Swordsman, may you rest in peace.

今になっても
僕の胸は君を尊敬する気持ちでいっぱいだ。
僕の決心は変わらない。

大なる剣士よ、安らかに眠りたまえ。

Sogar in diesem Augenblick ist mein Herz
erfüllt von Ehrfurcht vor dir.
Ich werde an meinem Glauben festhalten.

Großer Schwertkämpfer, ruhe in Frieden.

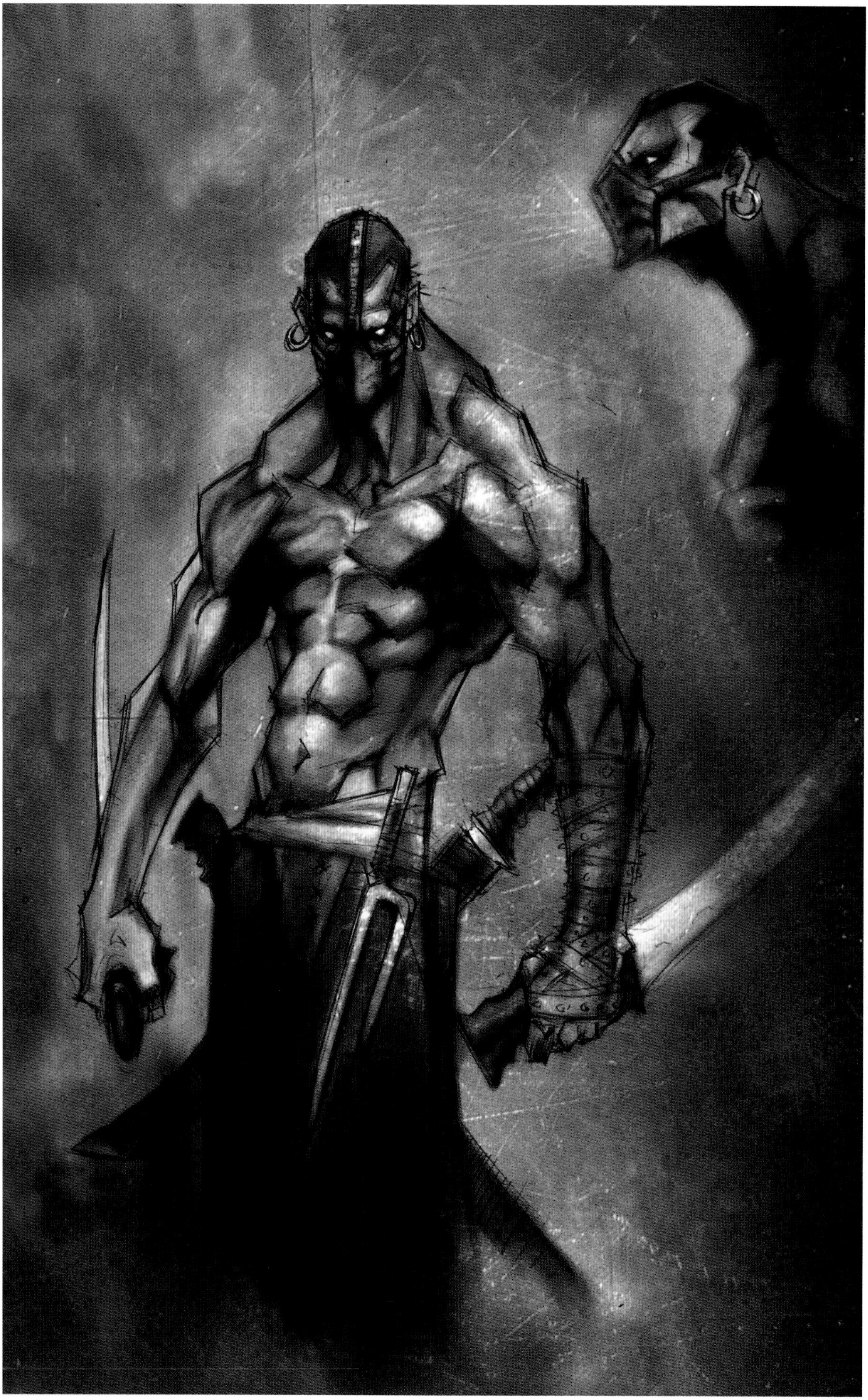

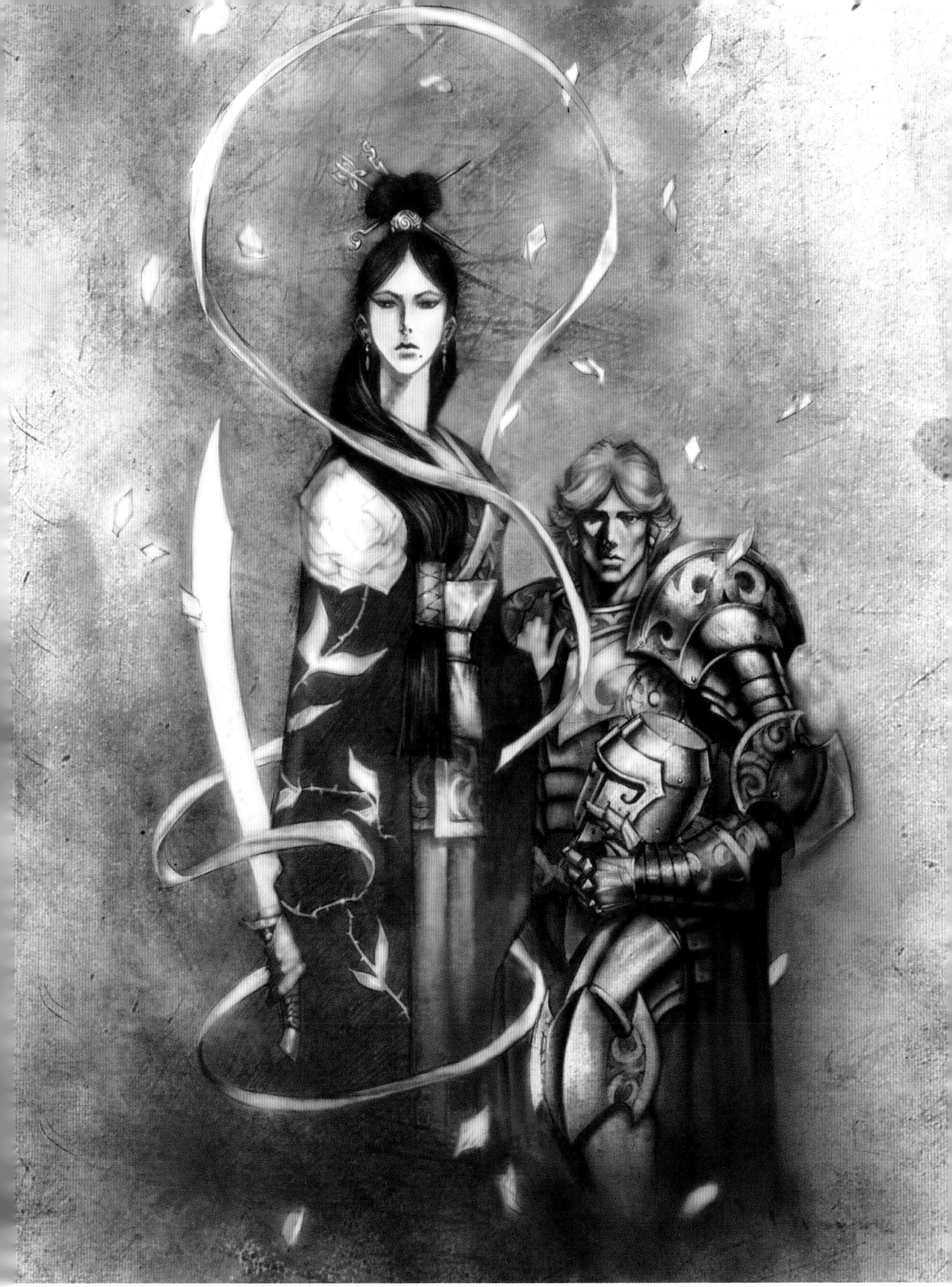

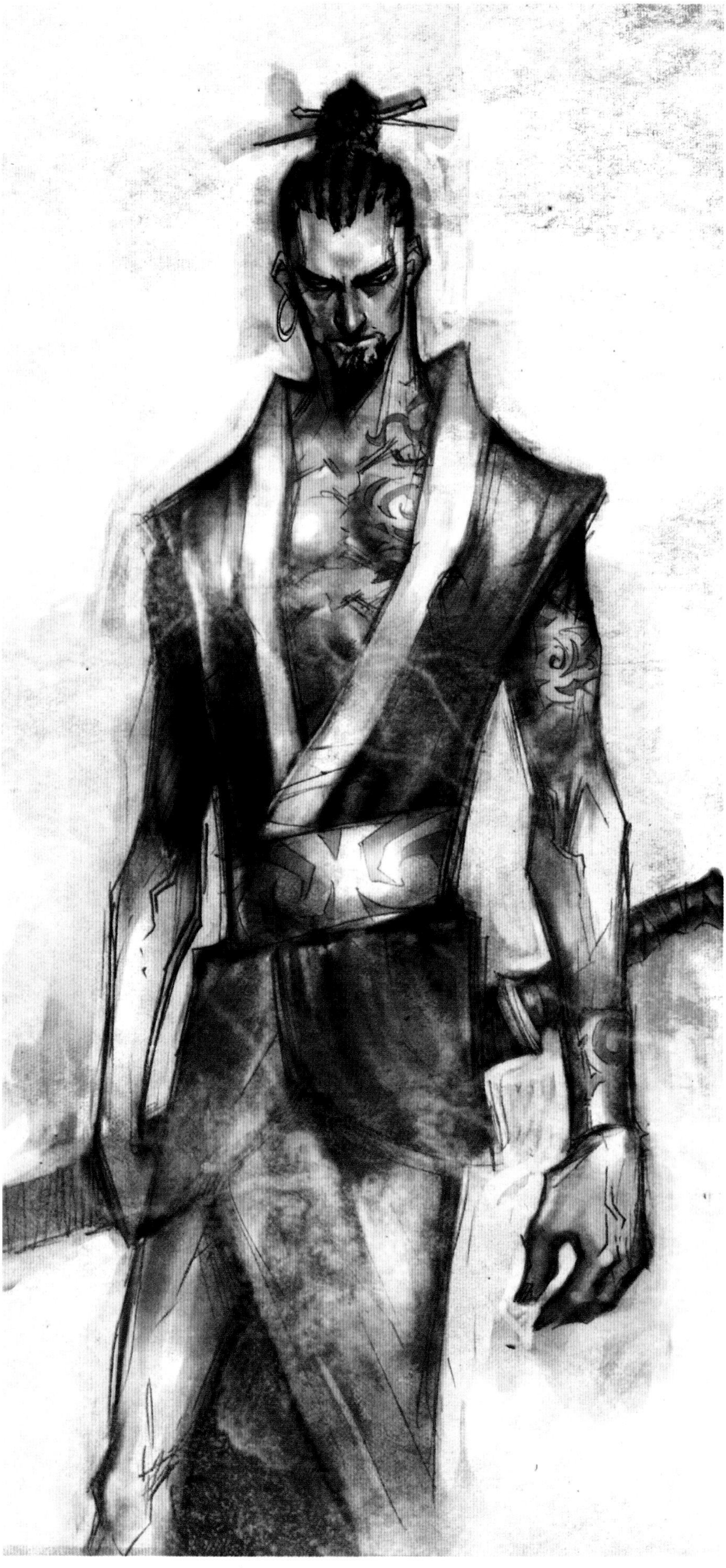

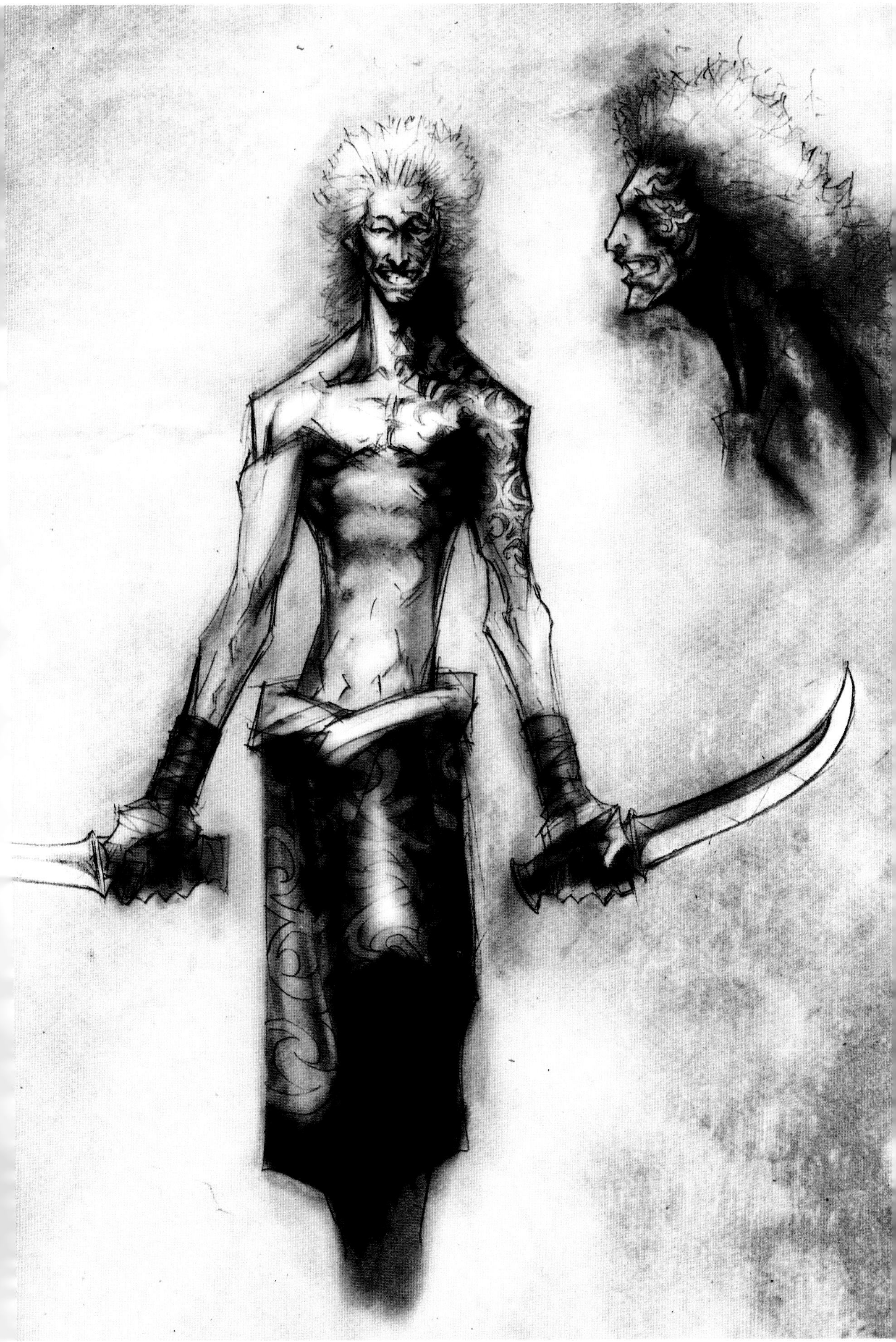

My yearning for all that is powerful…
力ある全てのものに対する願望...
Meine Sehnsucht nach all dem ist gewaltig...

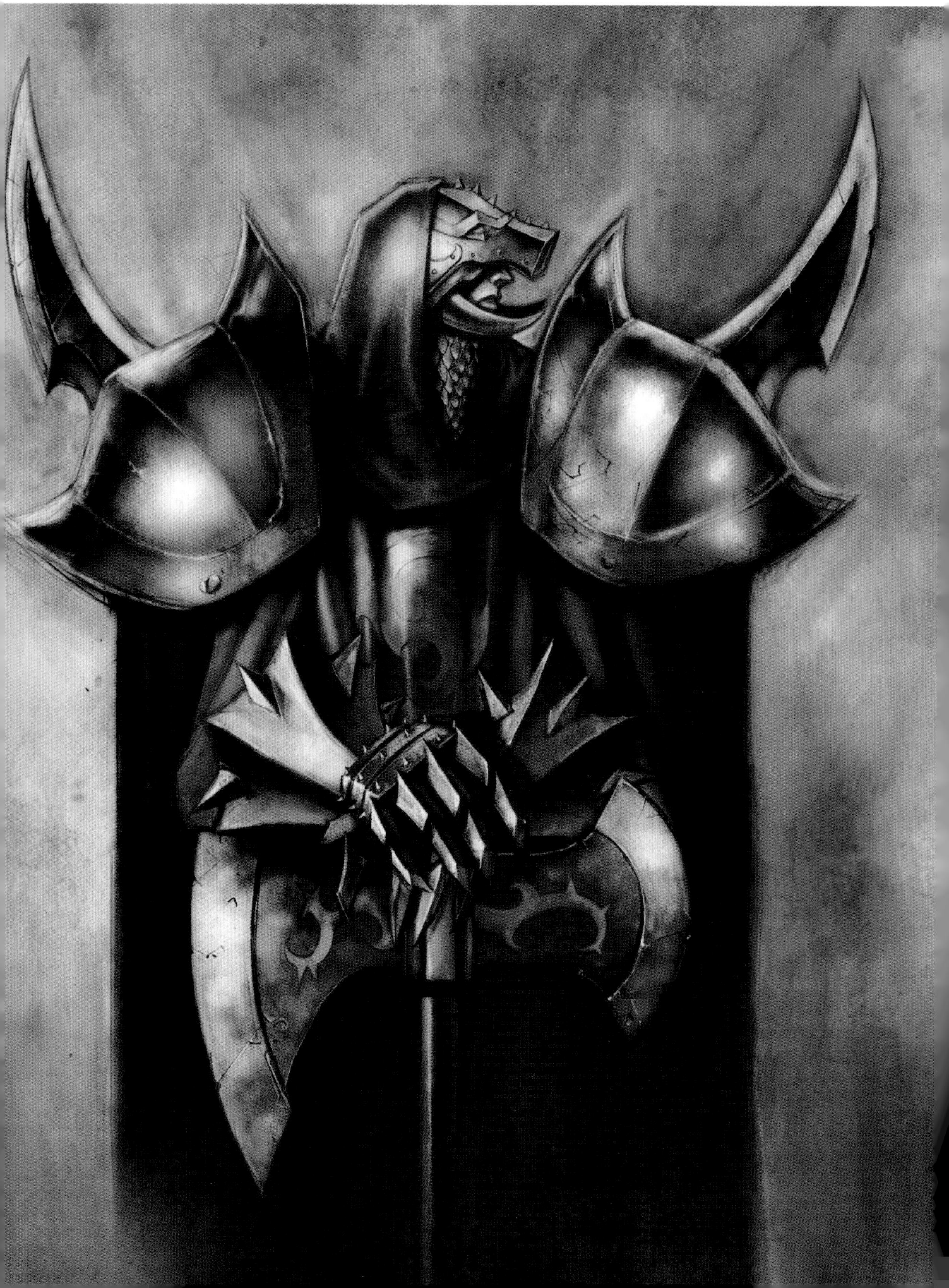

…is one of the reasons I draw.

…が、絵を書き続ける理由の一つ。

…sie ist einer der Gründe, warum ich zeichne.

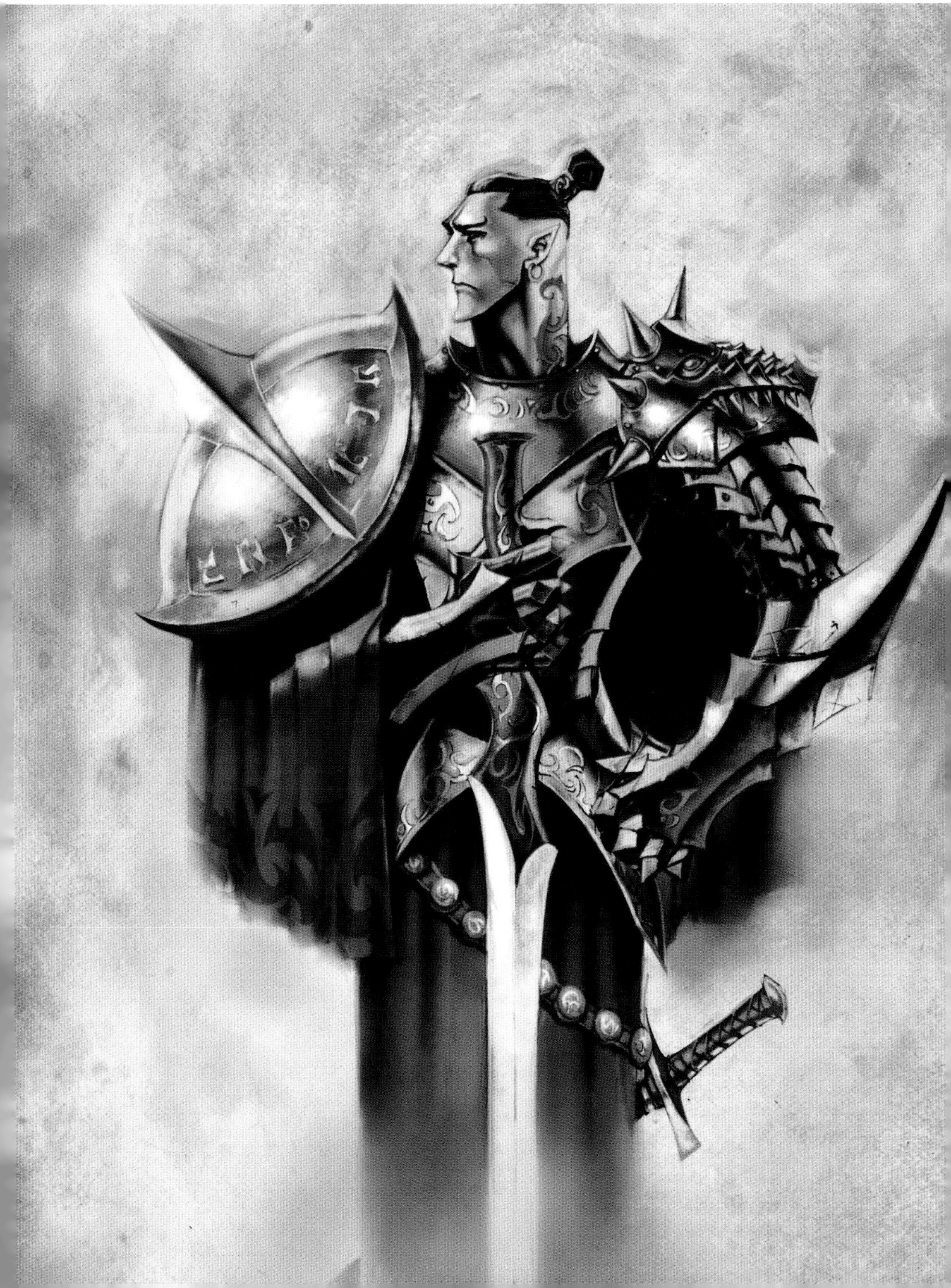

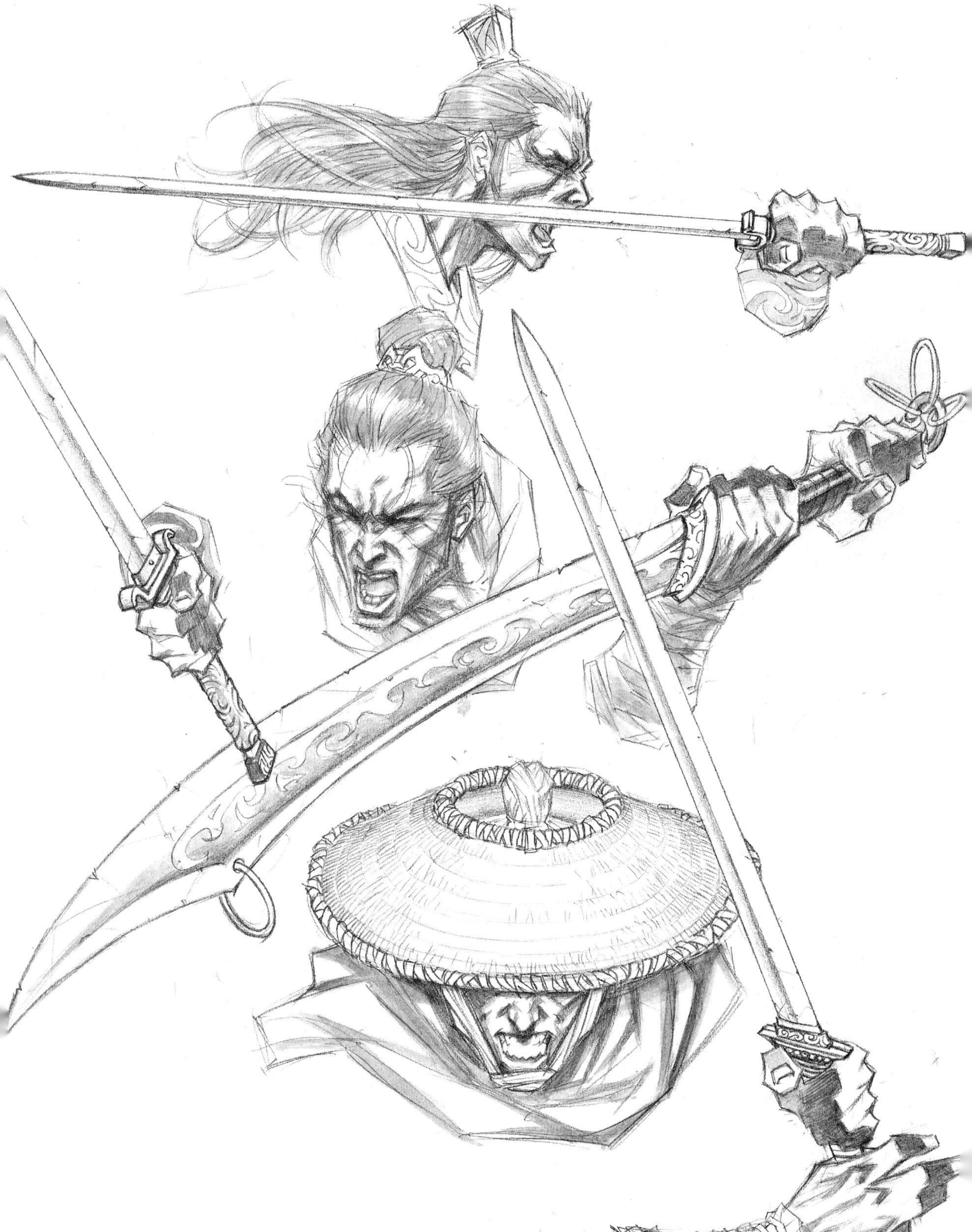

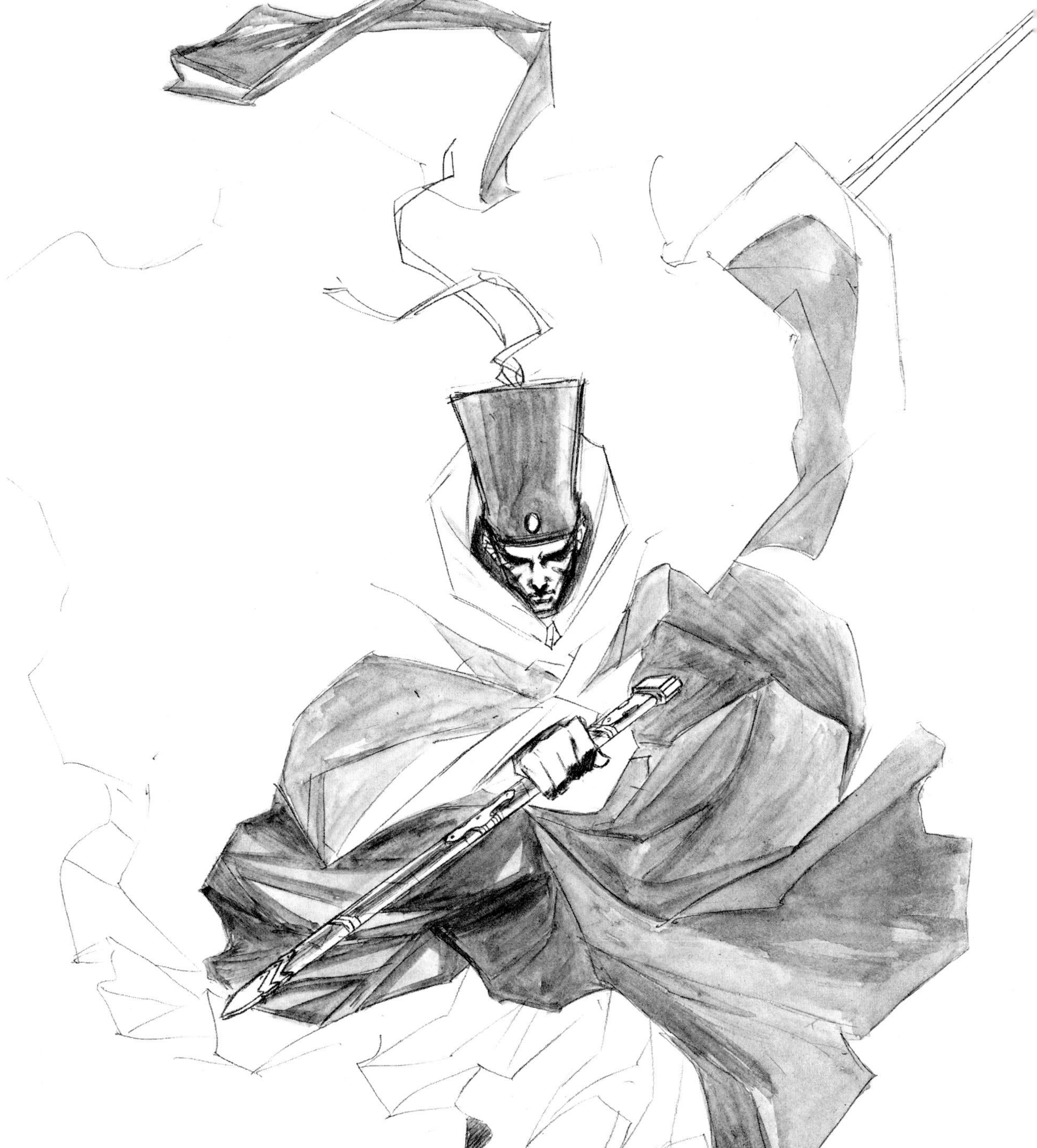

>>> chapter 2

第2章

>>> 2. Kapitel

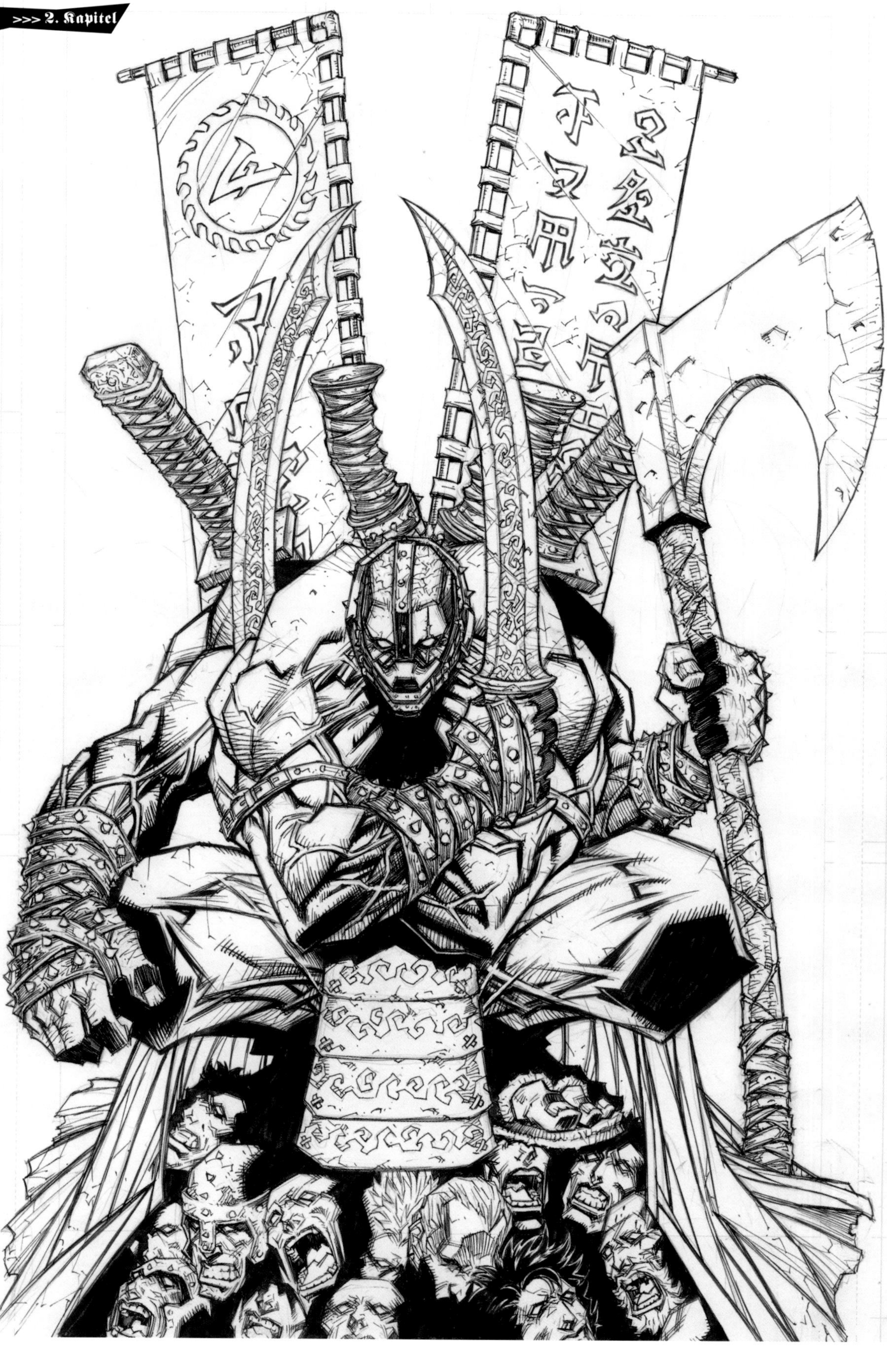

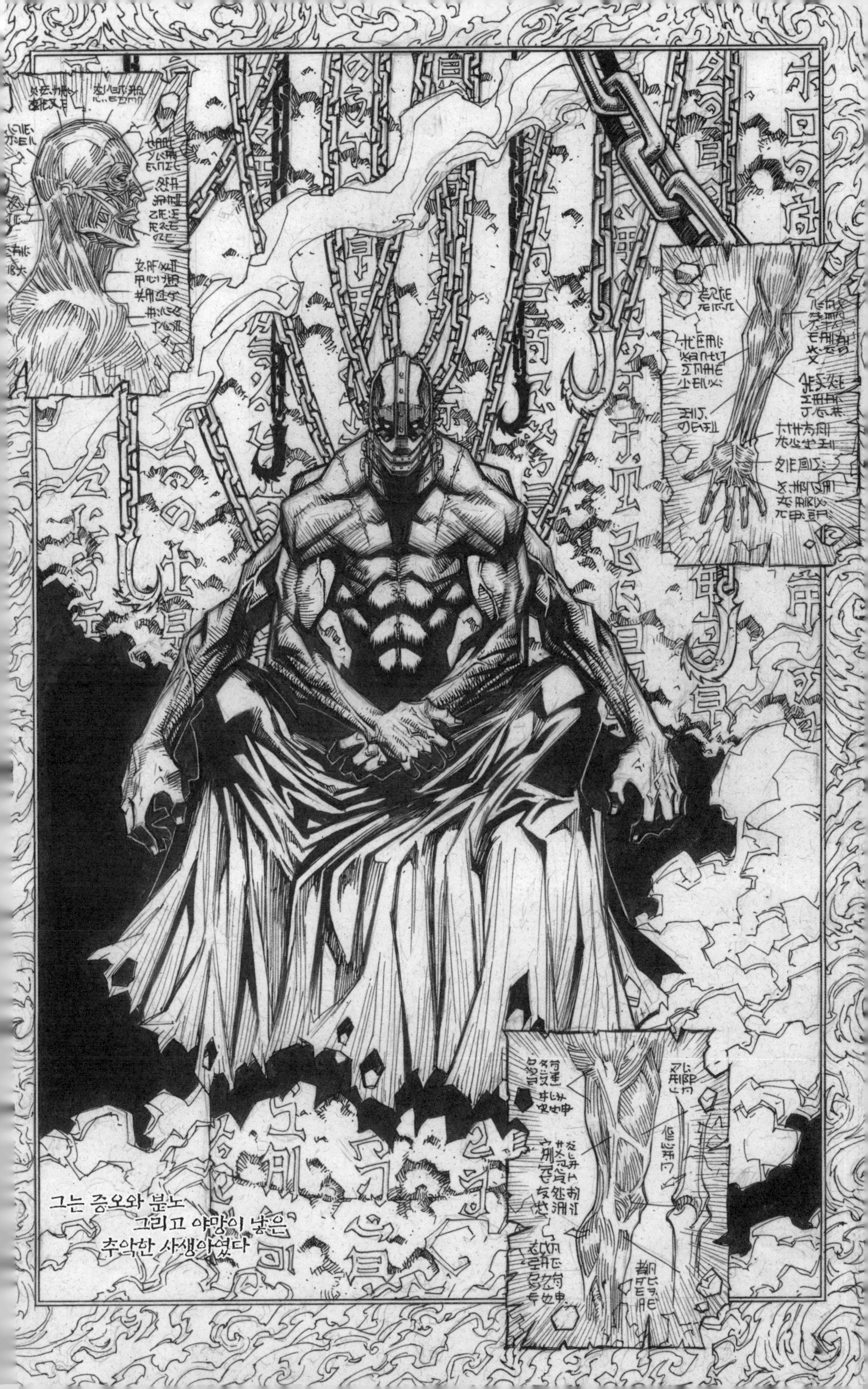
그는 증오와 분노
그리고 야망이 낳은
추악한 사생아였다

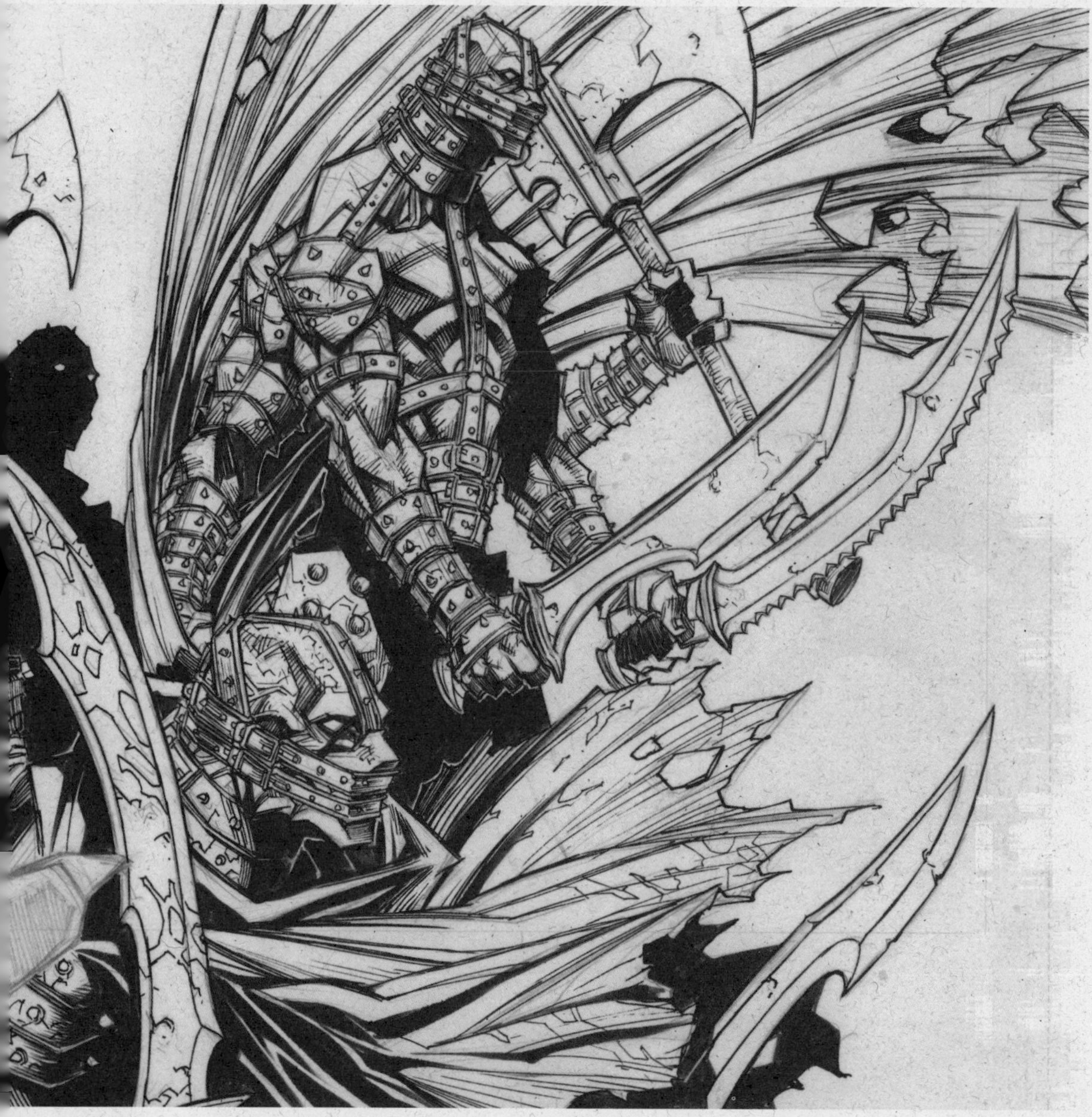

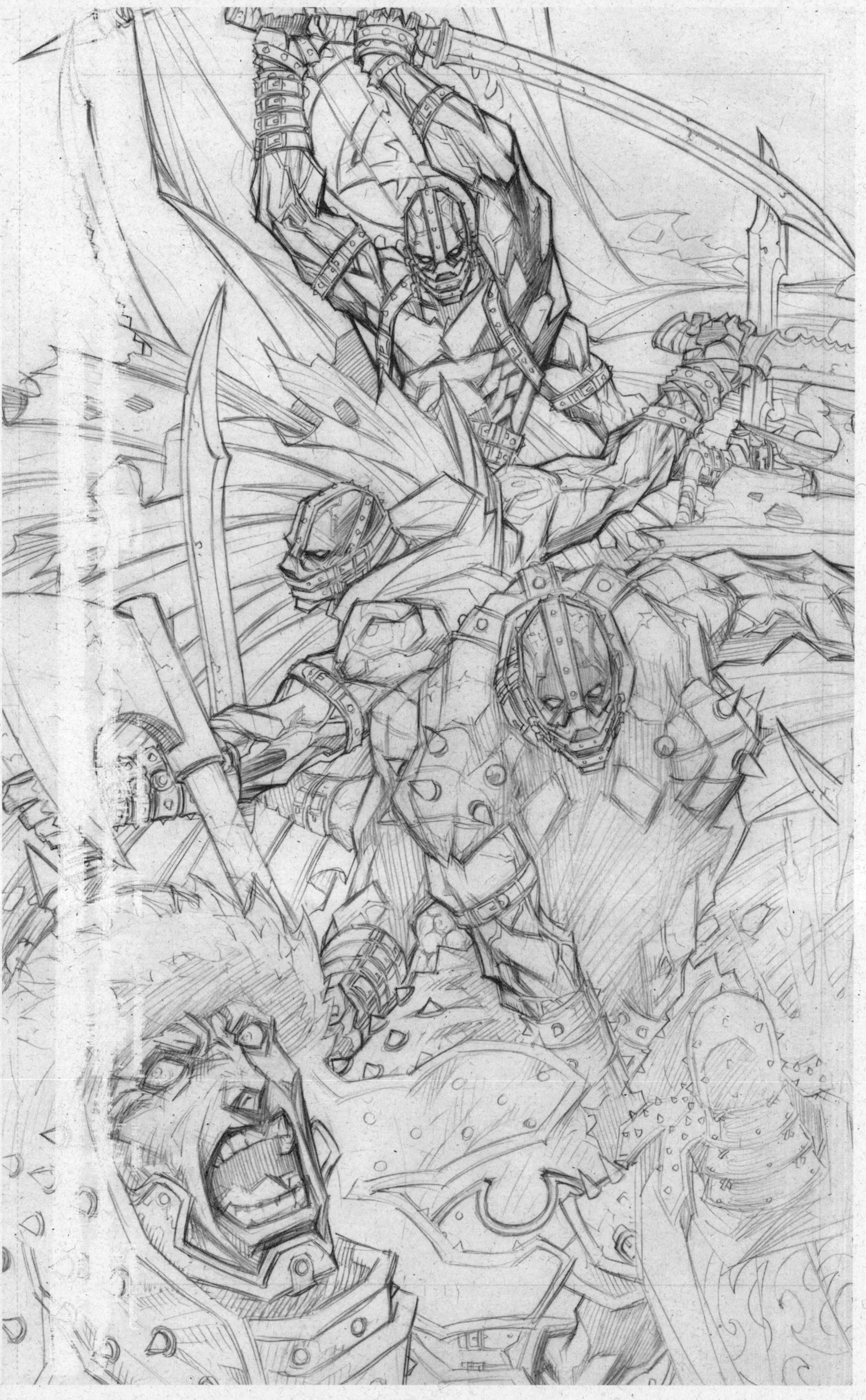

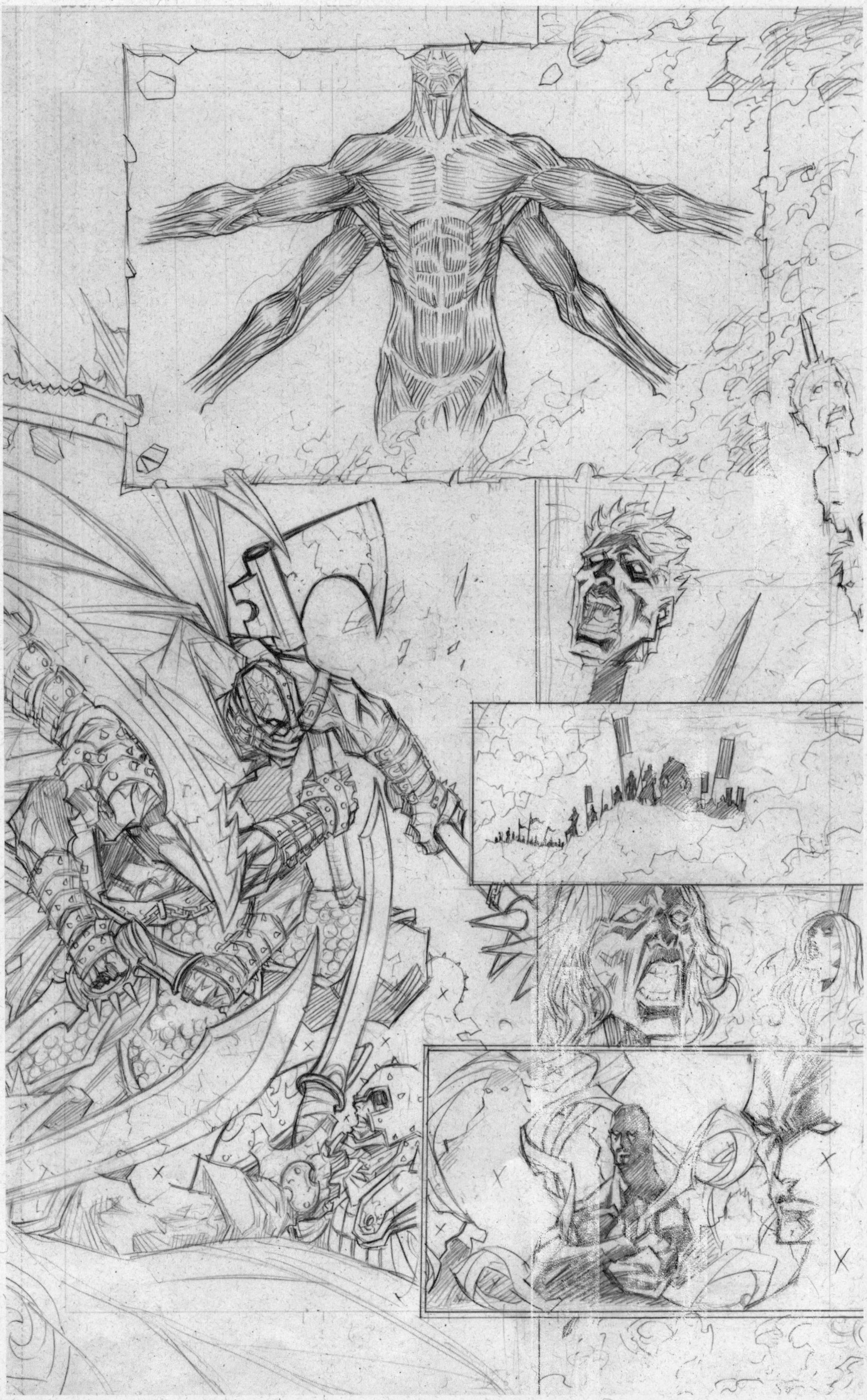

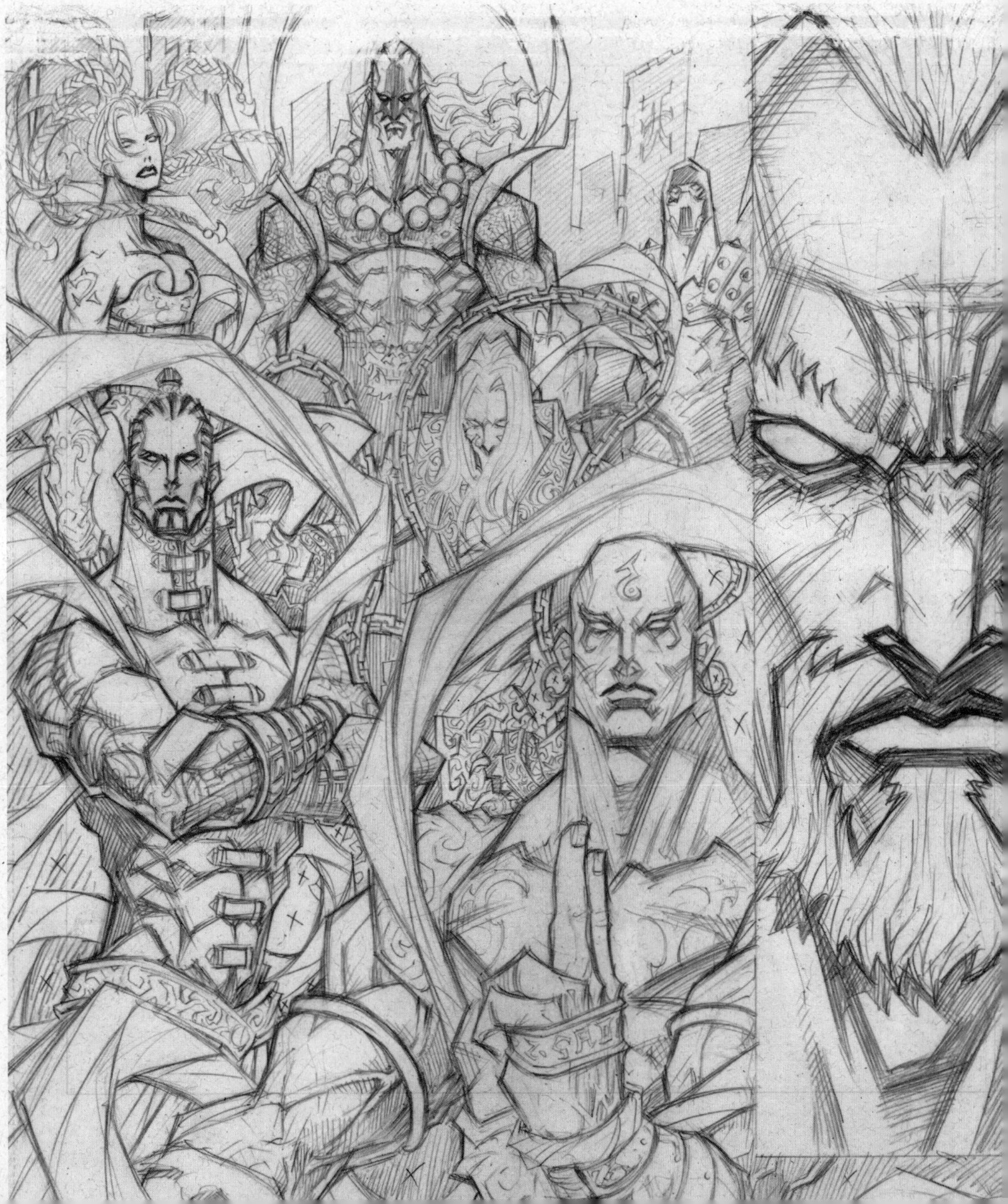

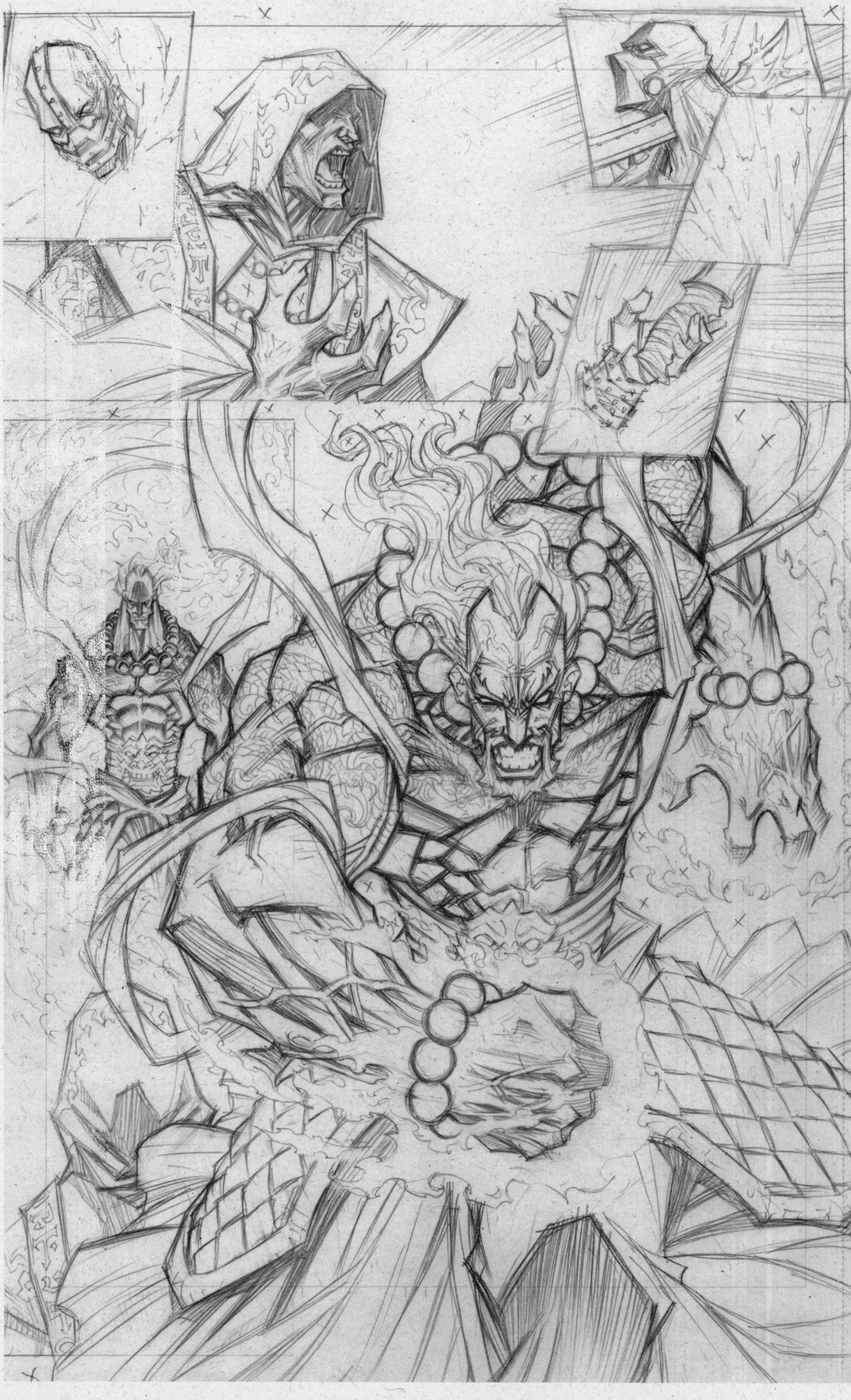

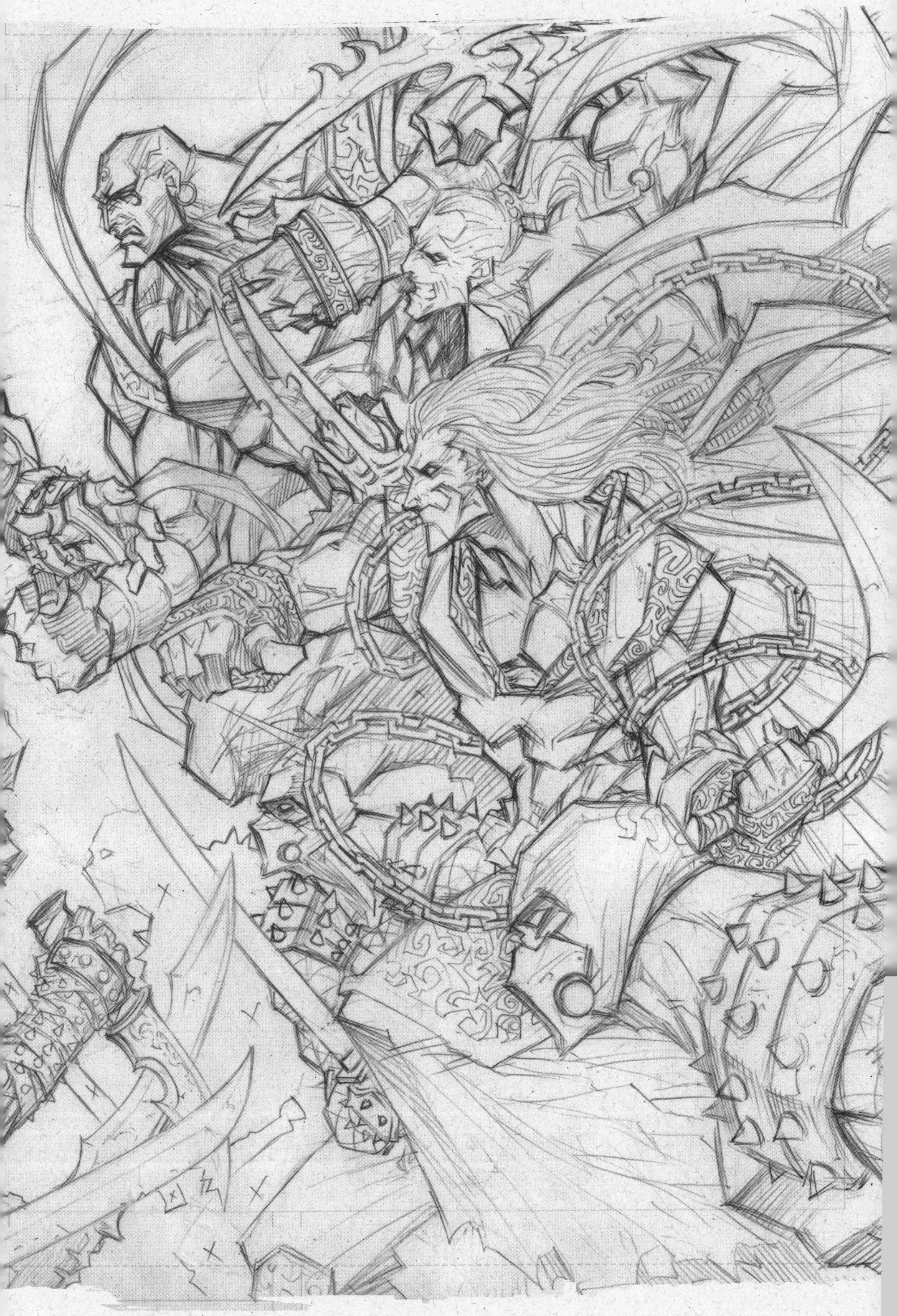

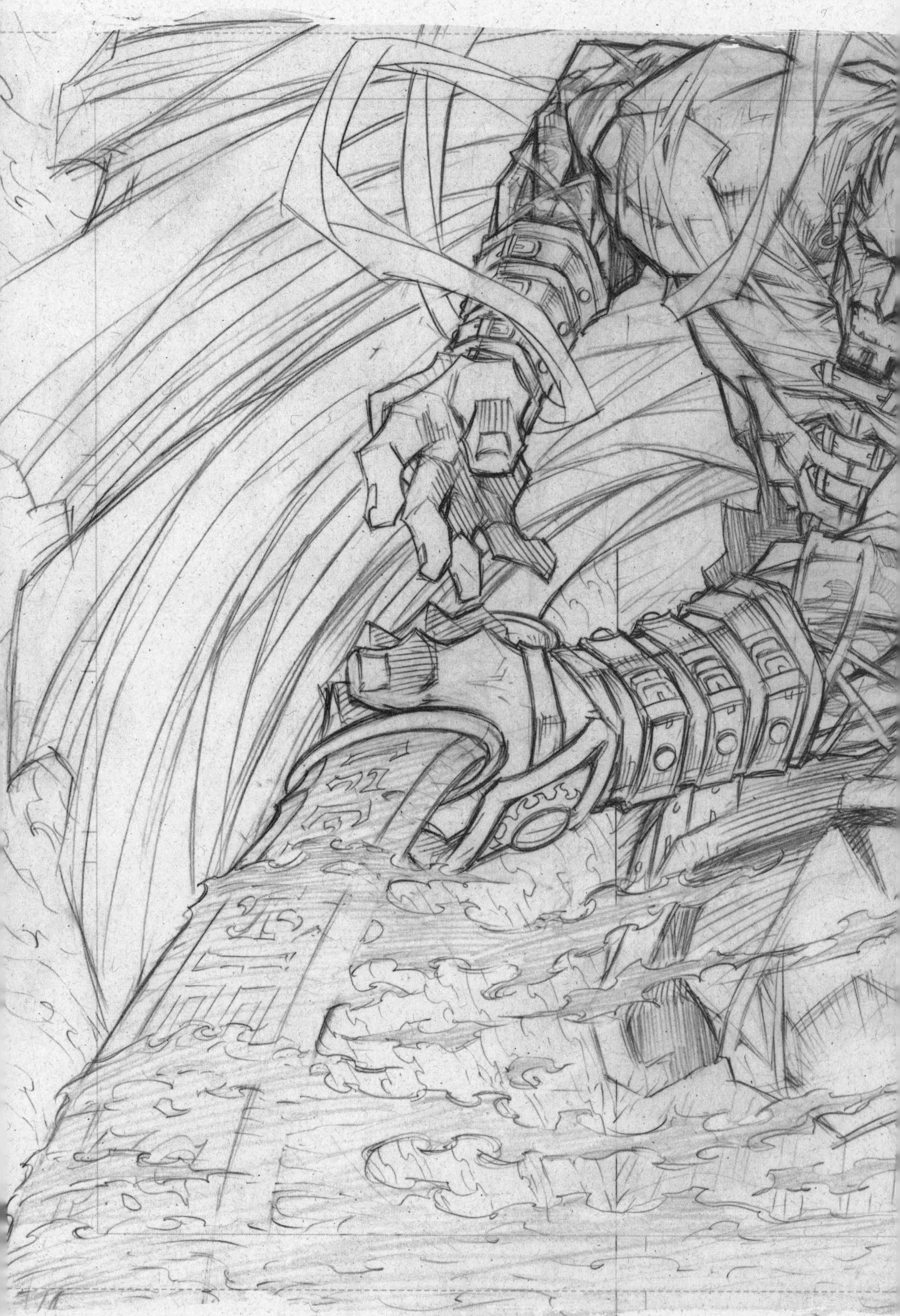

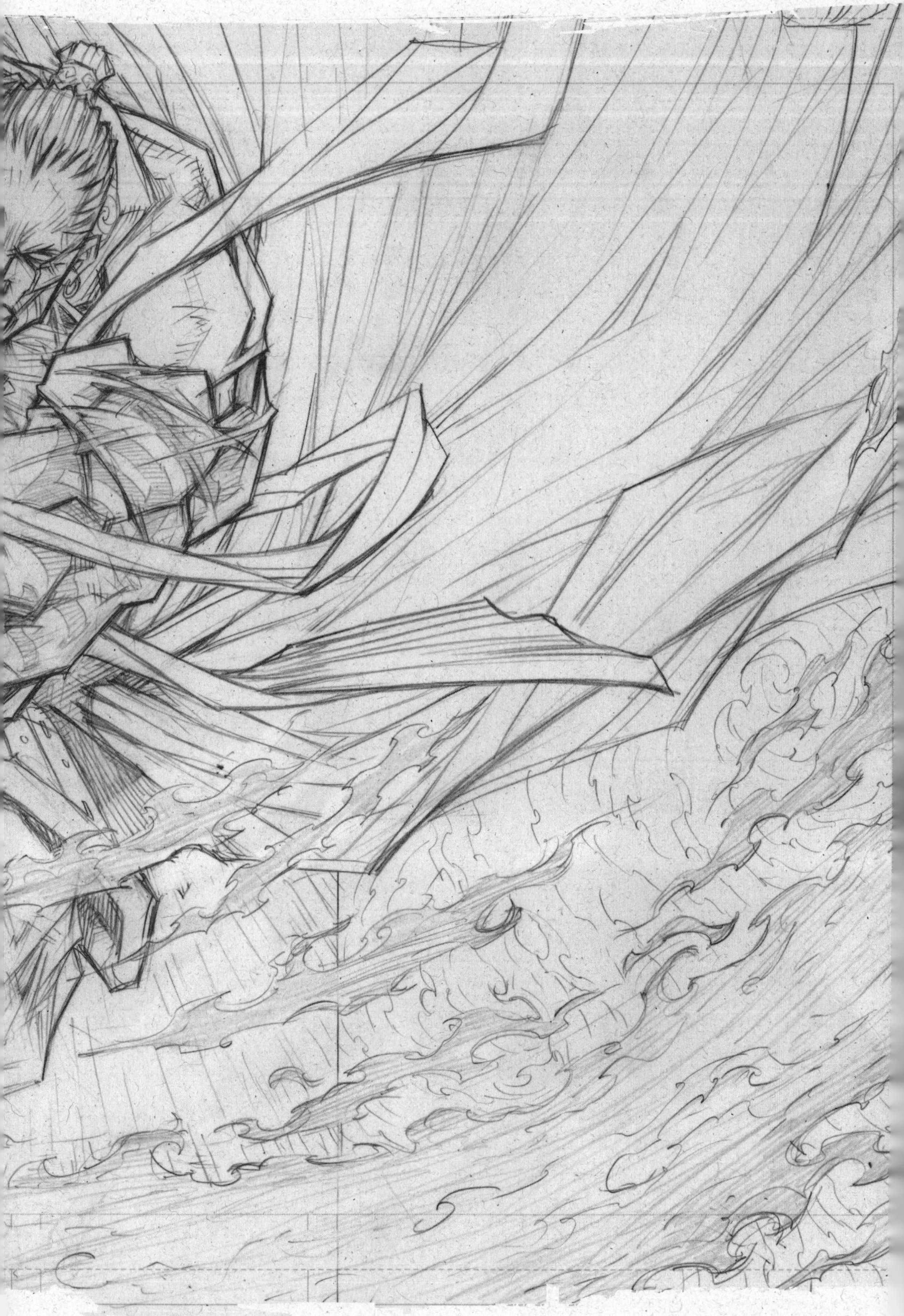

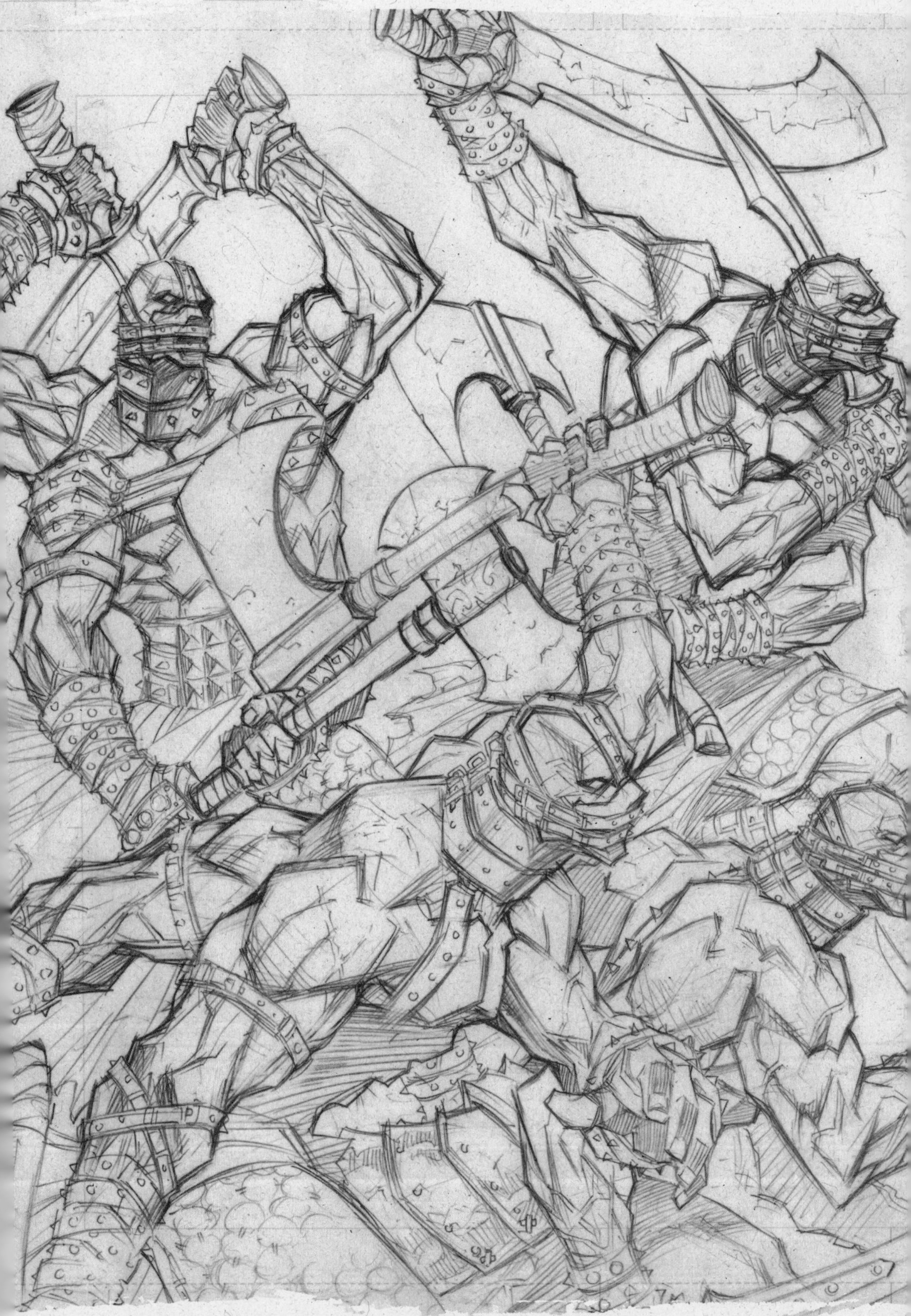

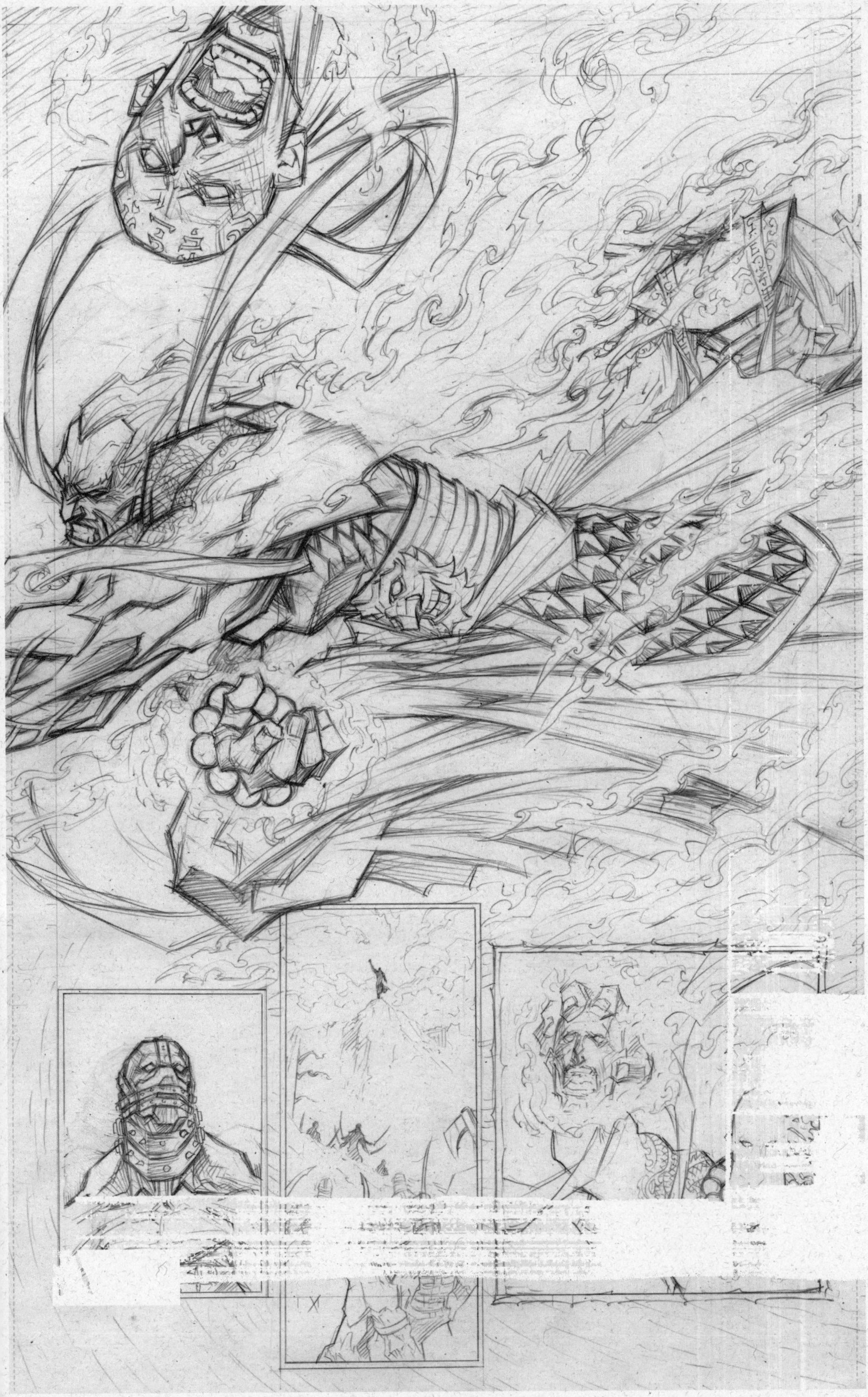

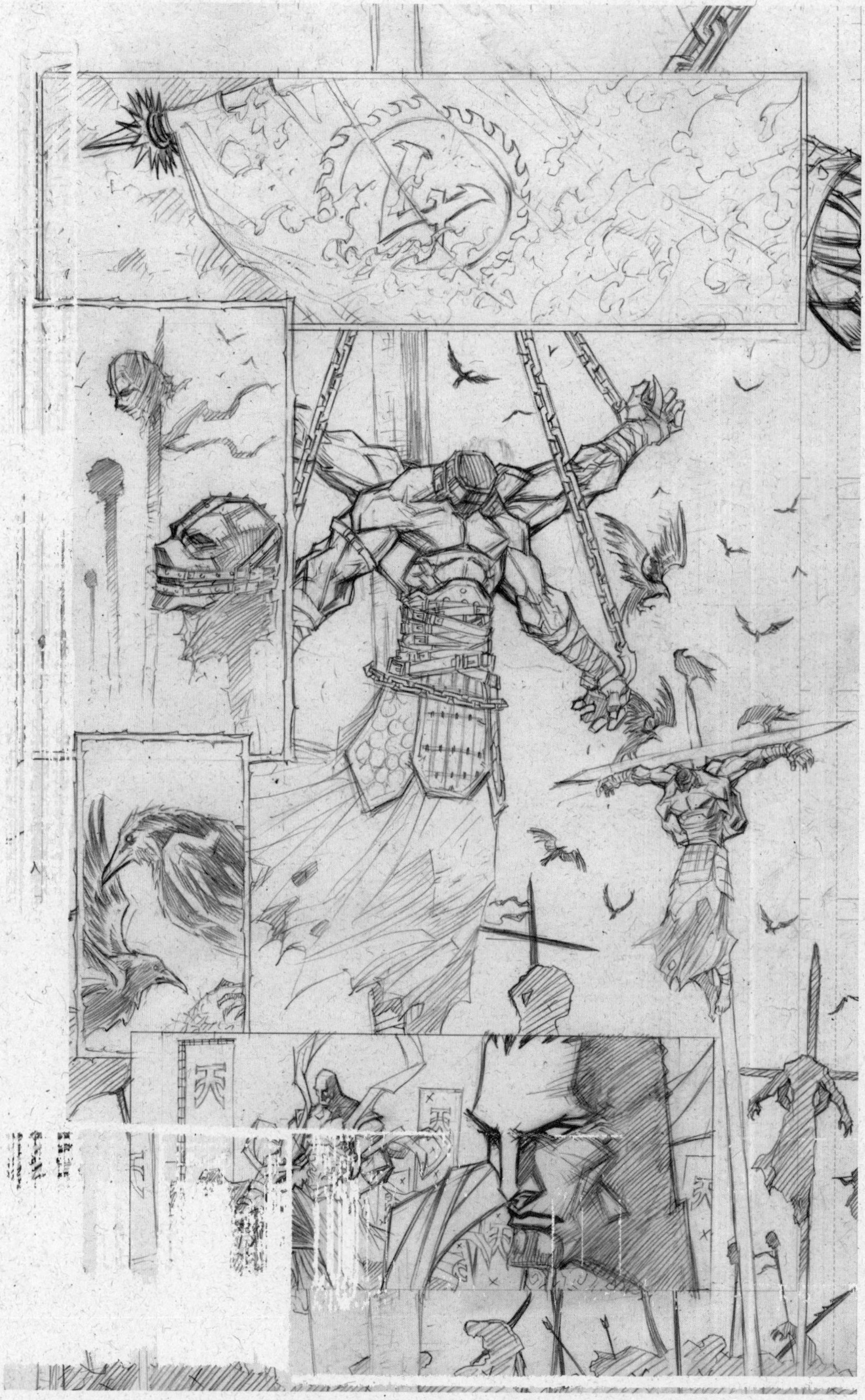

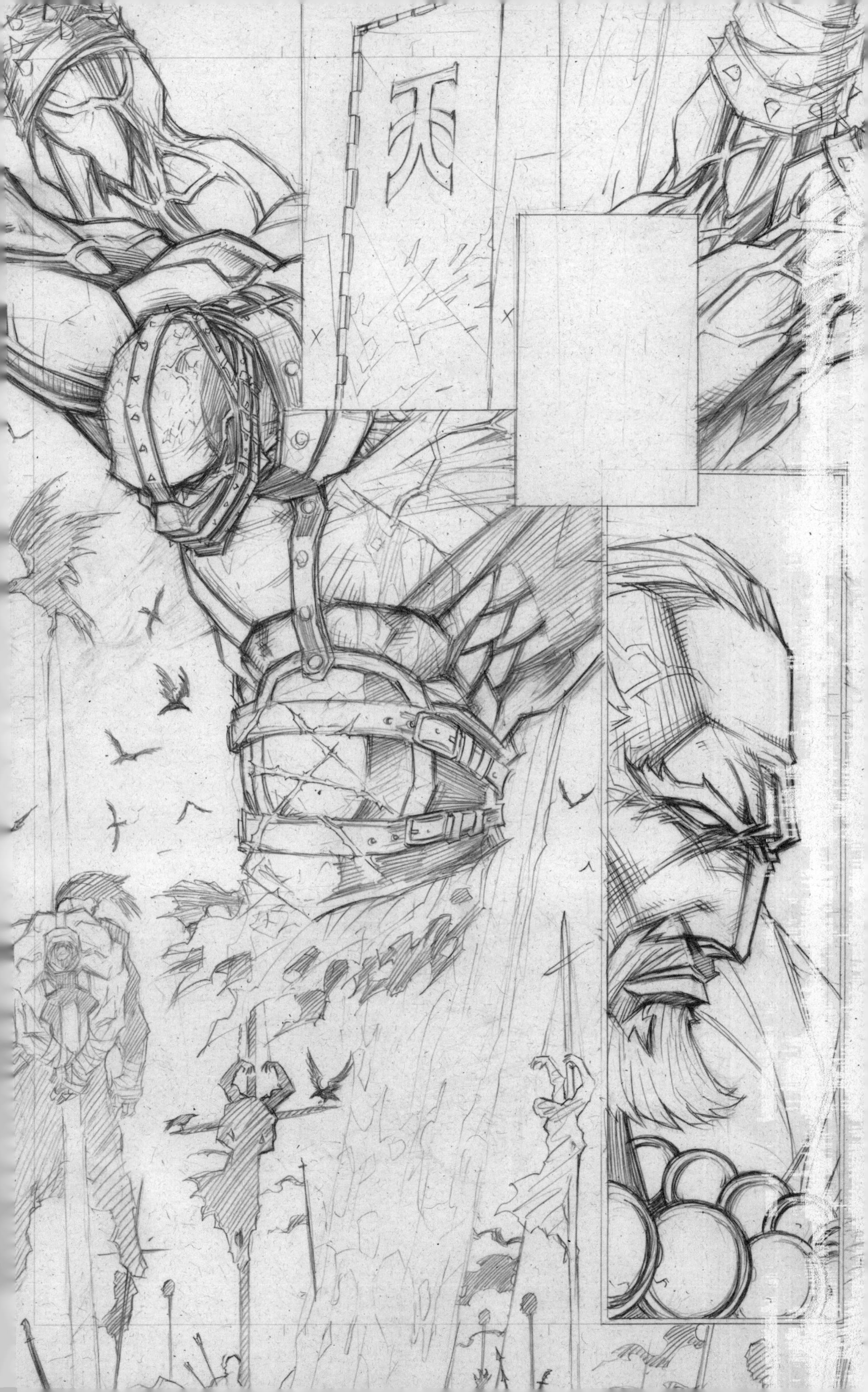
天

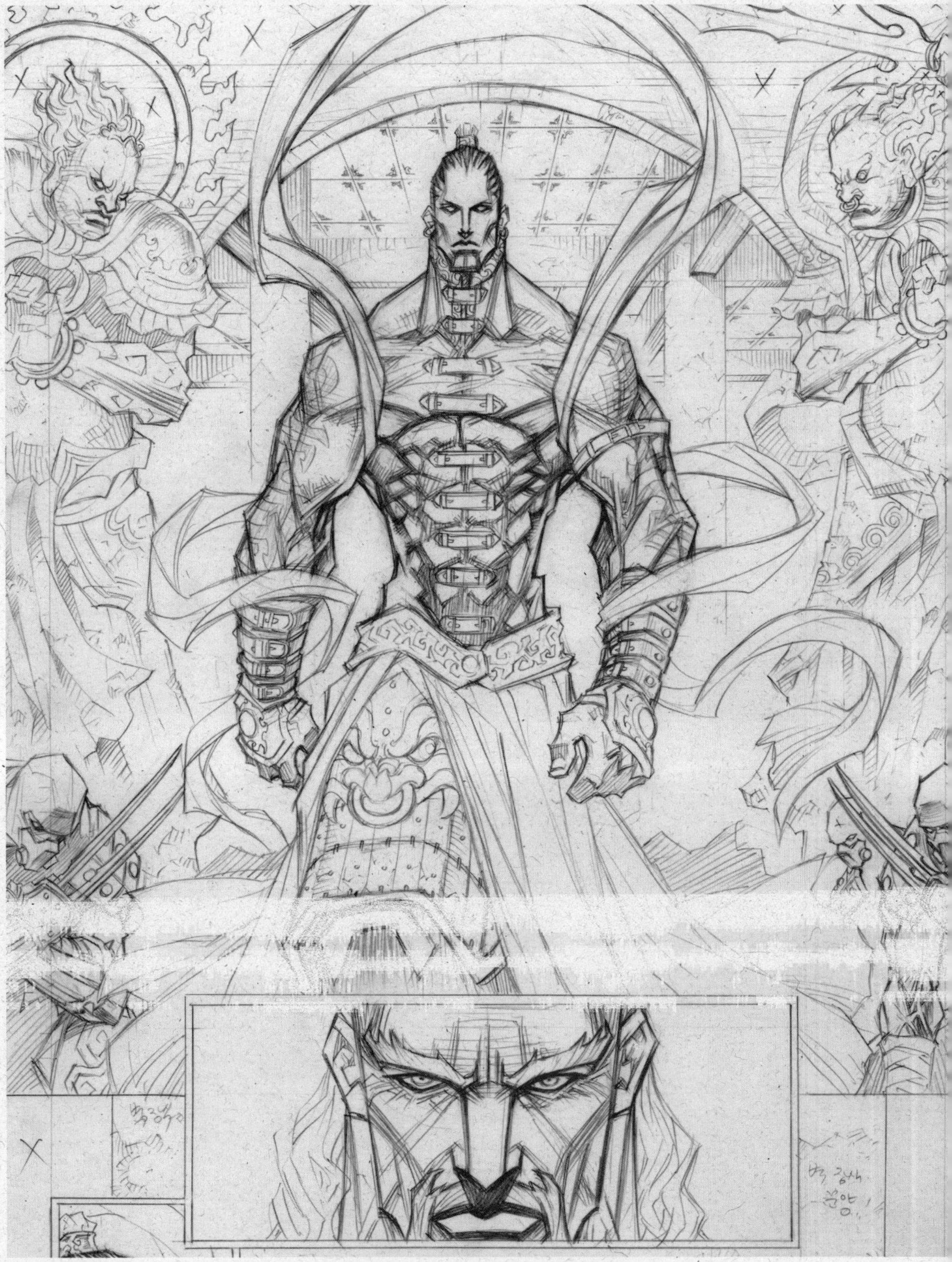

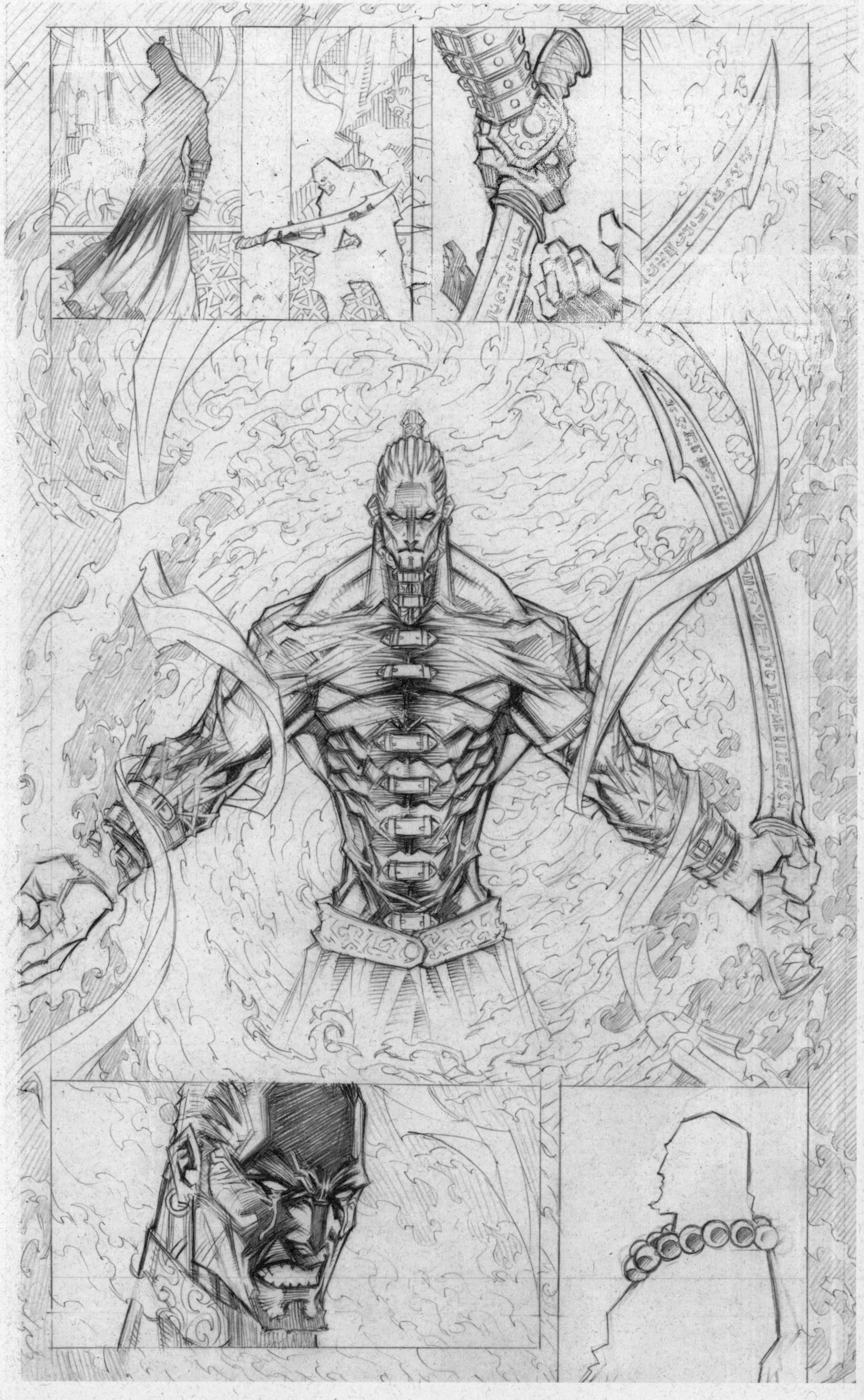

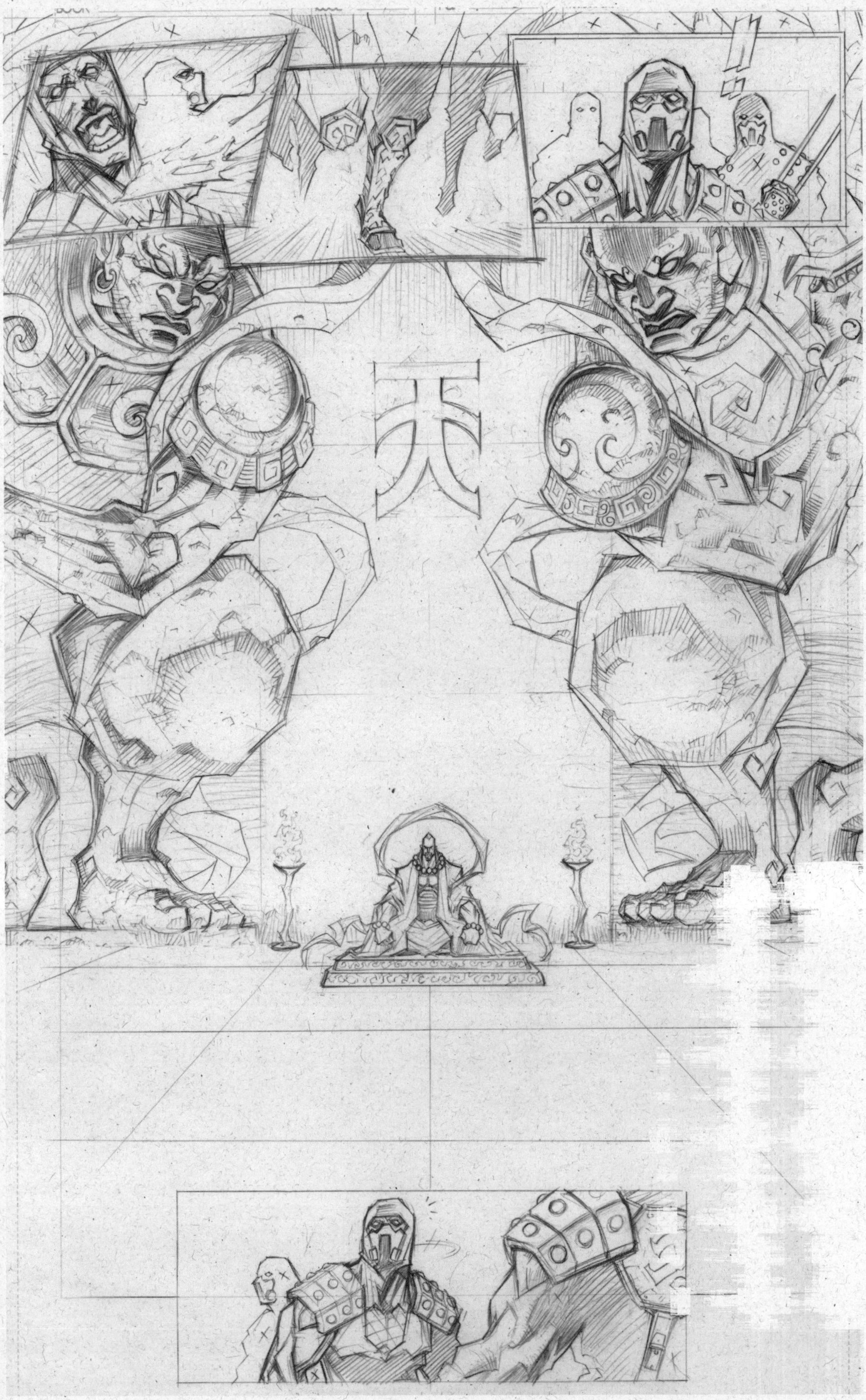
天

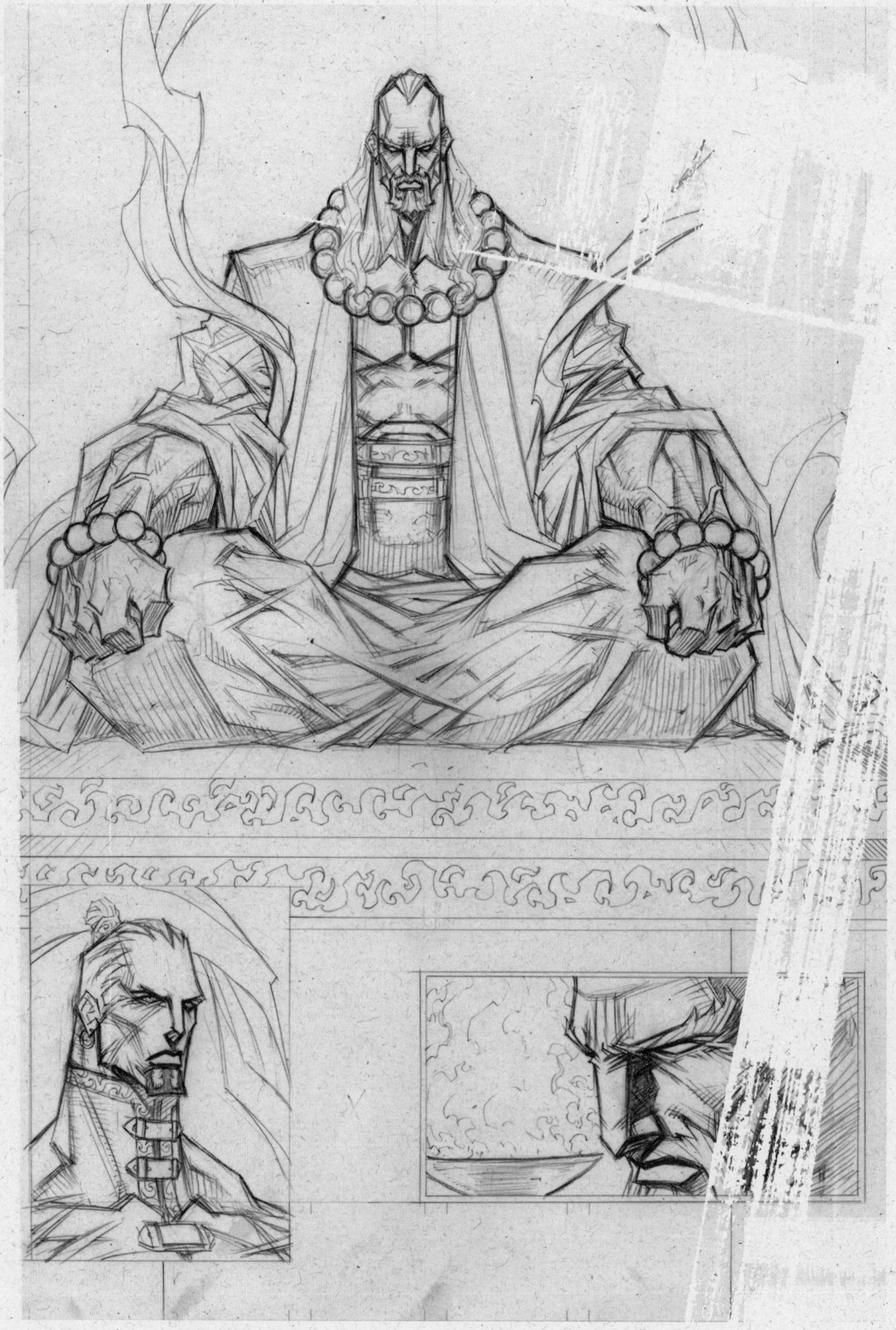

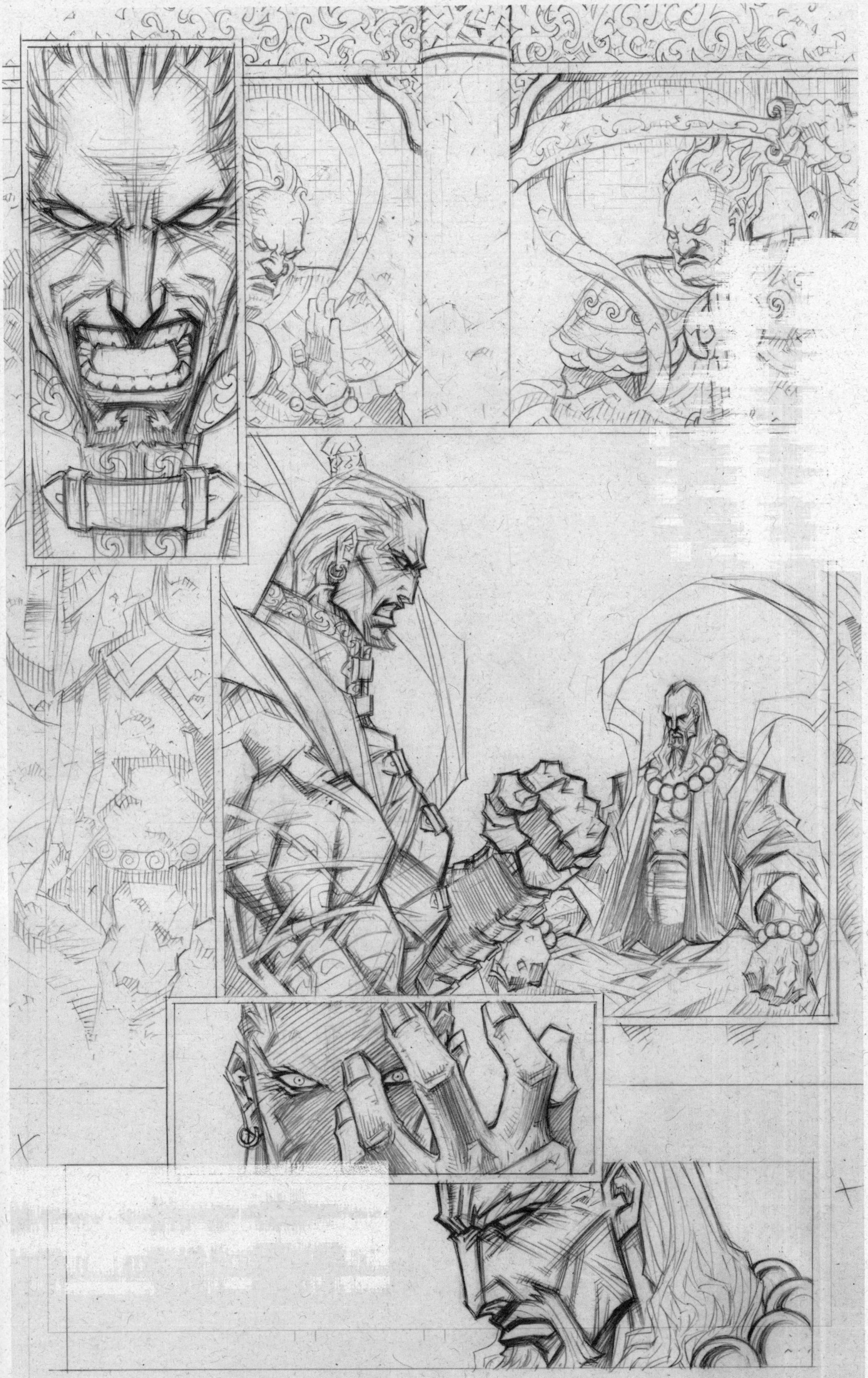

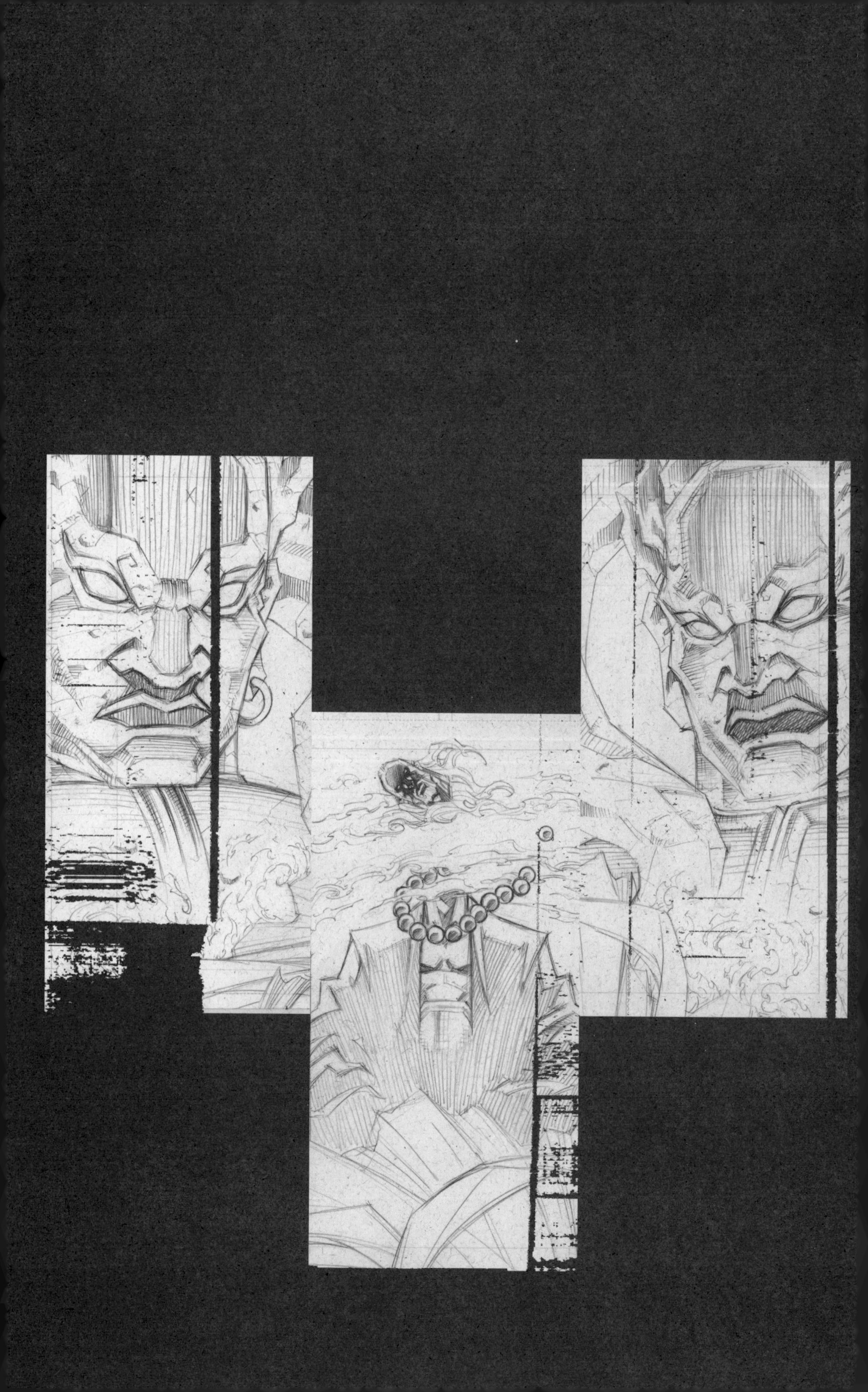

steel shadow hitman character

I have no memory of such things as names.

steel shadow 殺し屋キャラクター

名前などというものを覚えるための記憶力は無い。

Stahlschatten-Killer Character

An solche Dinge wie Namen kann
ich mich nicht erinnern.

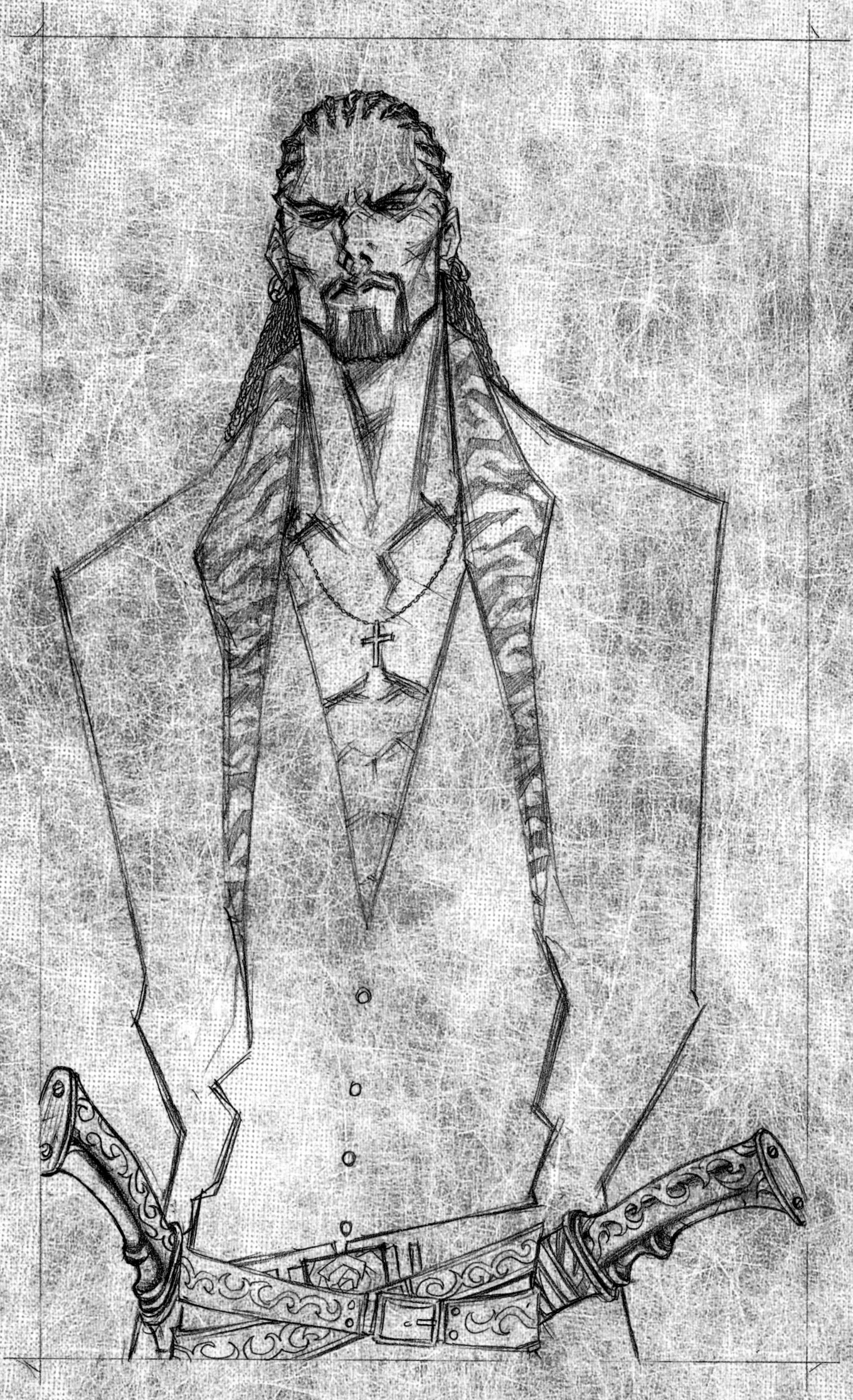

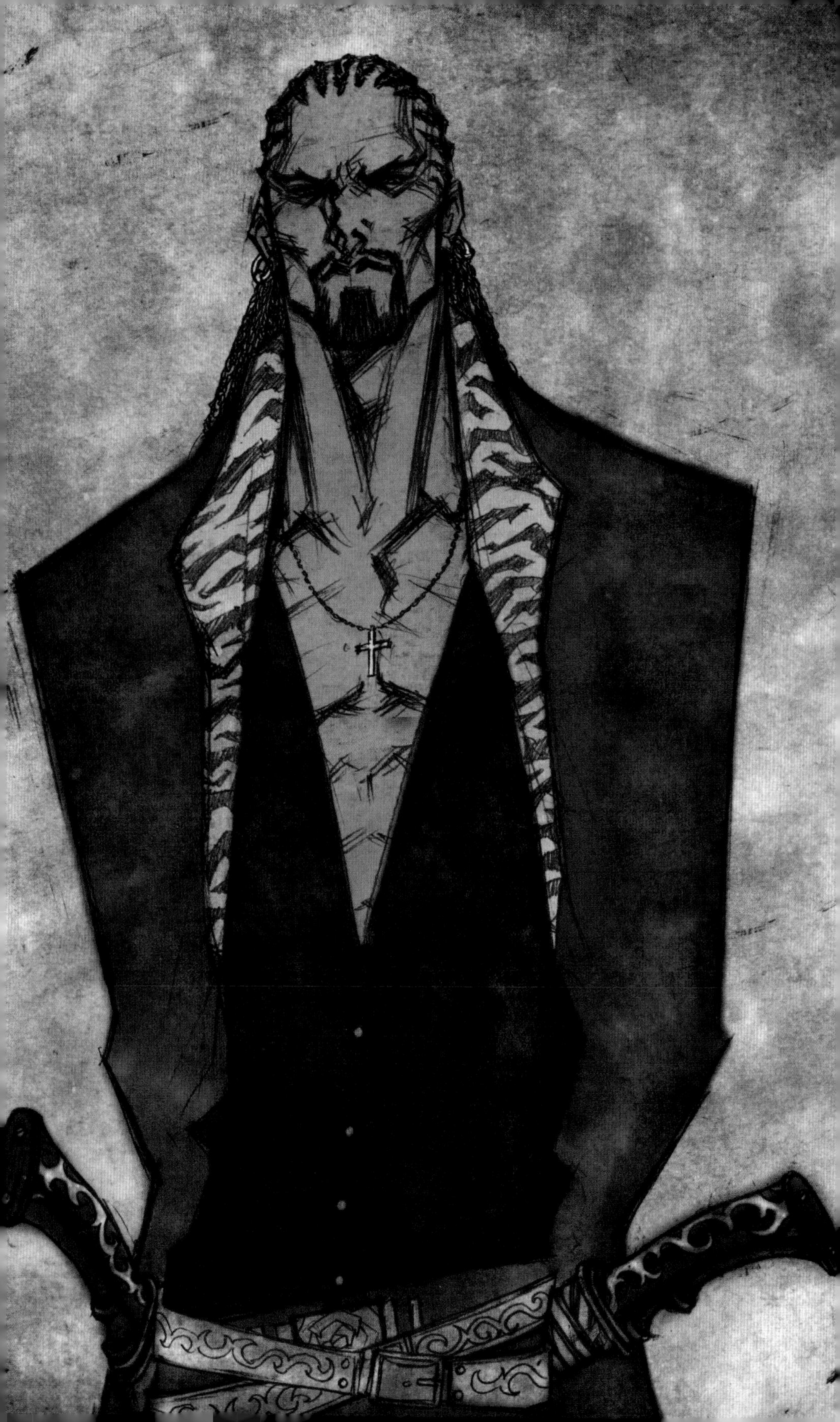

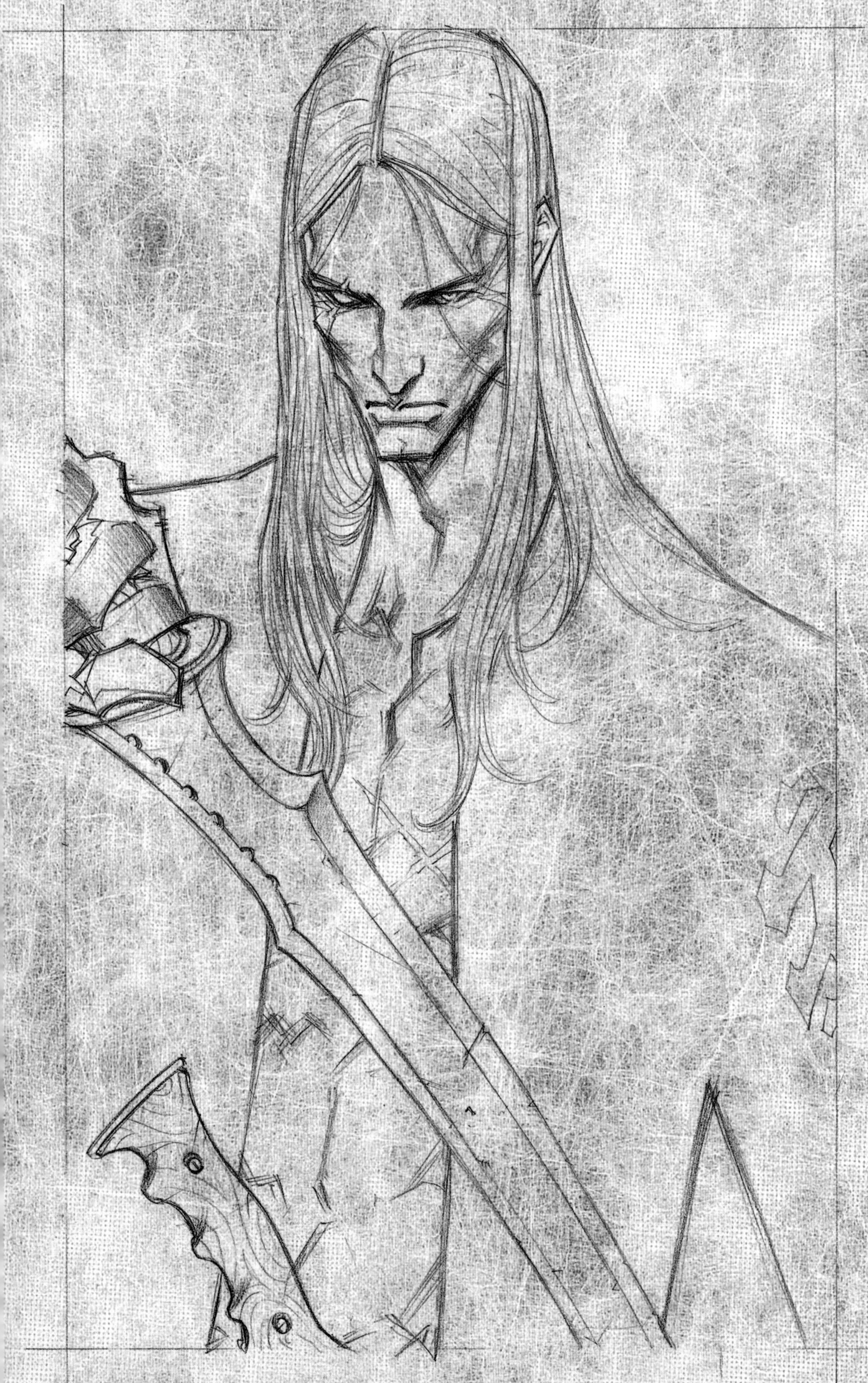

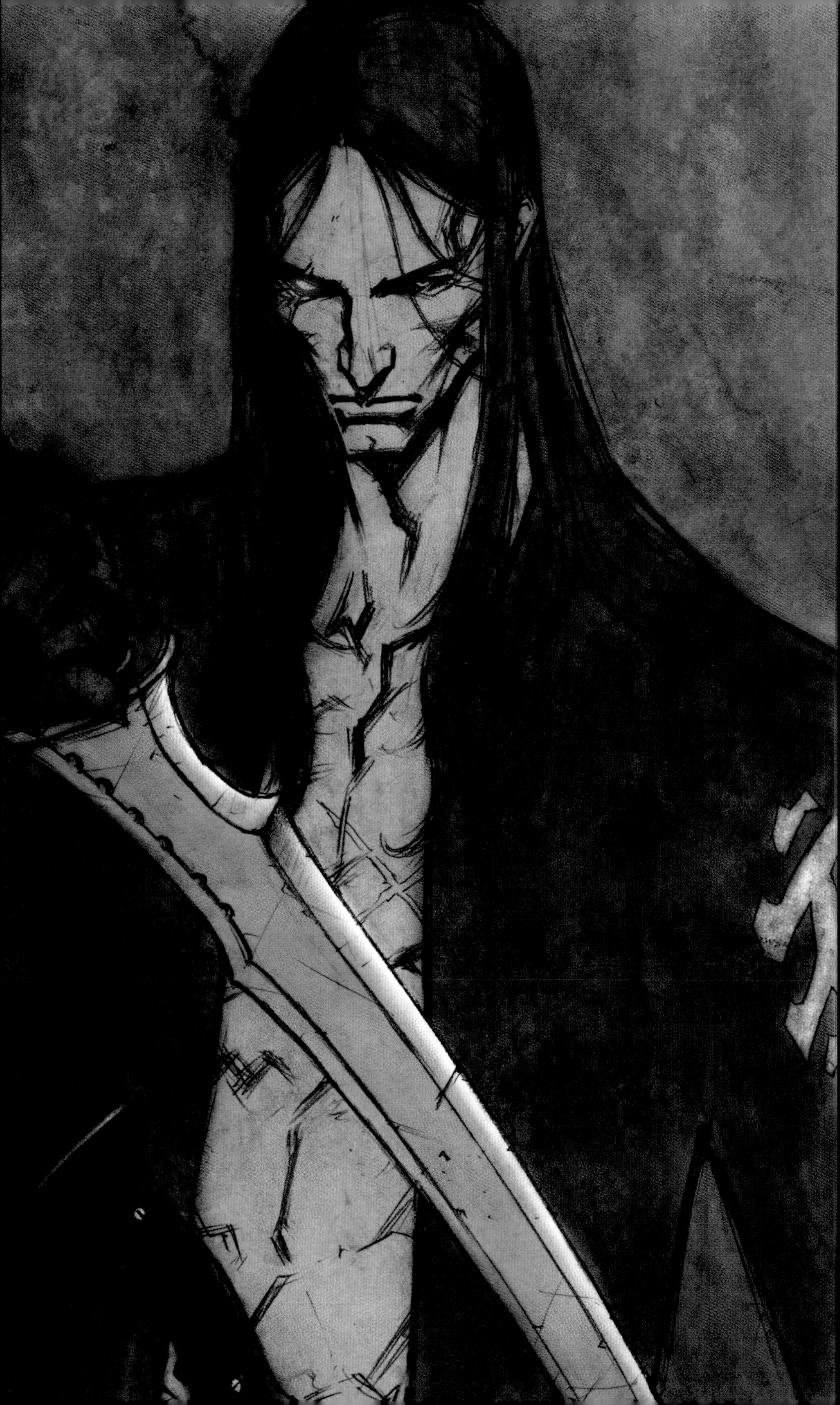

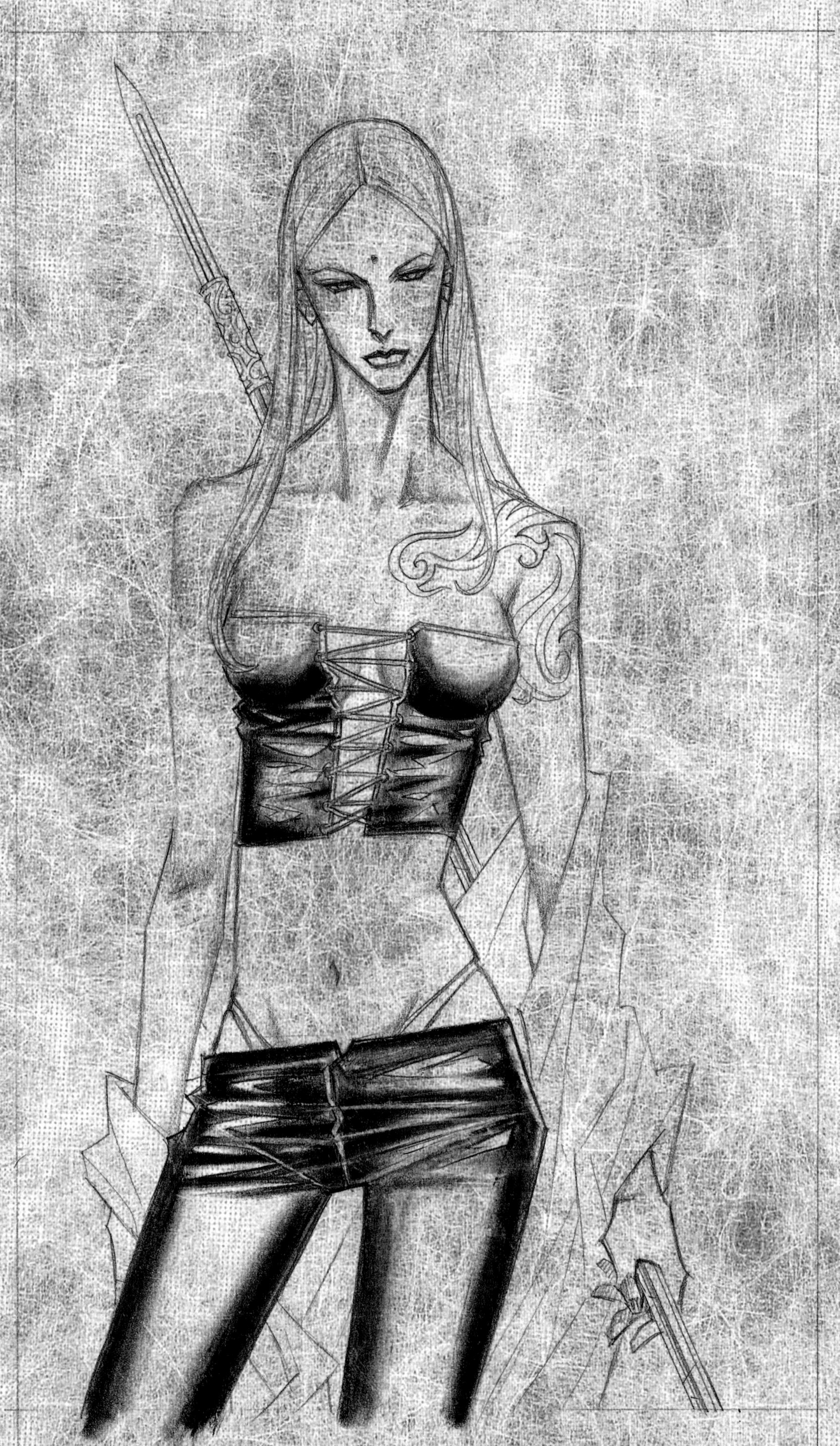

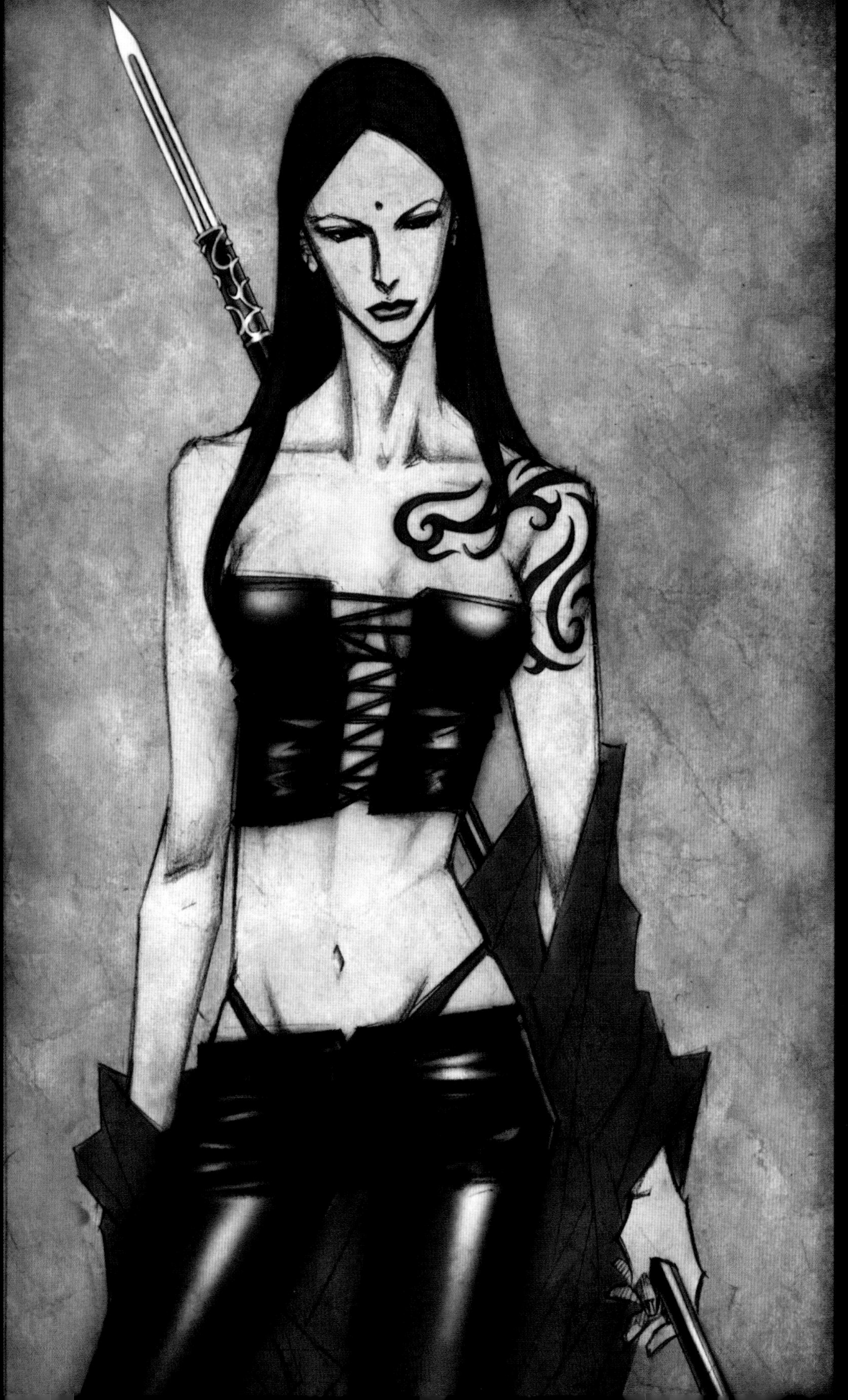

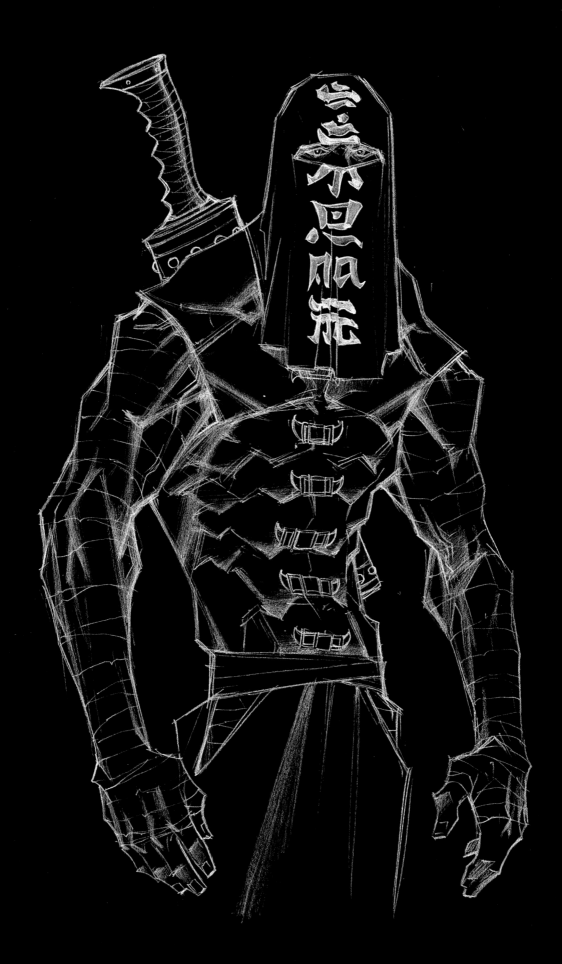

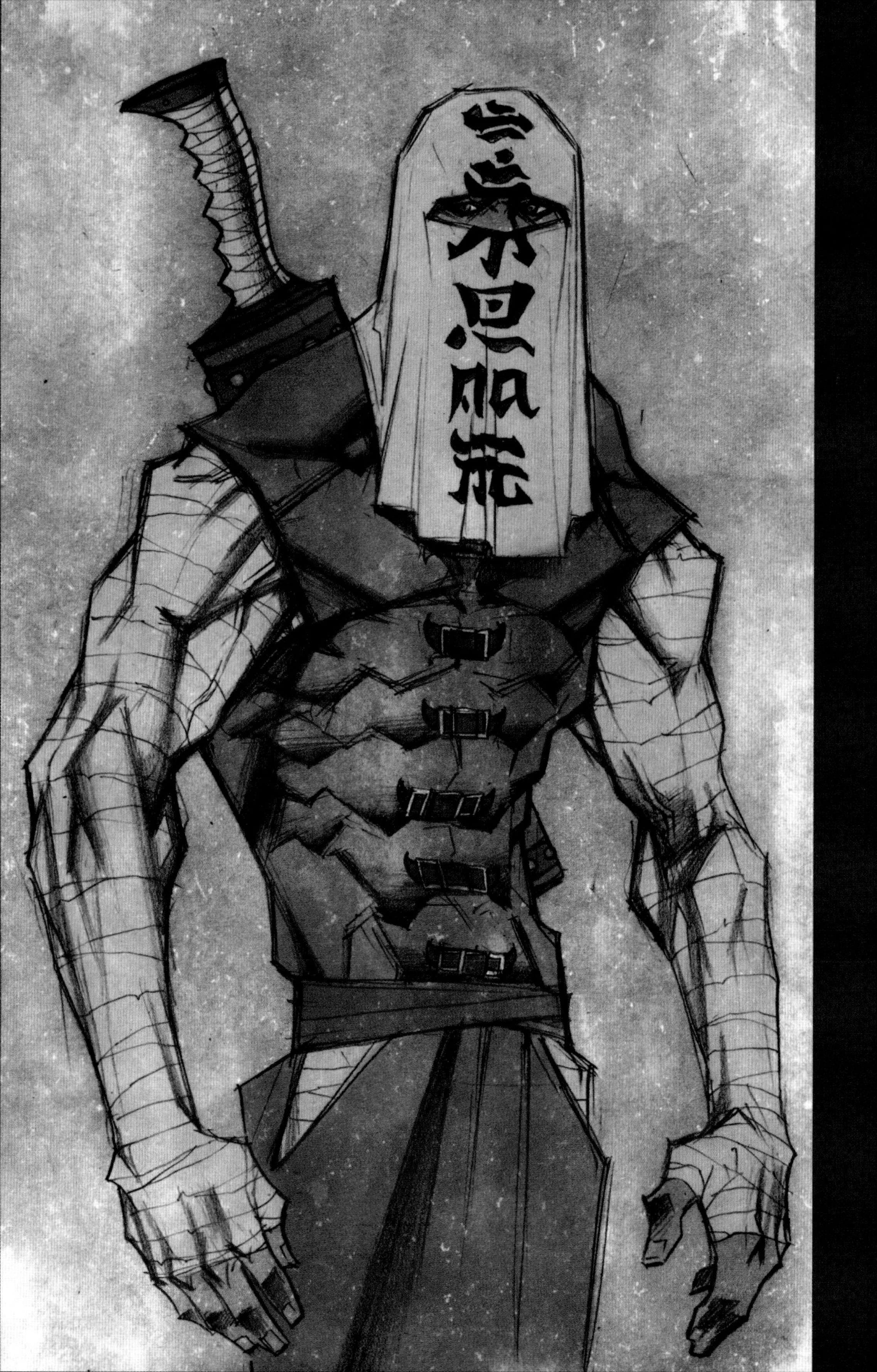

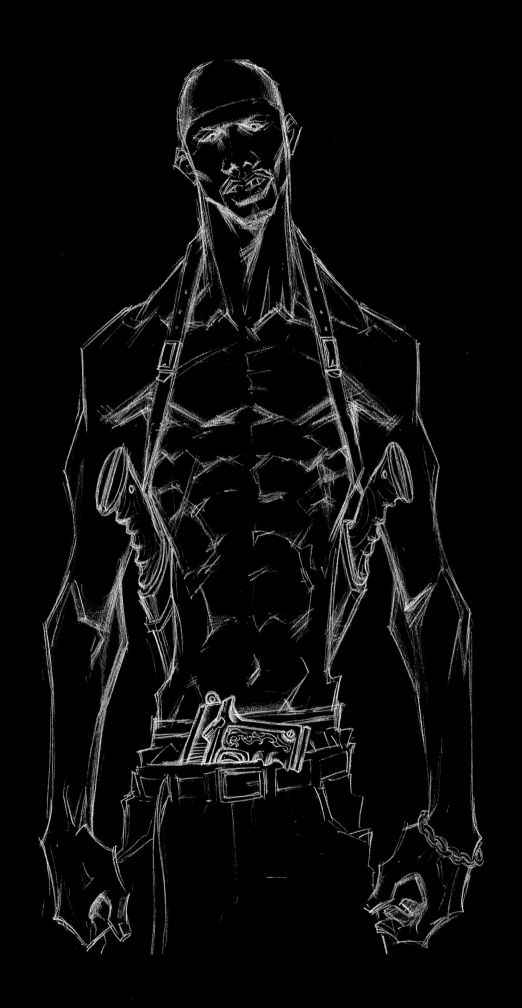

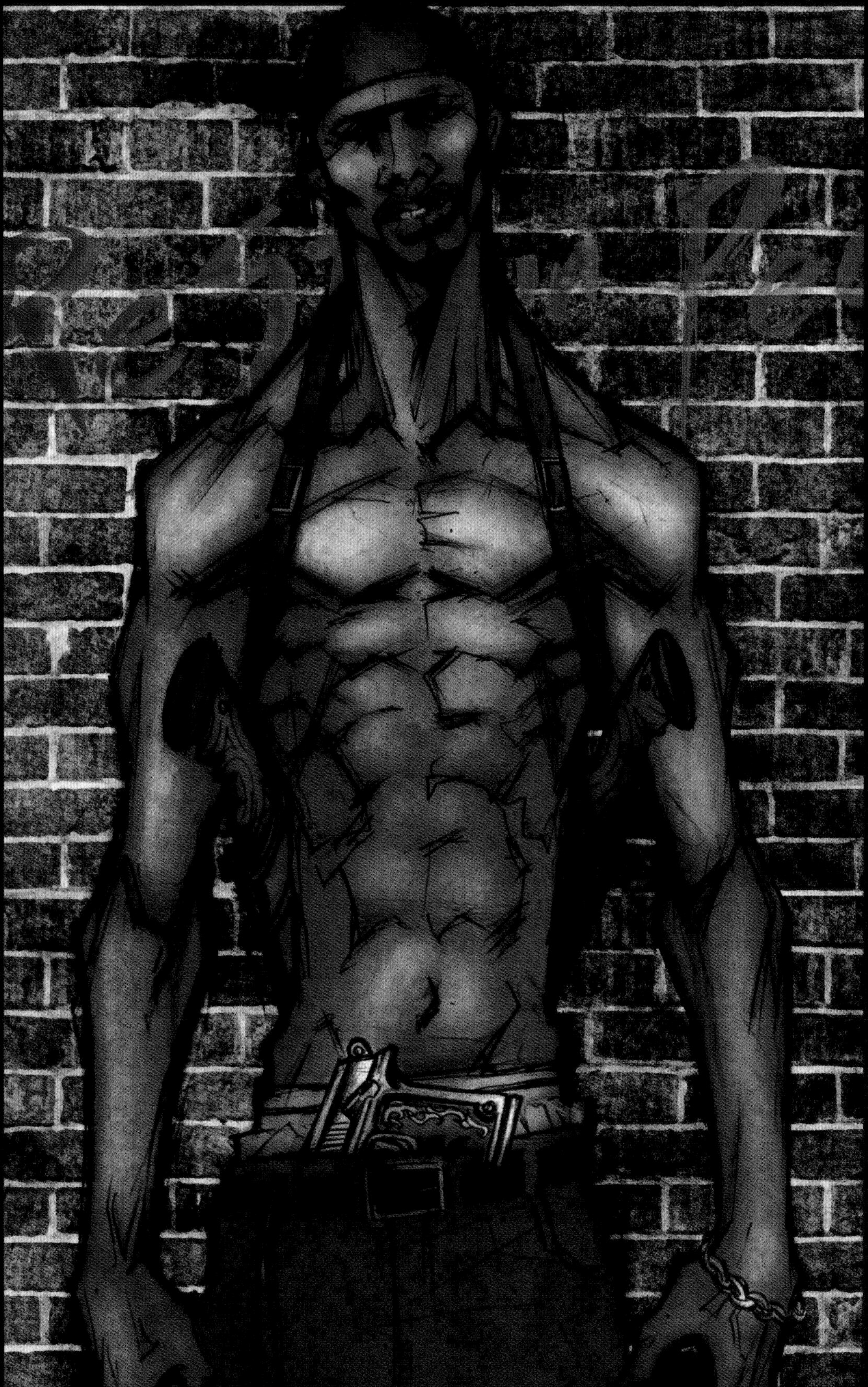

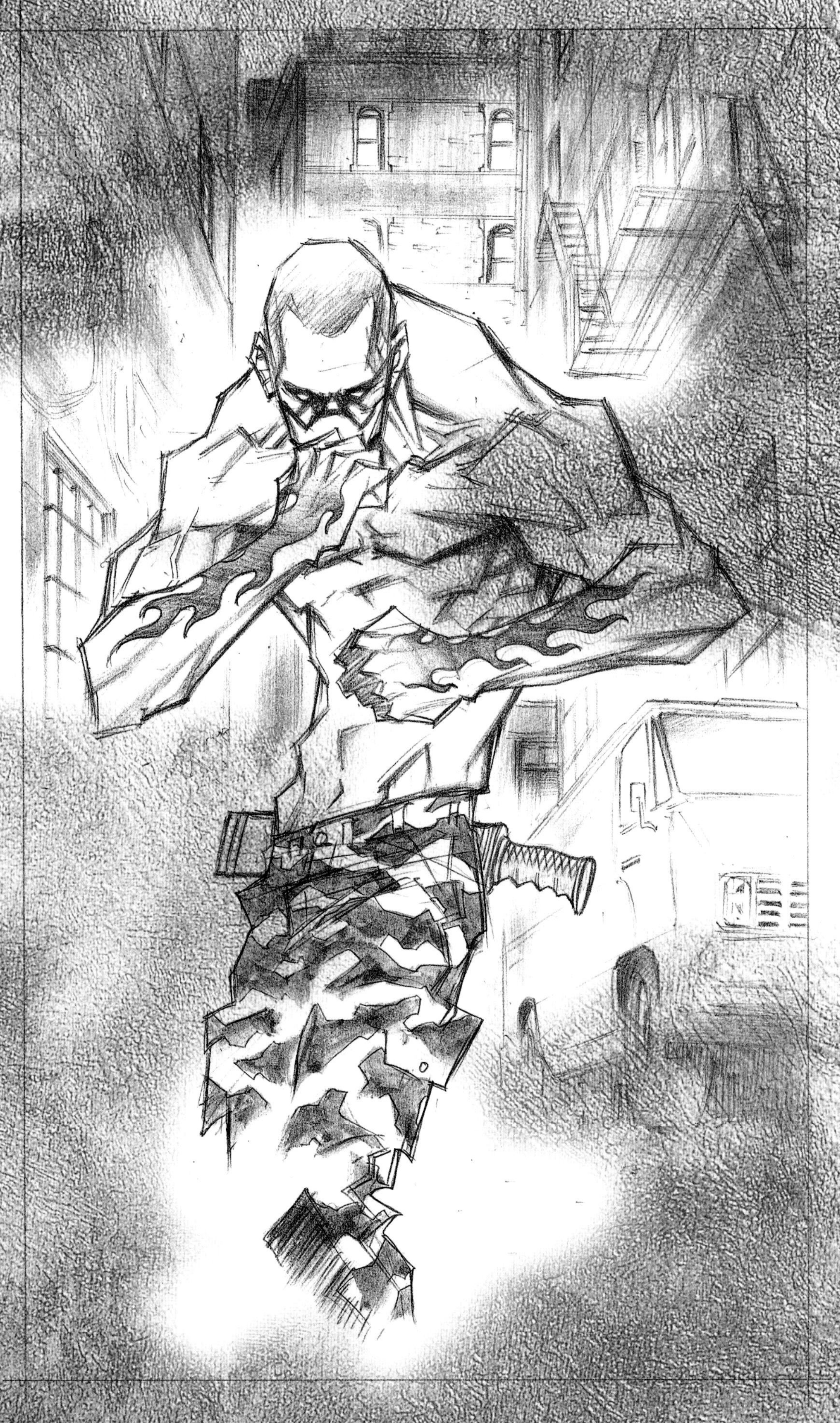

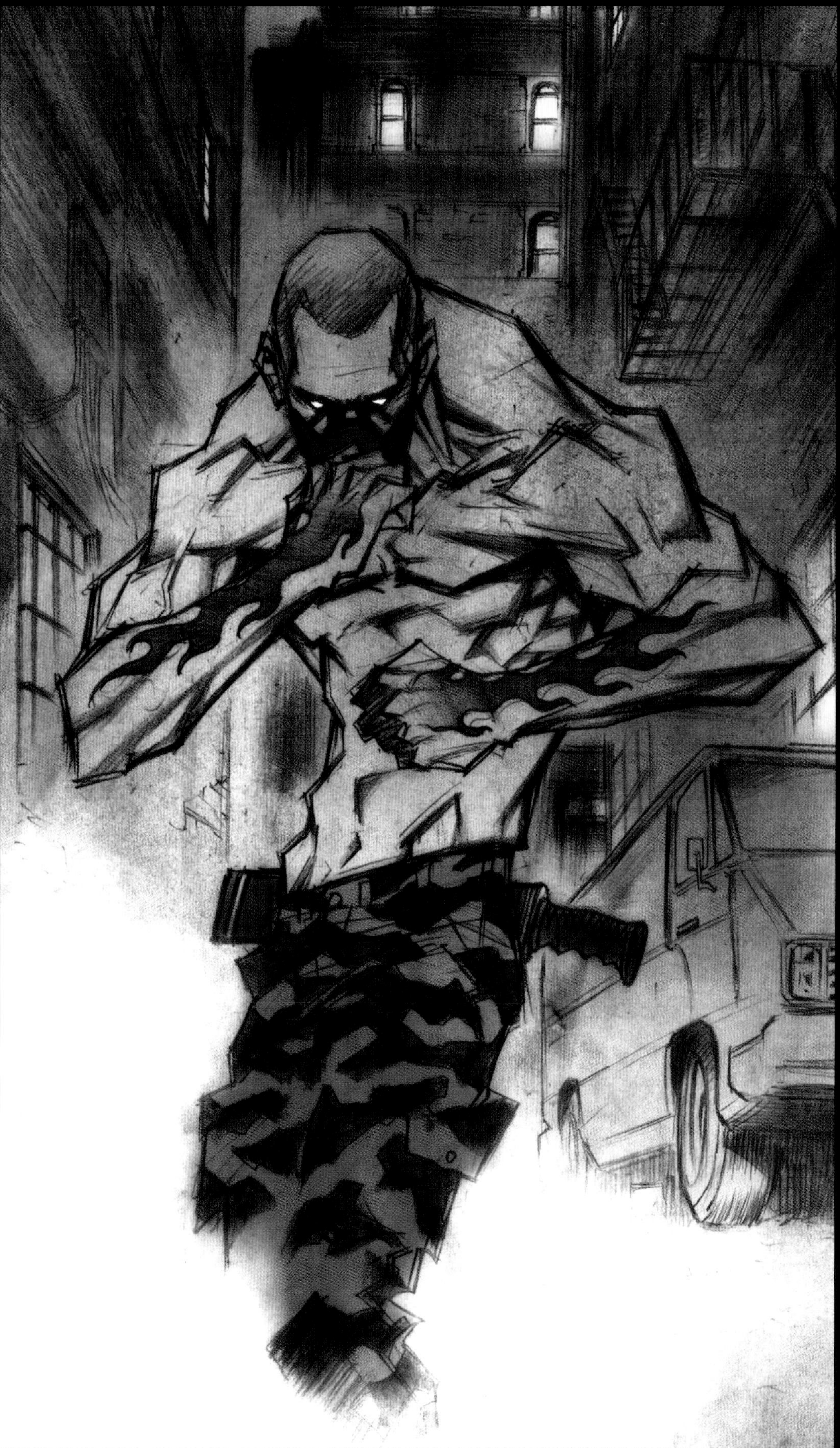

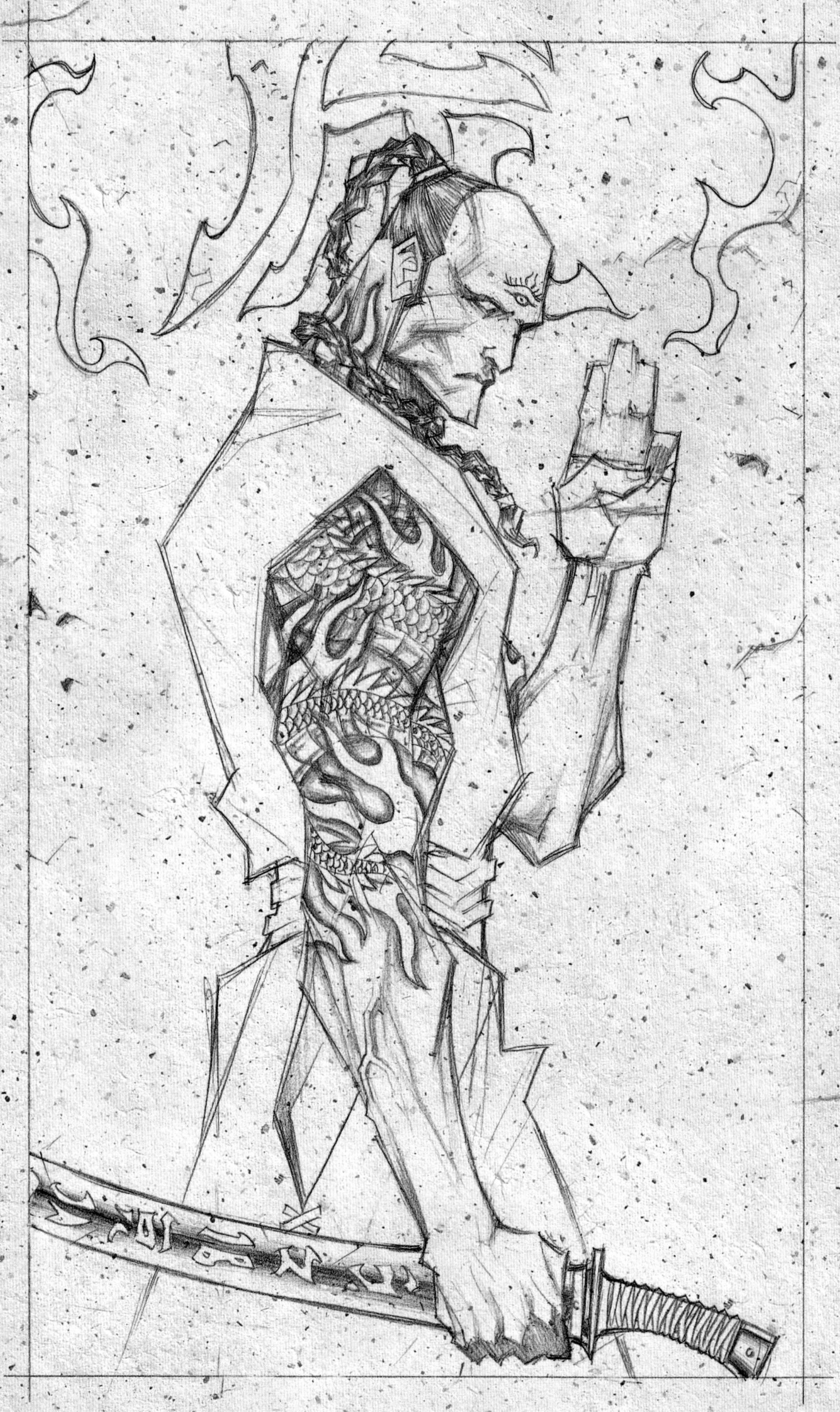

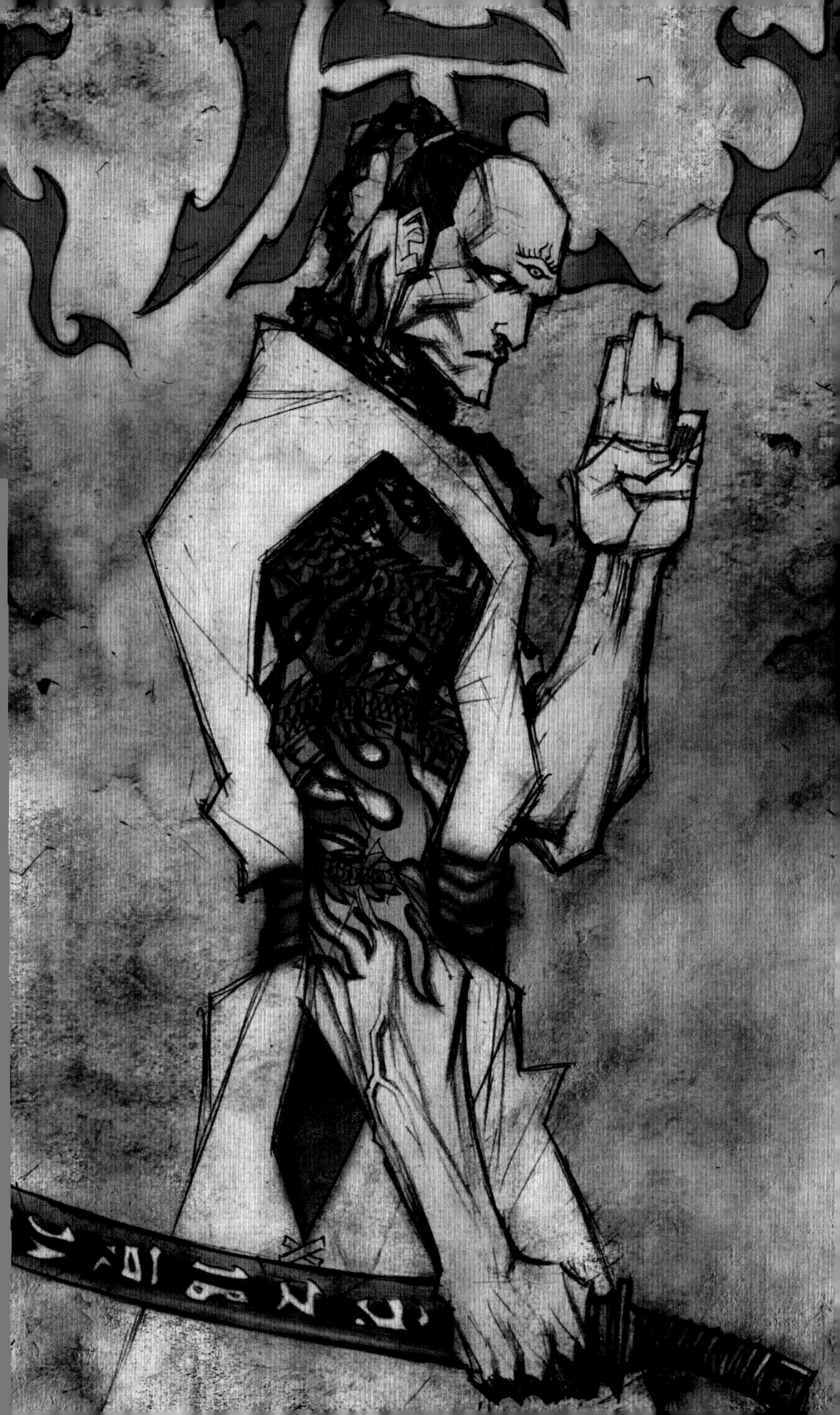

rough sketch

Your names,
    like all those that have gone before, will soon
disappear from memory.

下絵
君の名前も、過去の人々
    と同じように、すぐに記憶から無く
なるだろう。

Handskizze

Eure Namen werden wie alle,
    die vor euch gingen, bald aus
meinem Gedächtnis verschwinden.

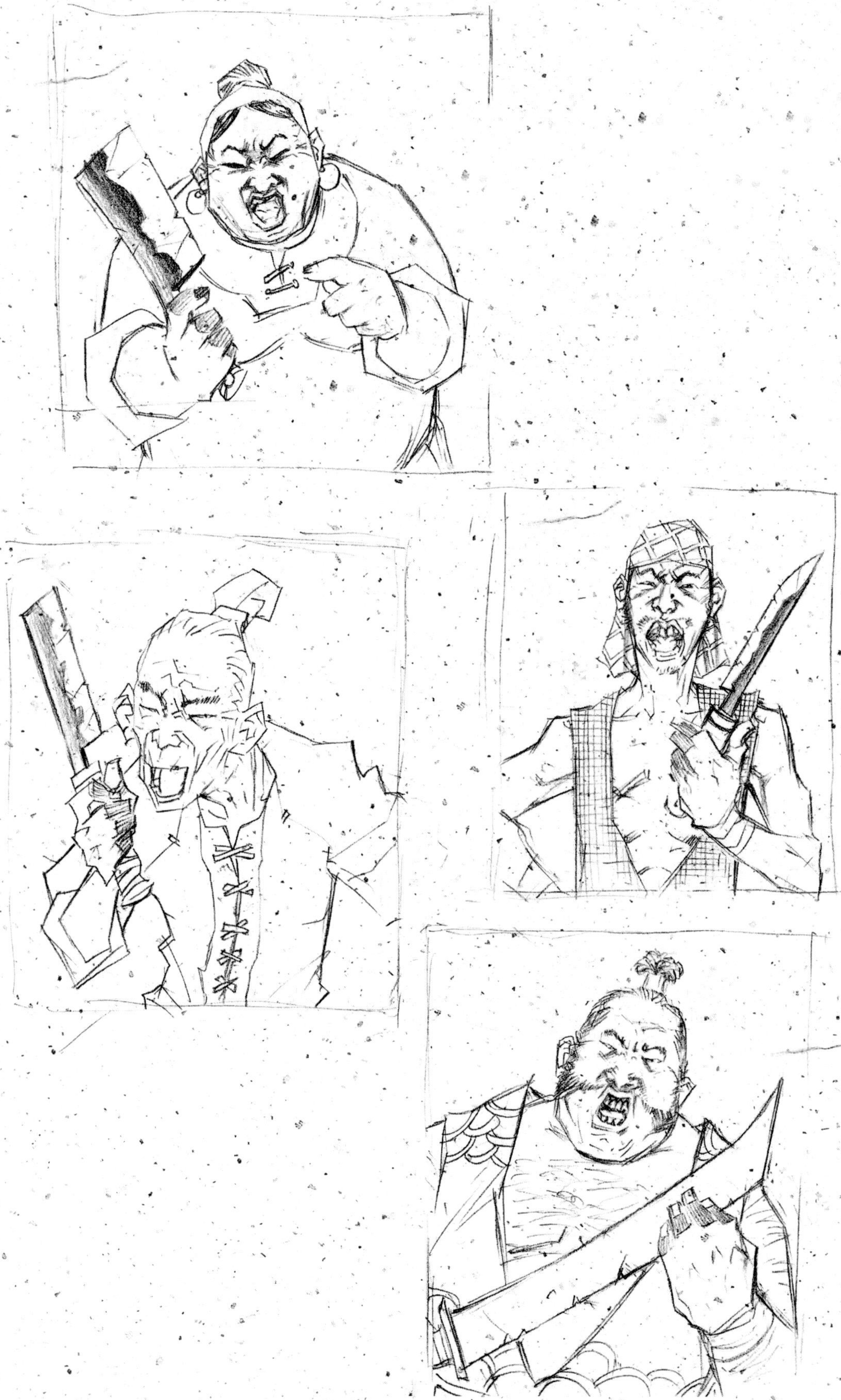

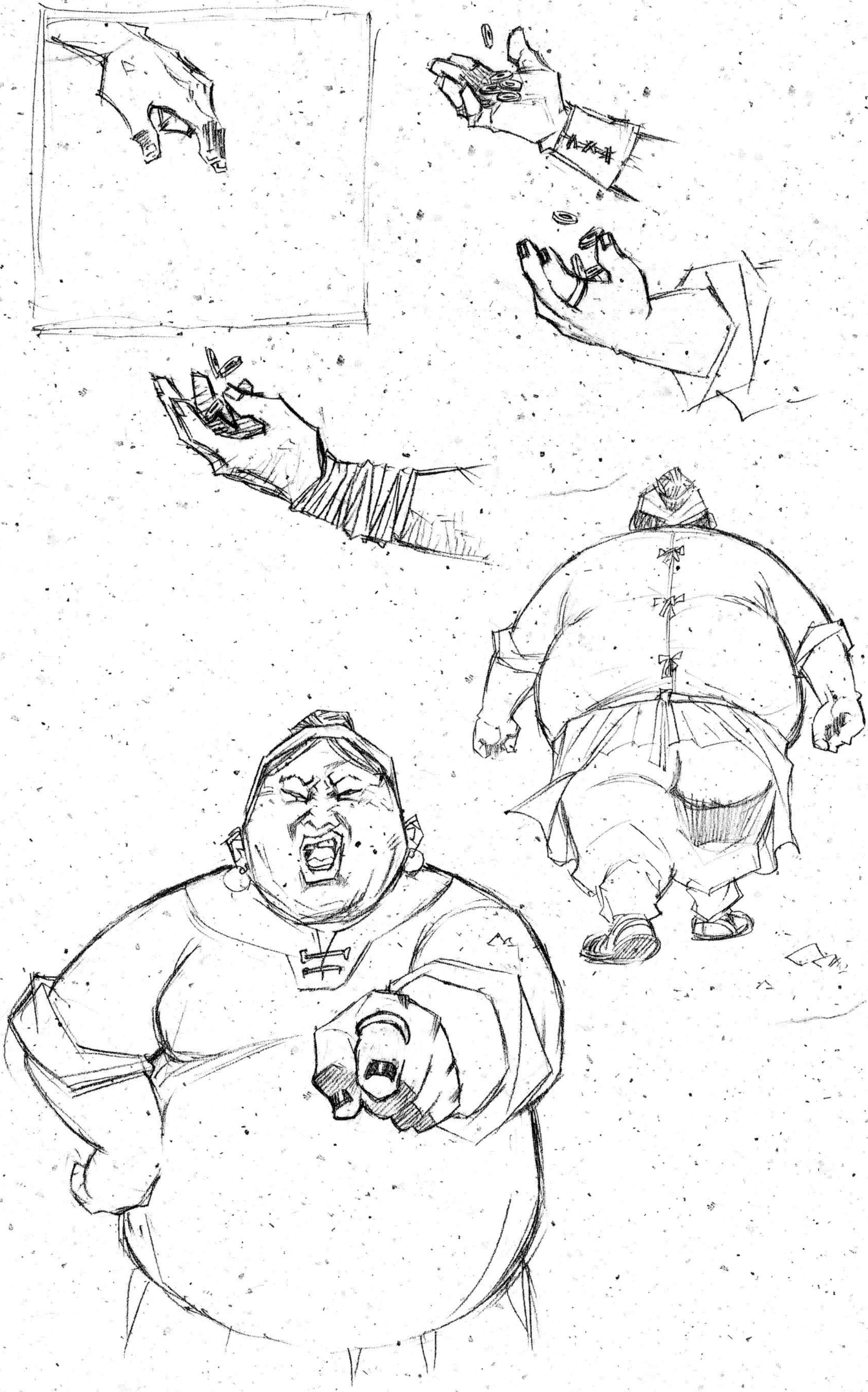

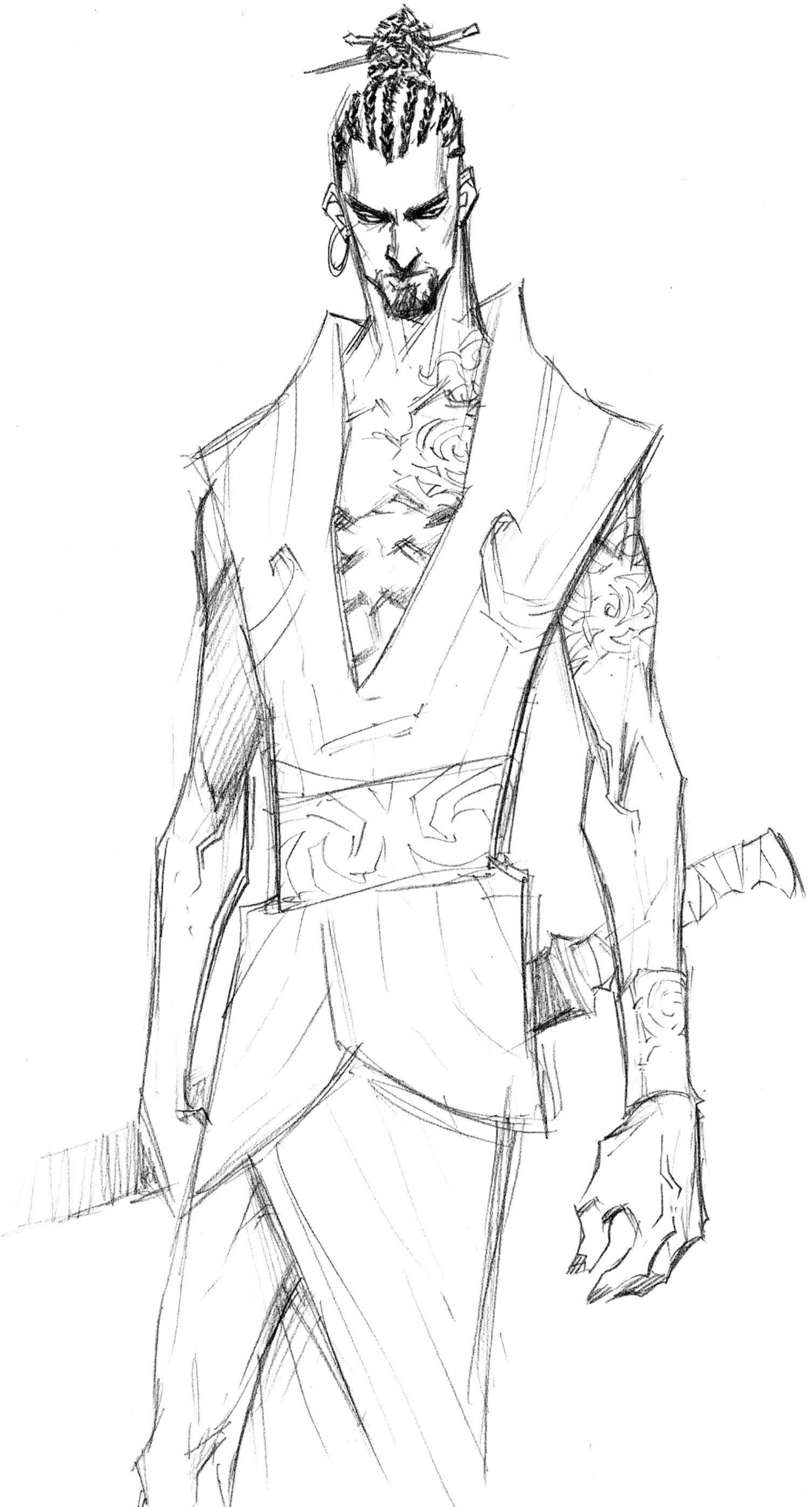

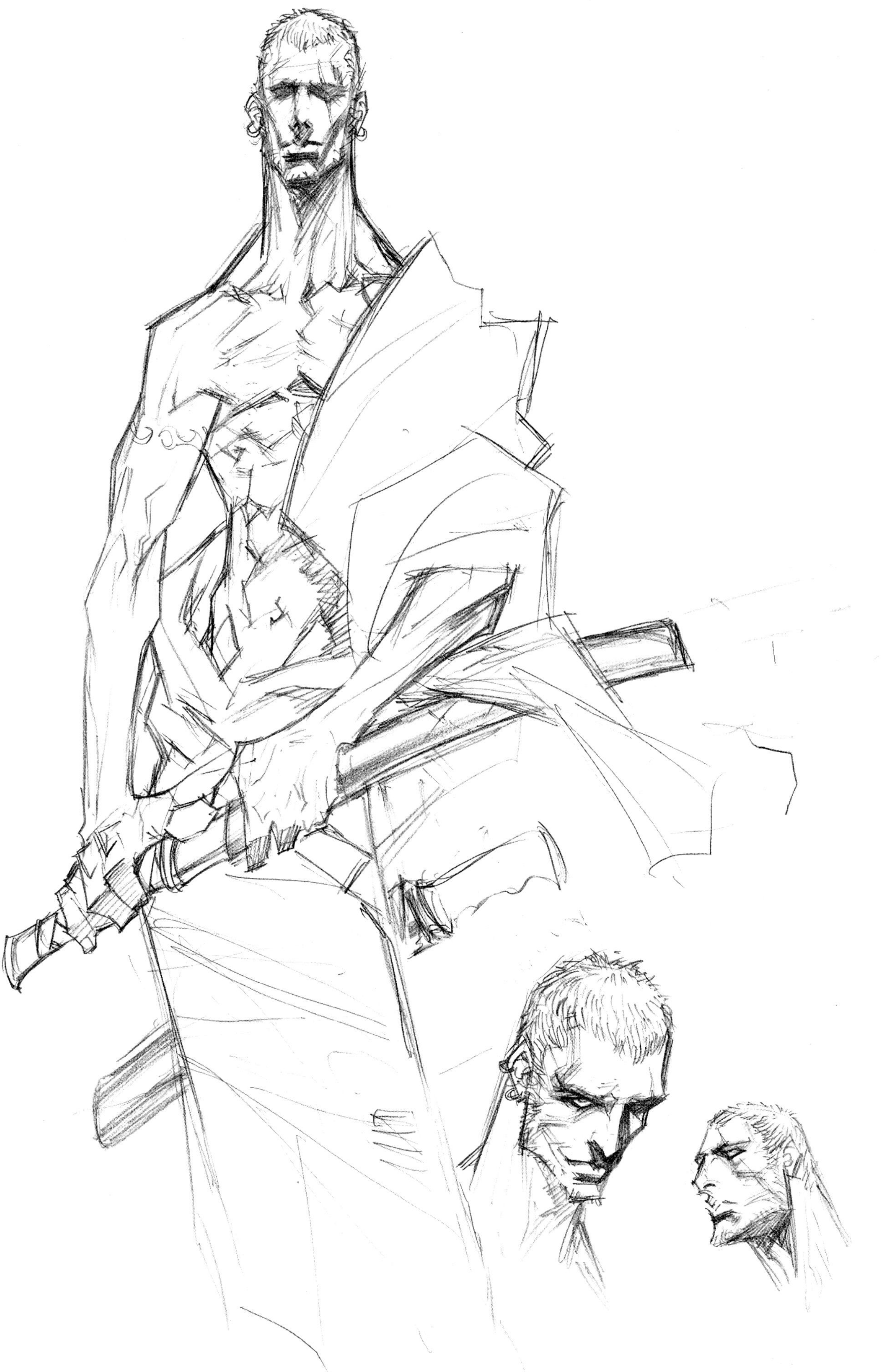

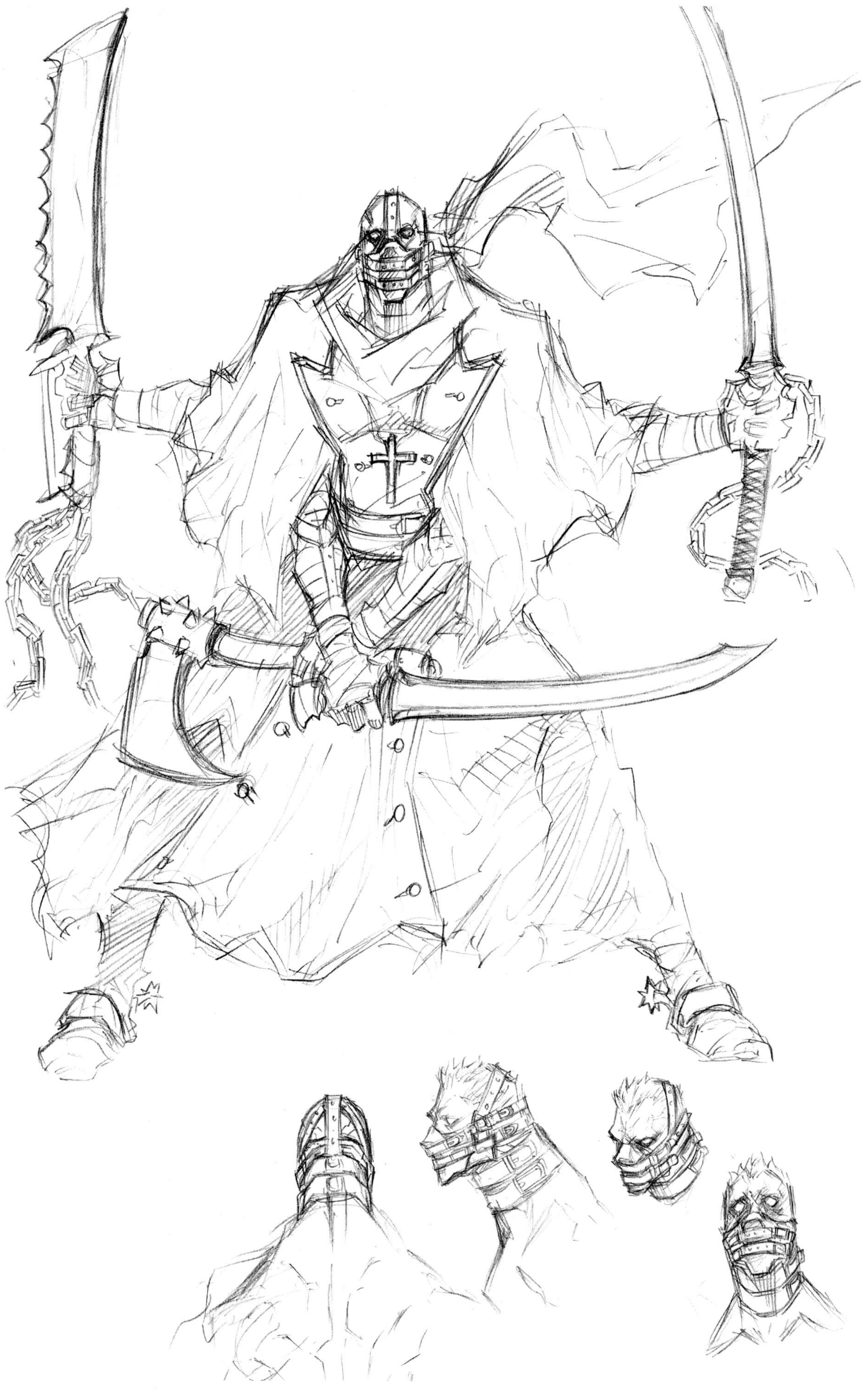

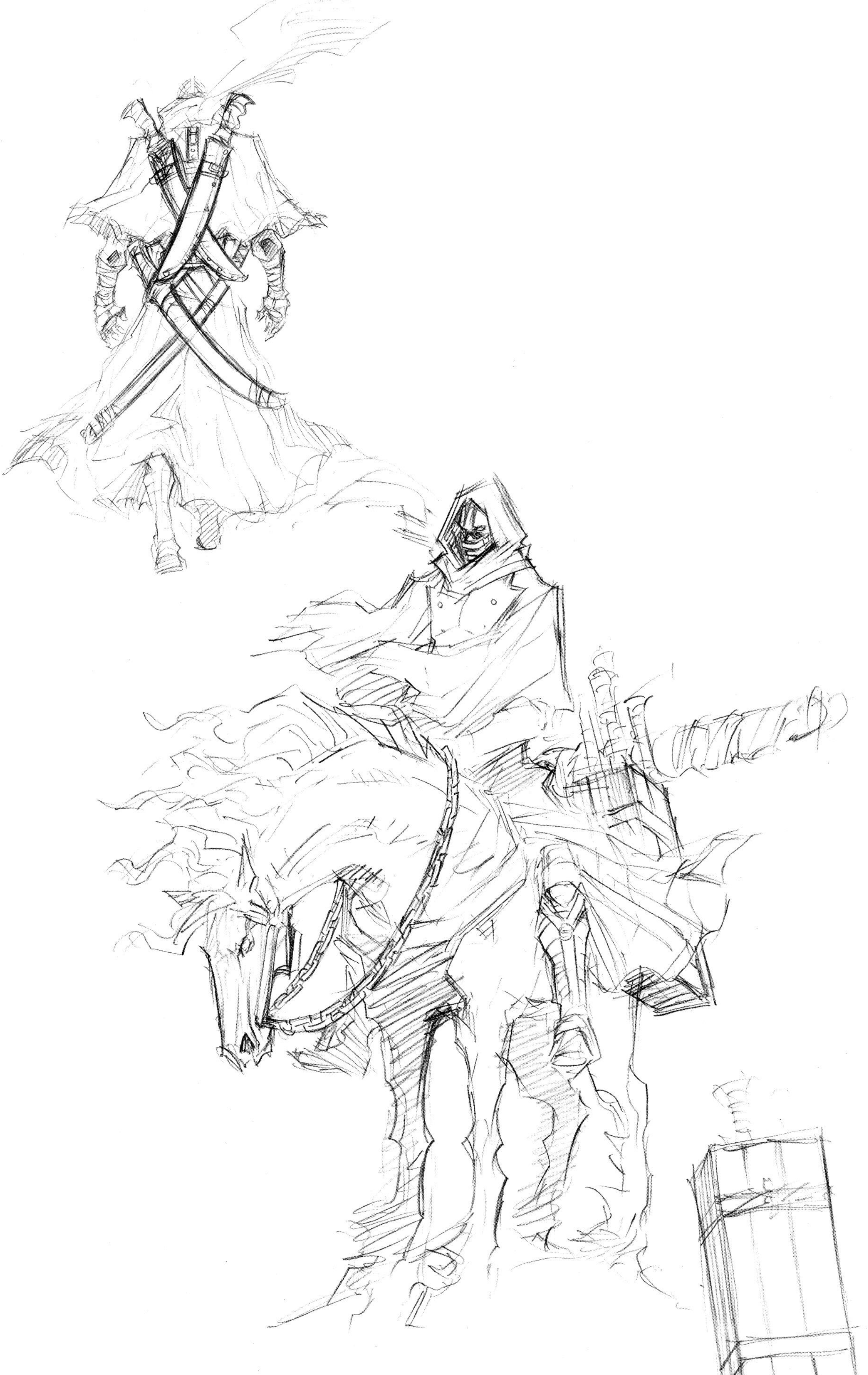

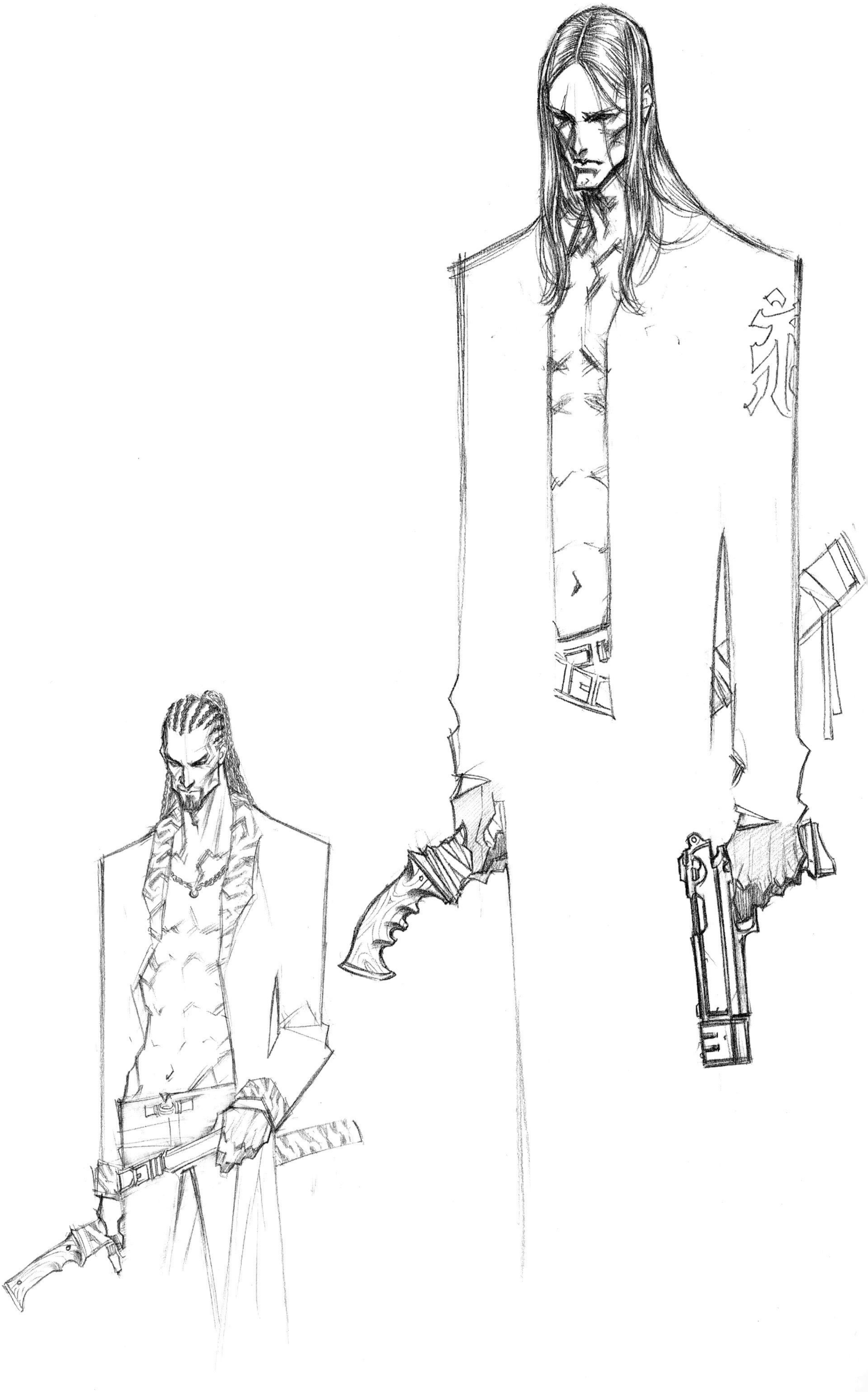

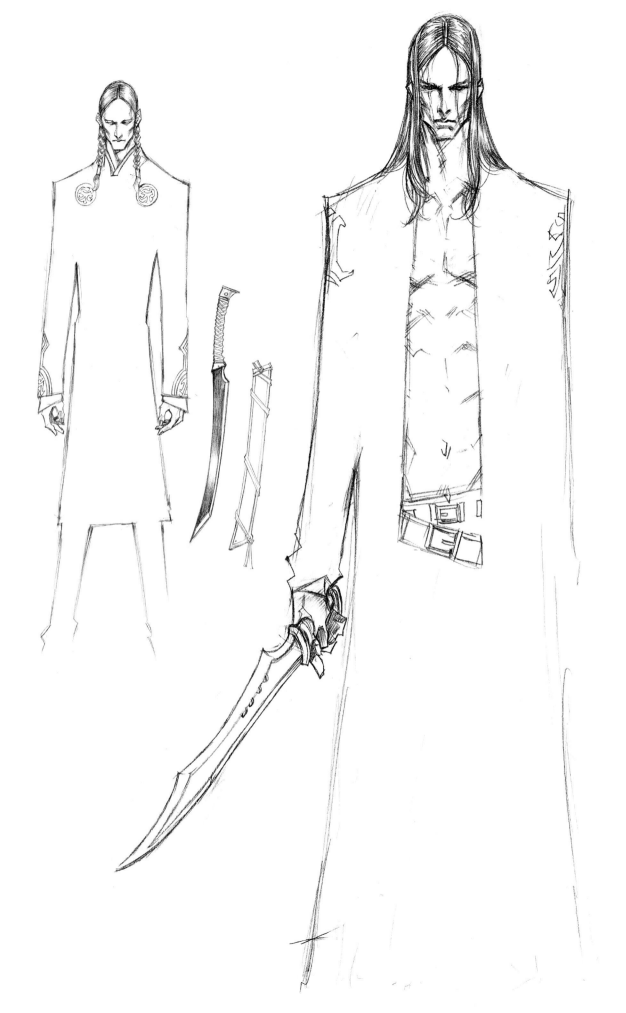

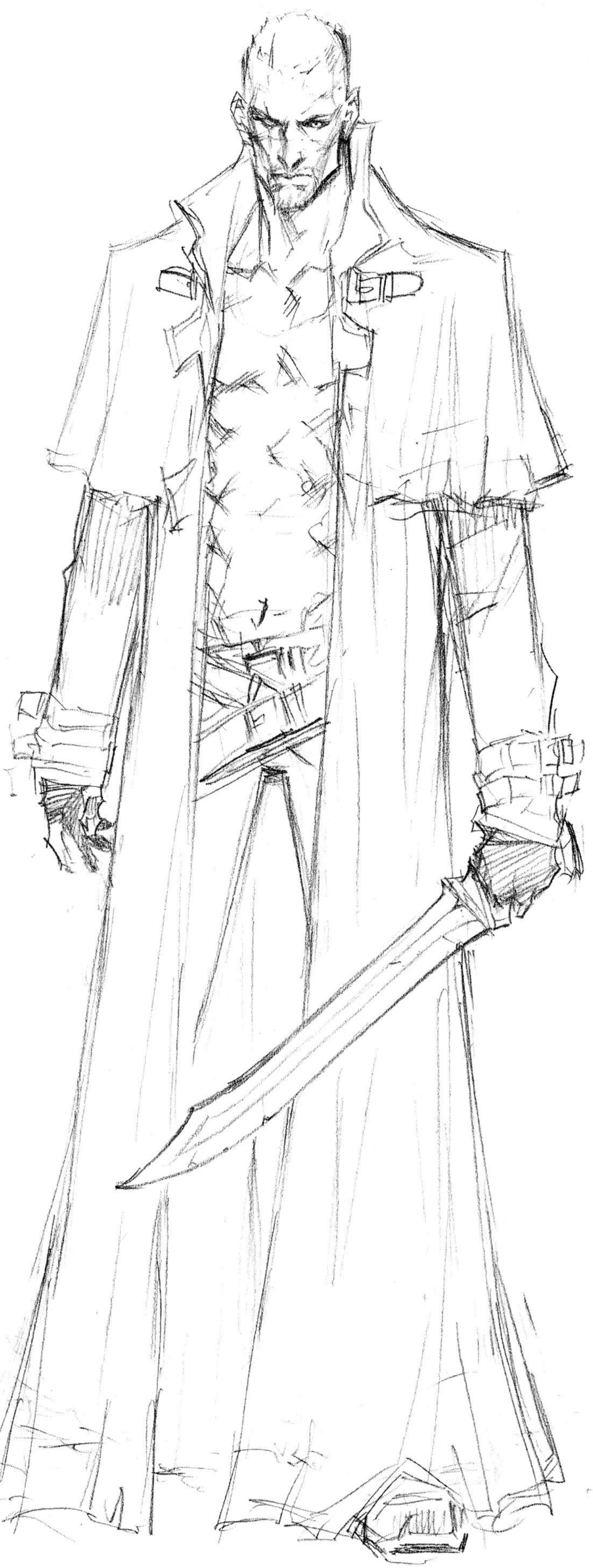

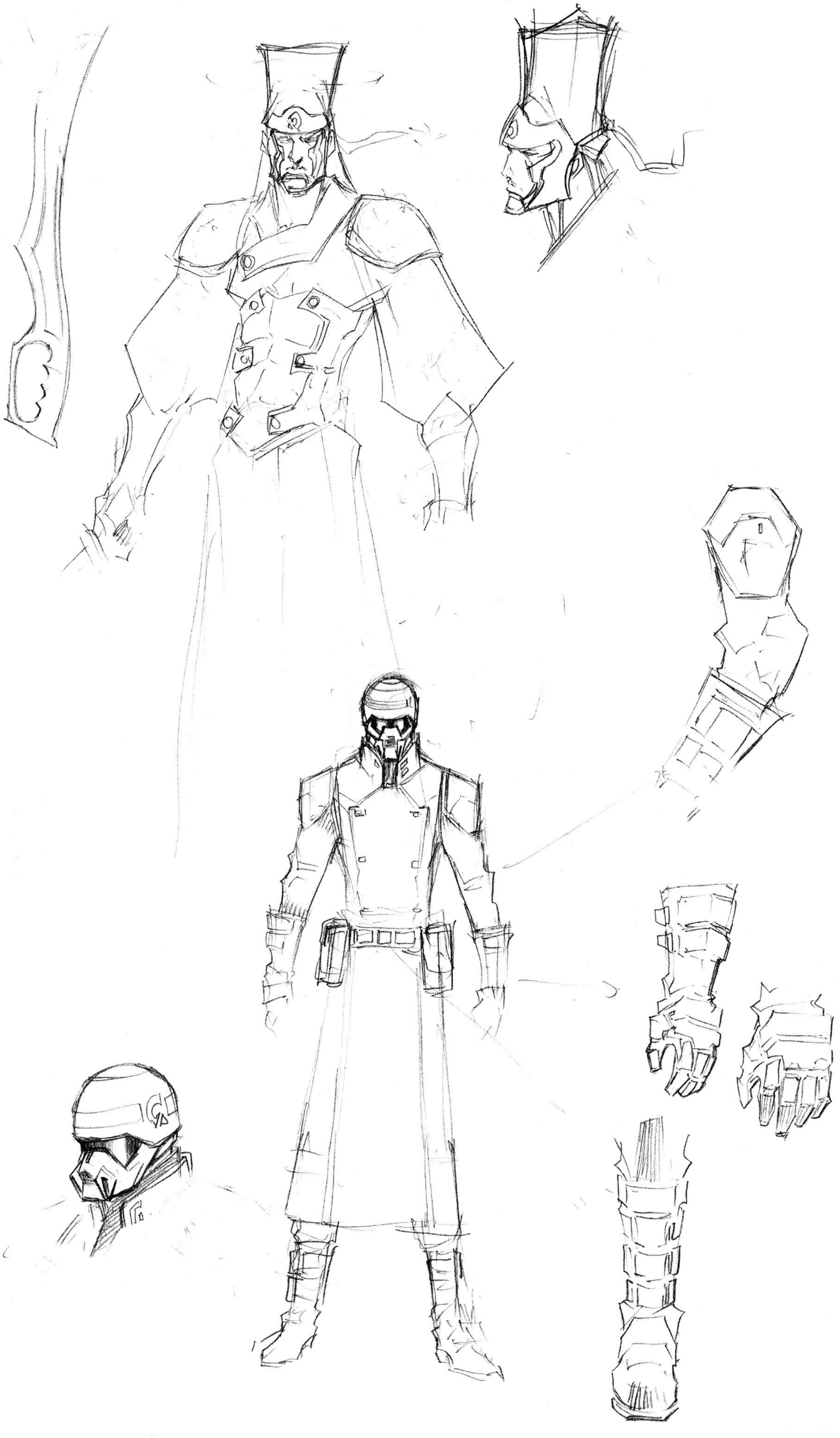

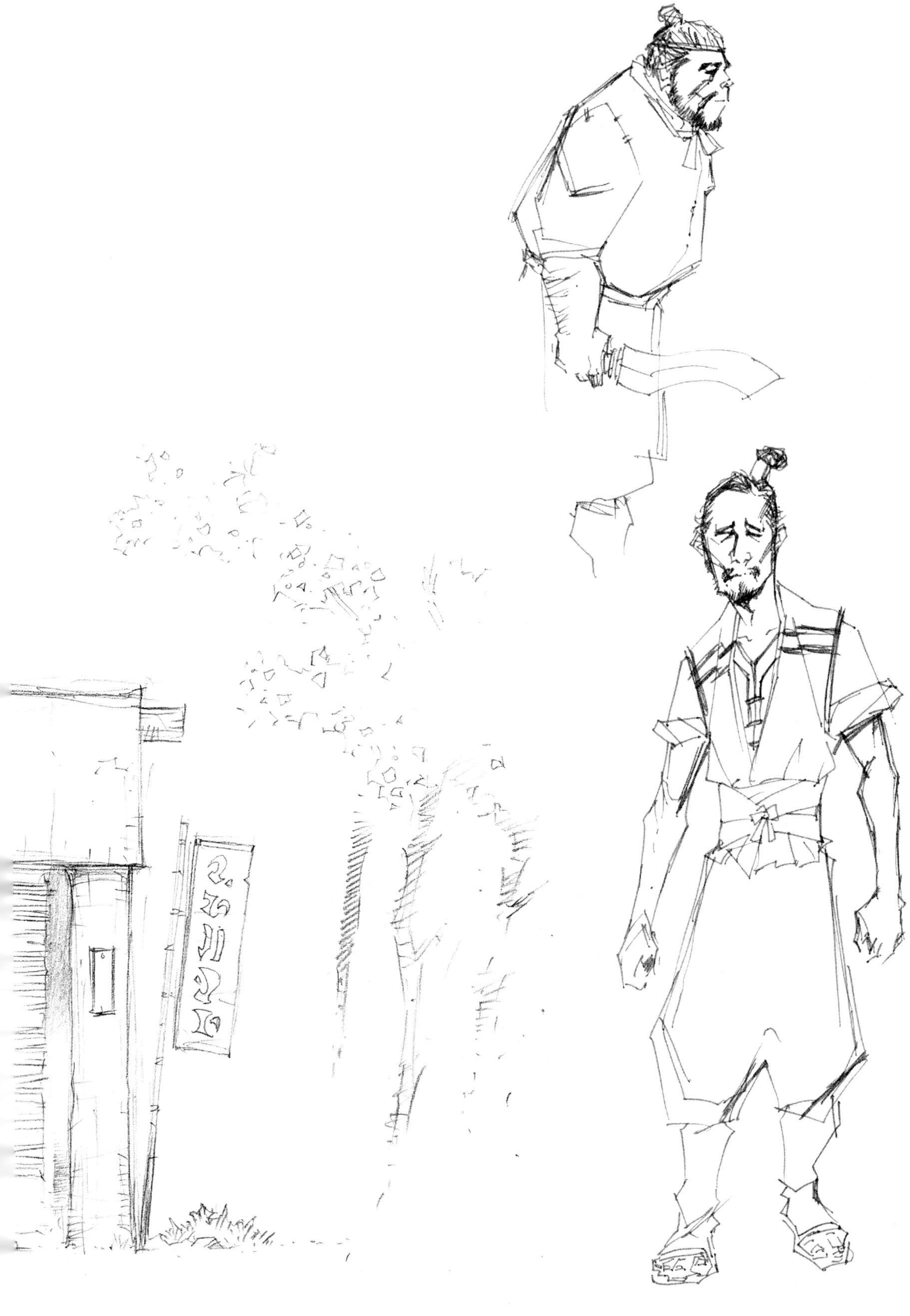

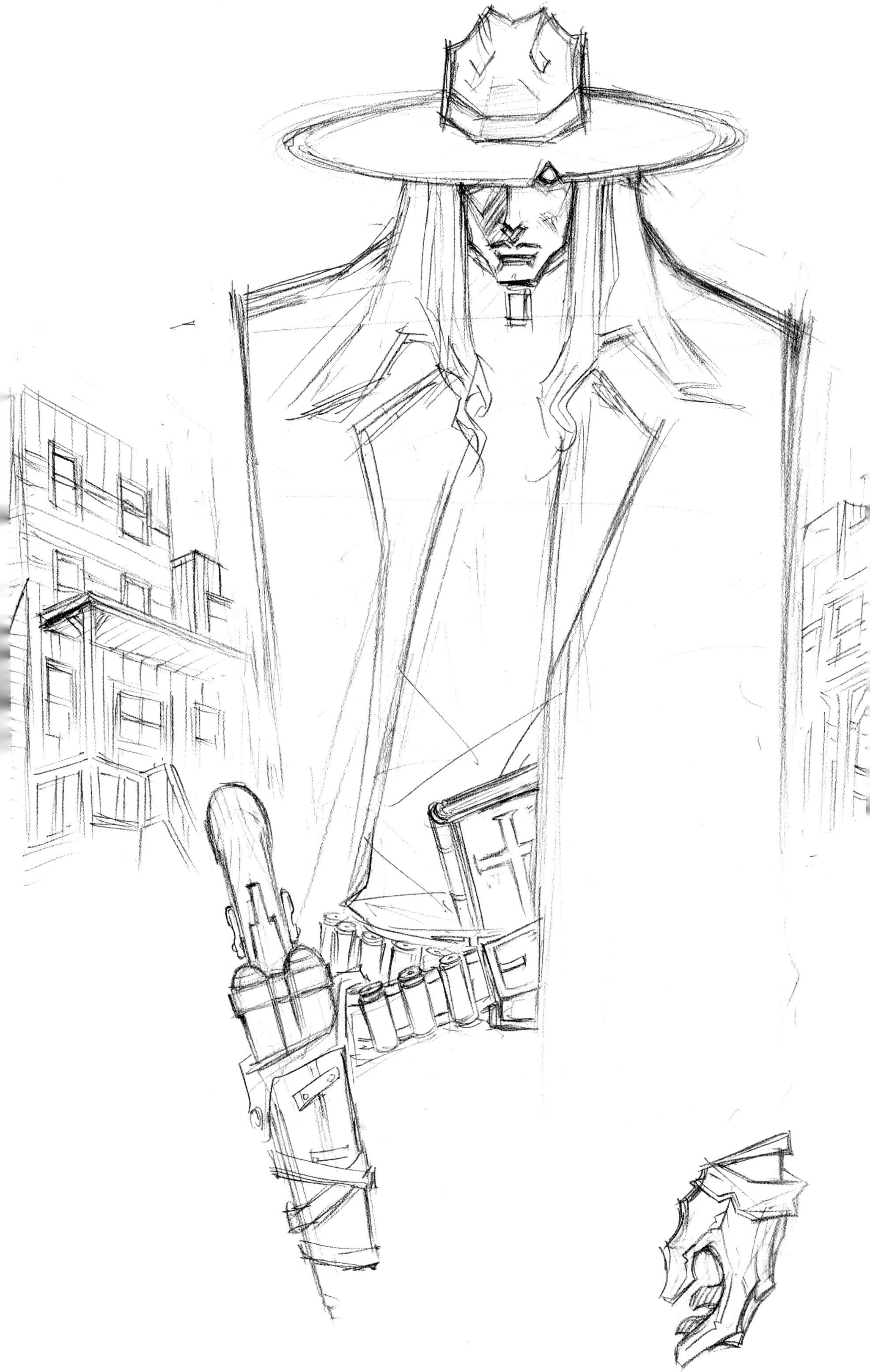

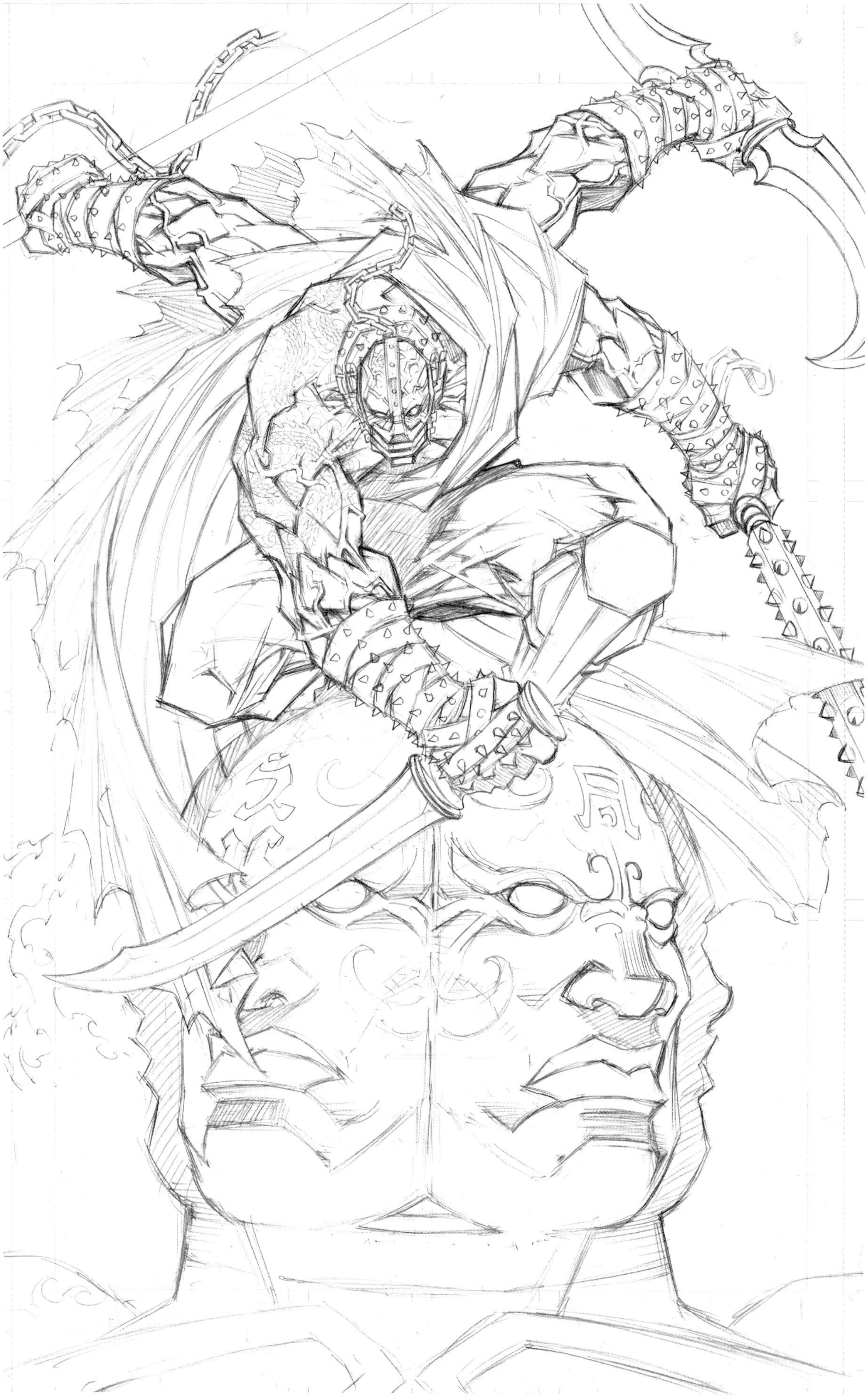

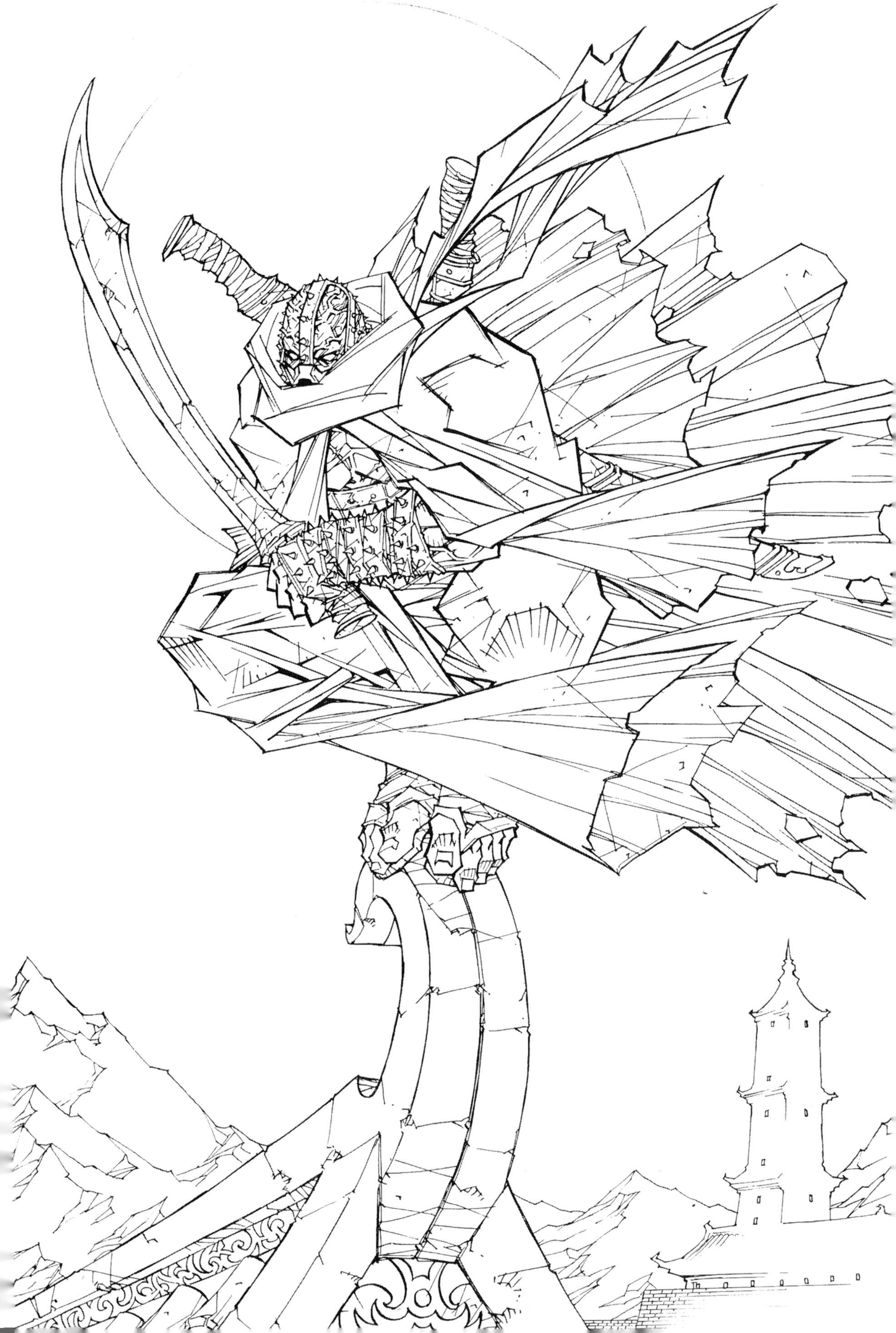

Those who wield the sword
   will pay with their lives!

剣を用いるものは、命でツケを払ってもらおう!

Jene, die das Schwert führen,
   werden mit ihrem Leben bezahlen!

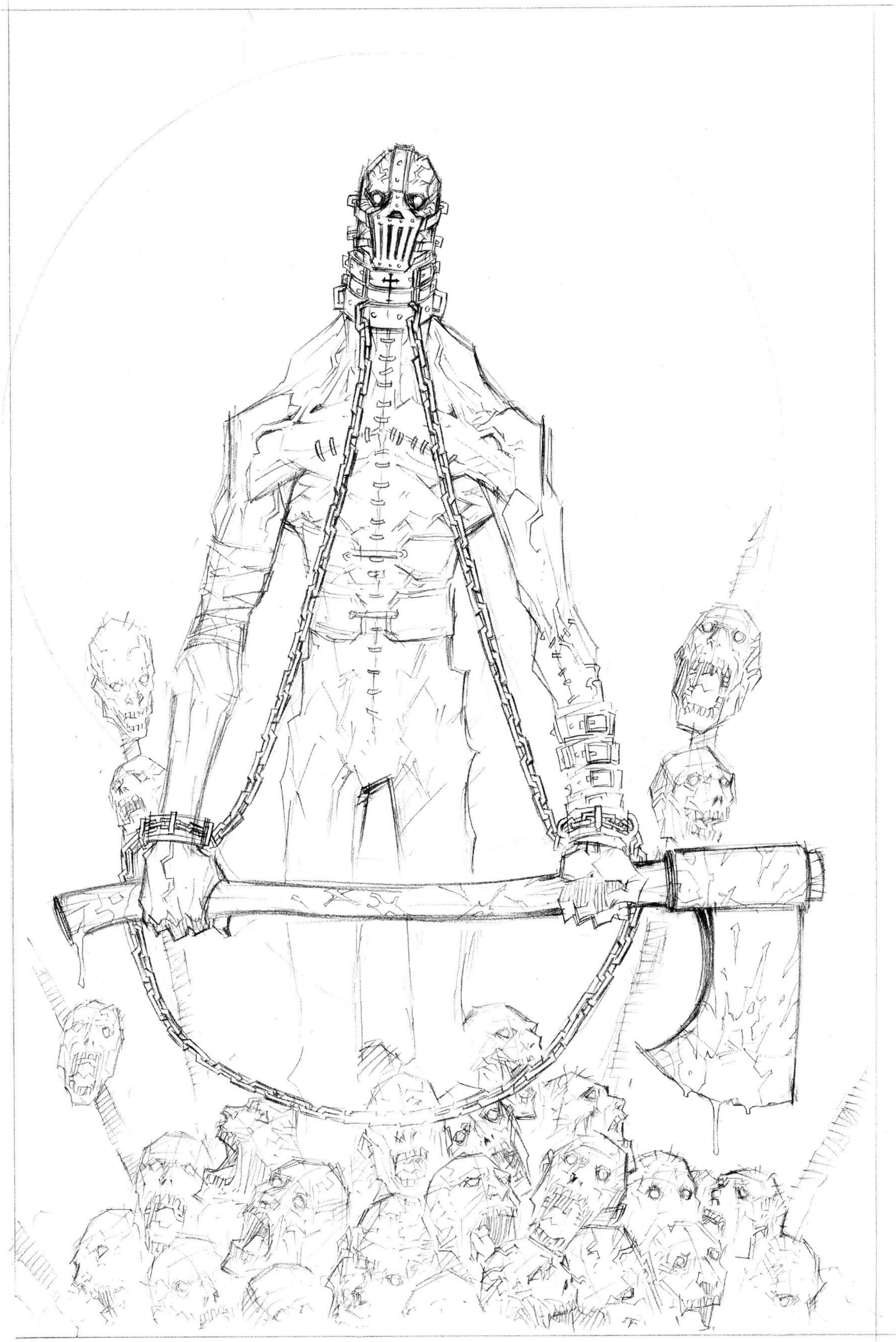

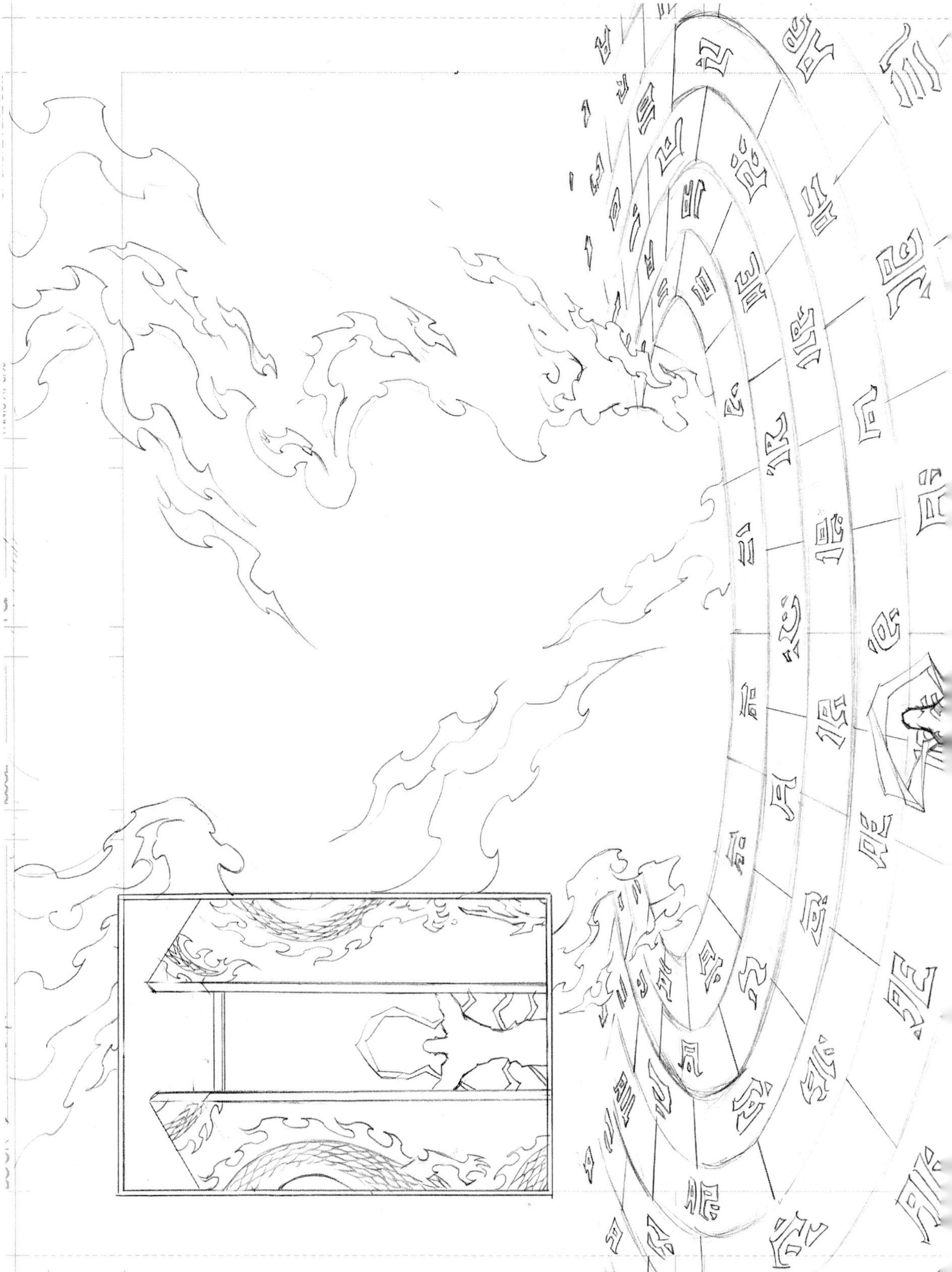

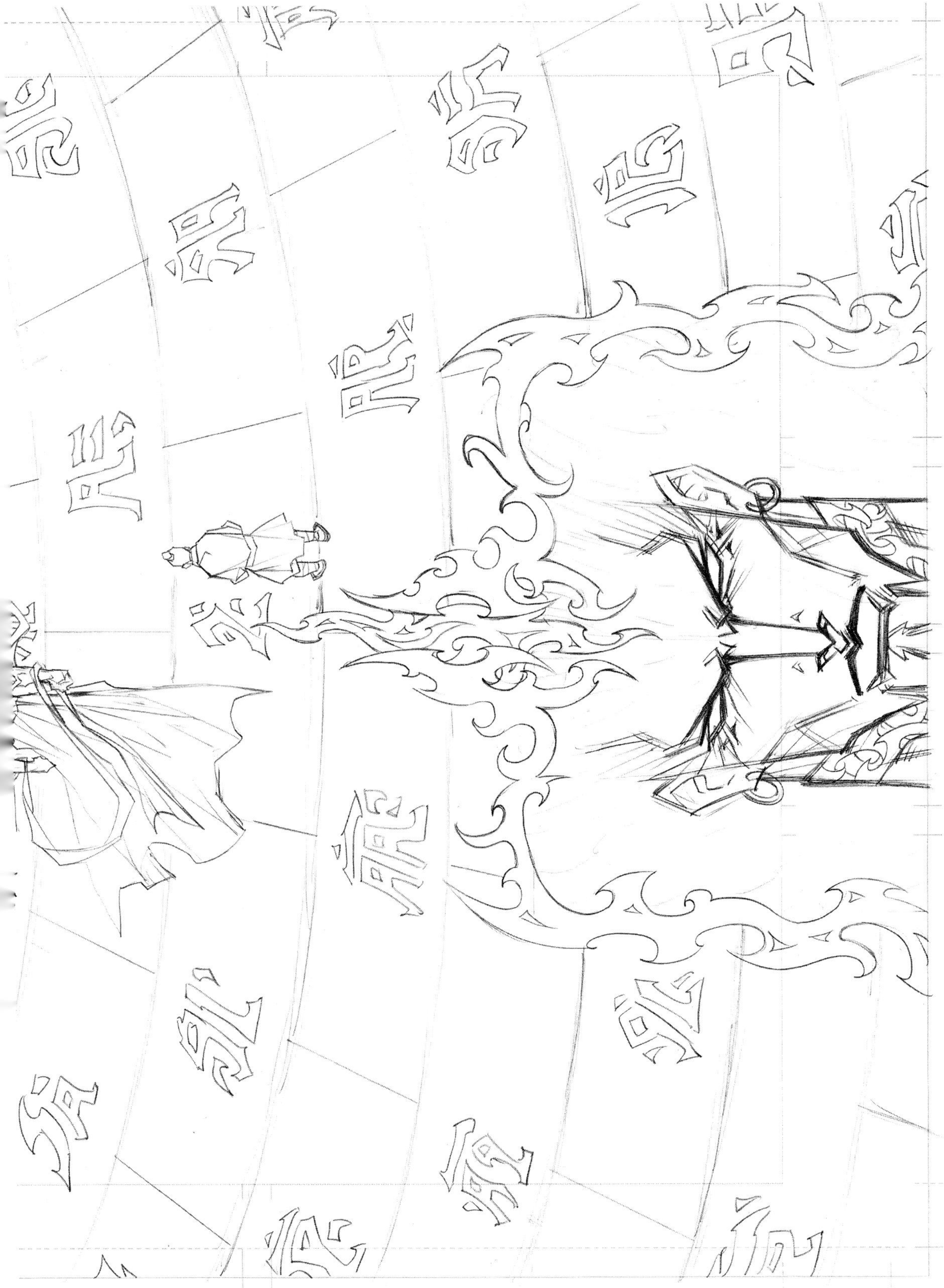

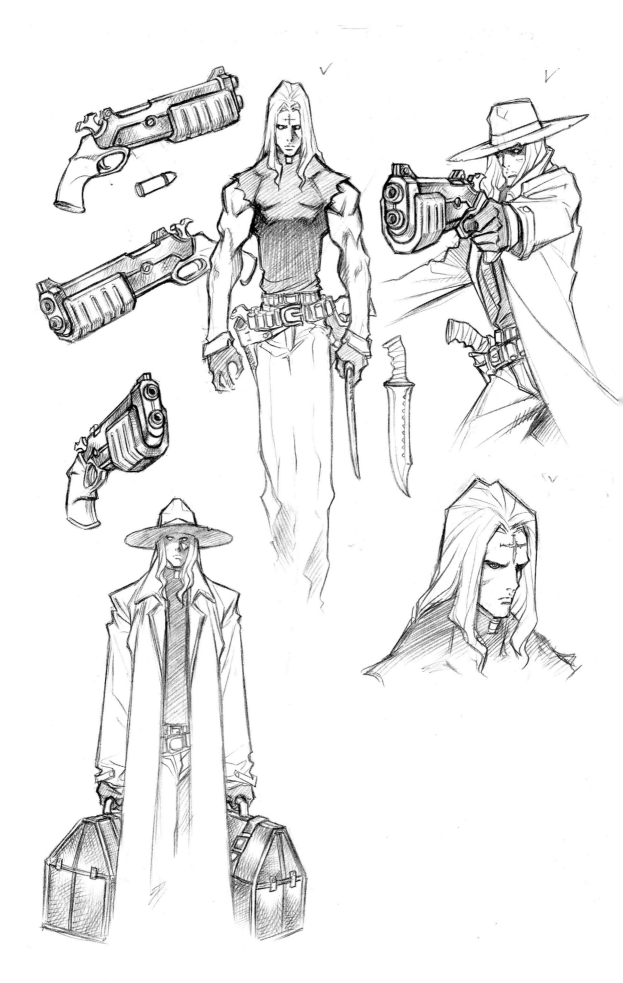

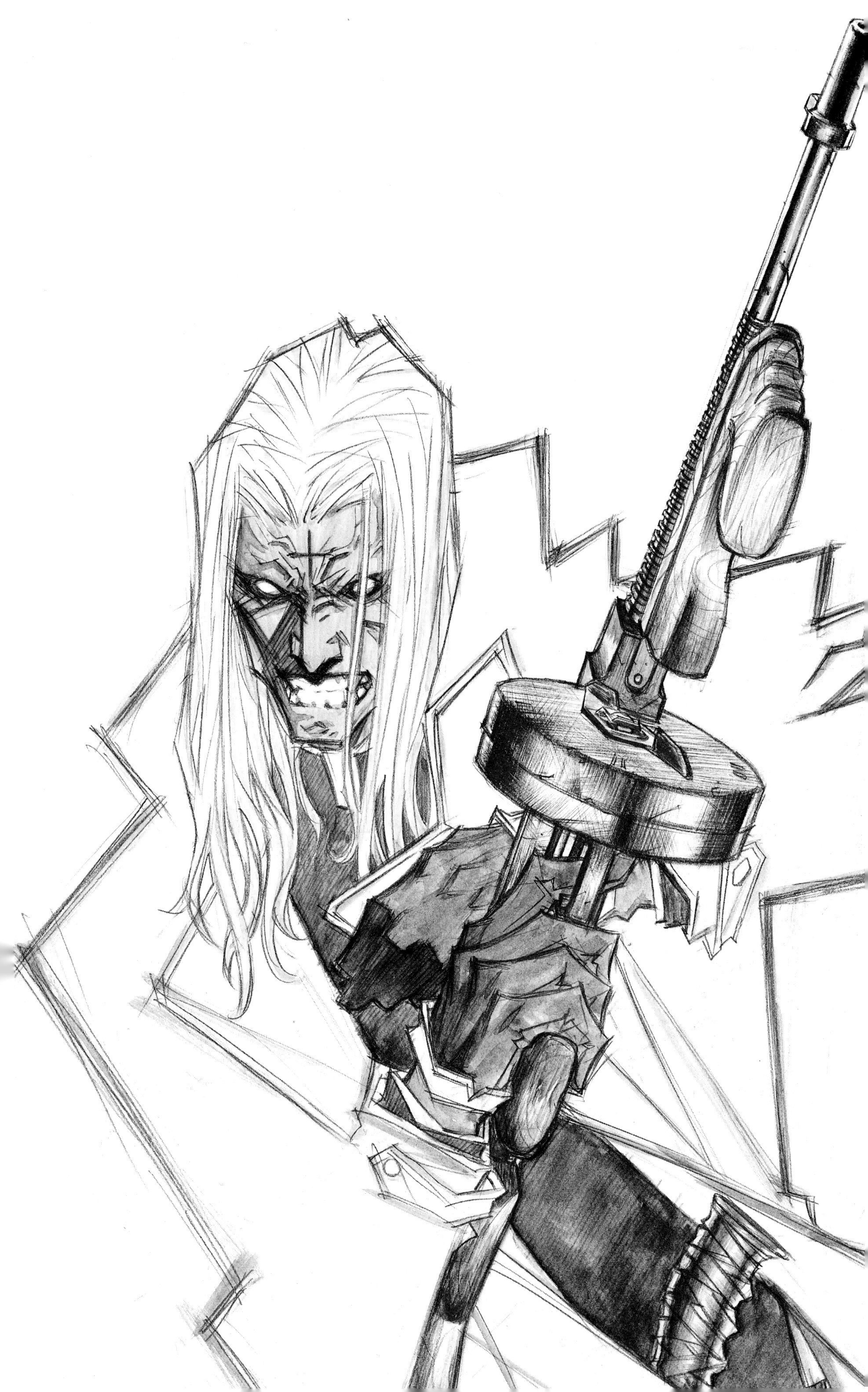

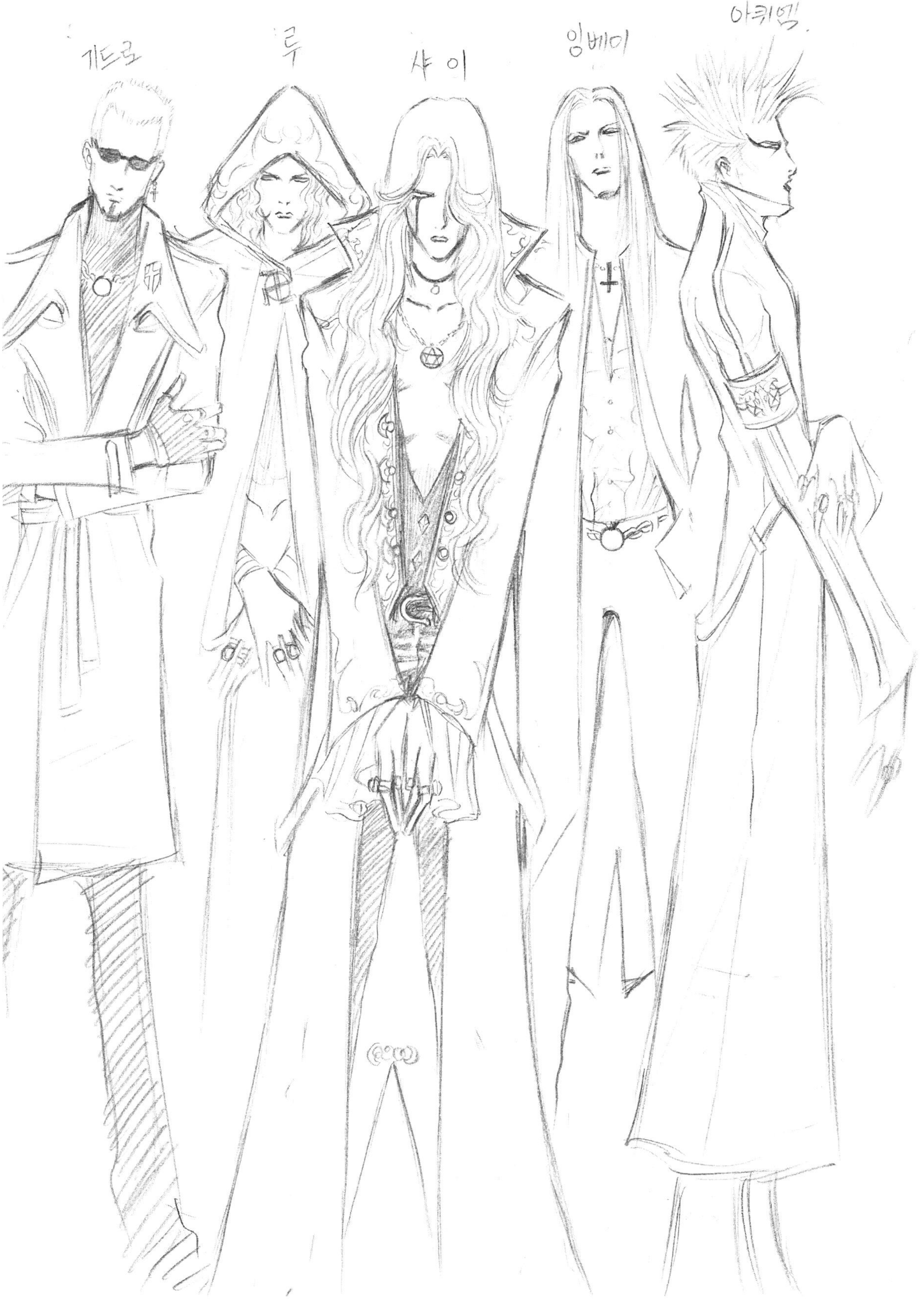
기드로
루
샤이
잉베이
아퀴엘

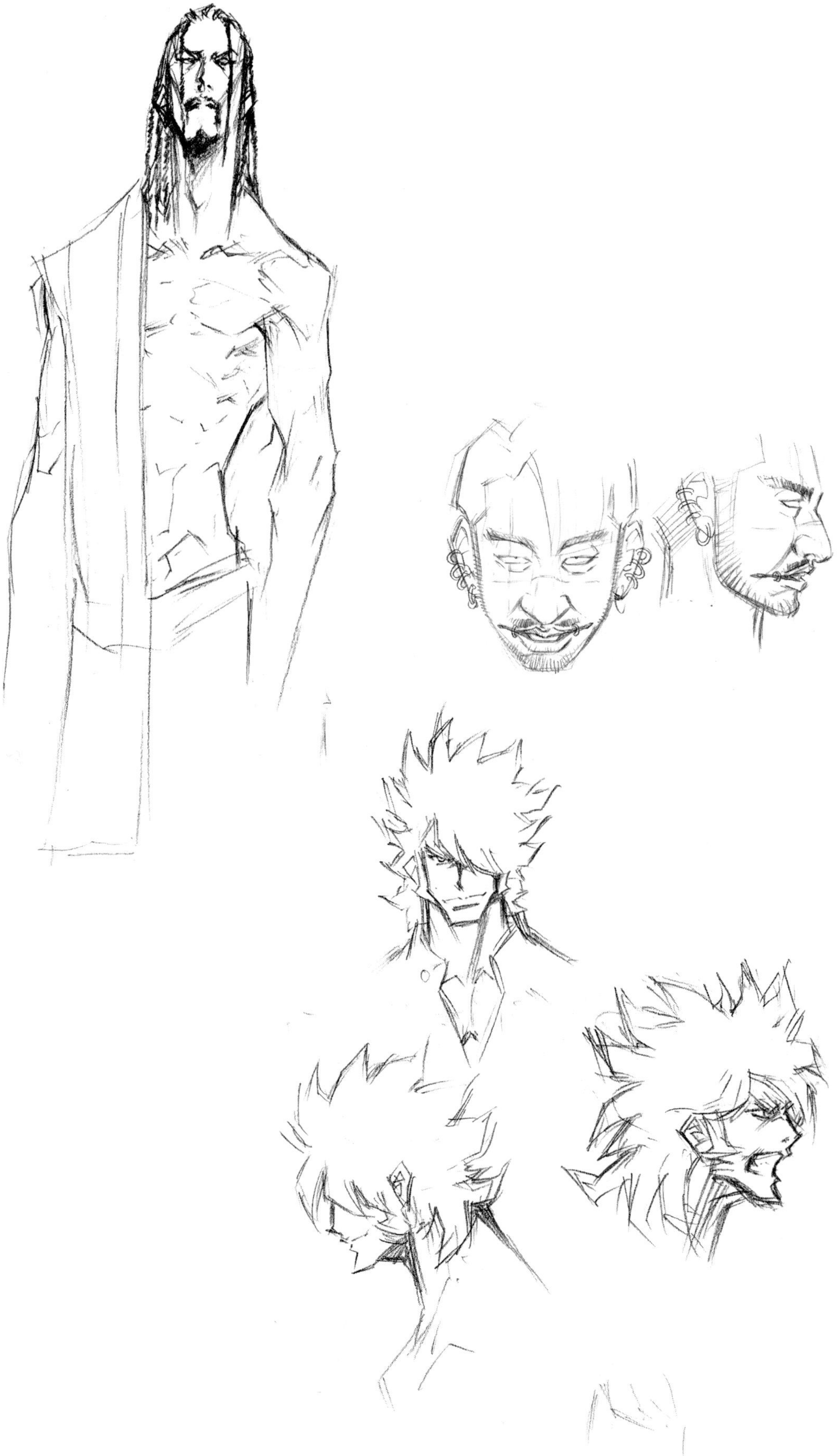

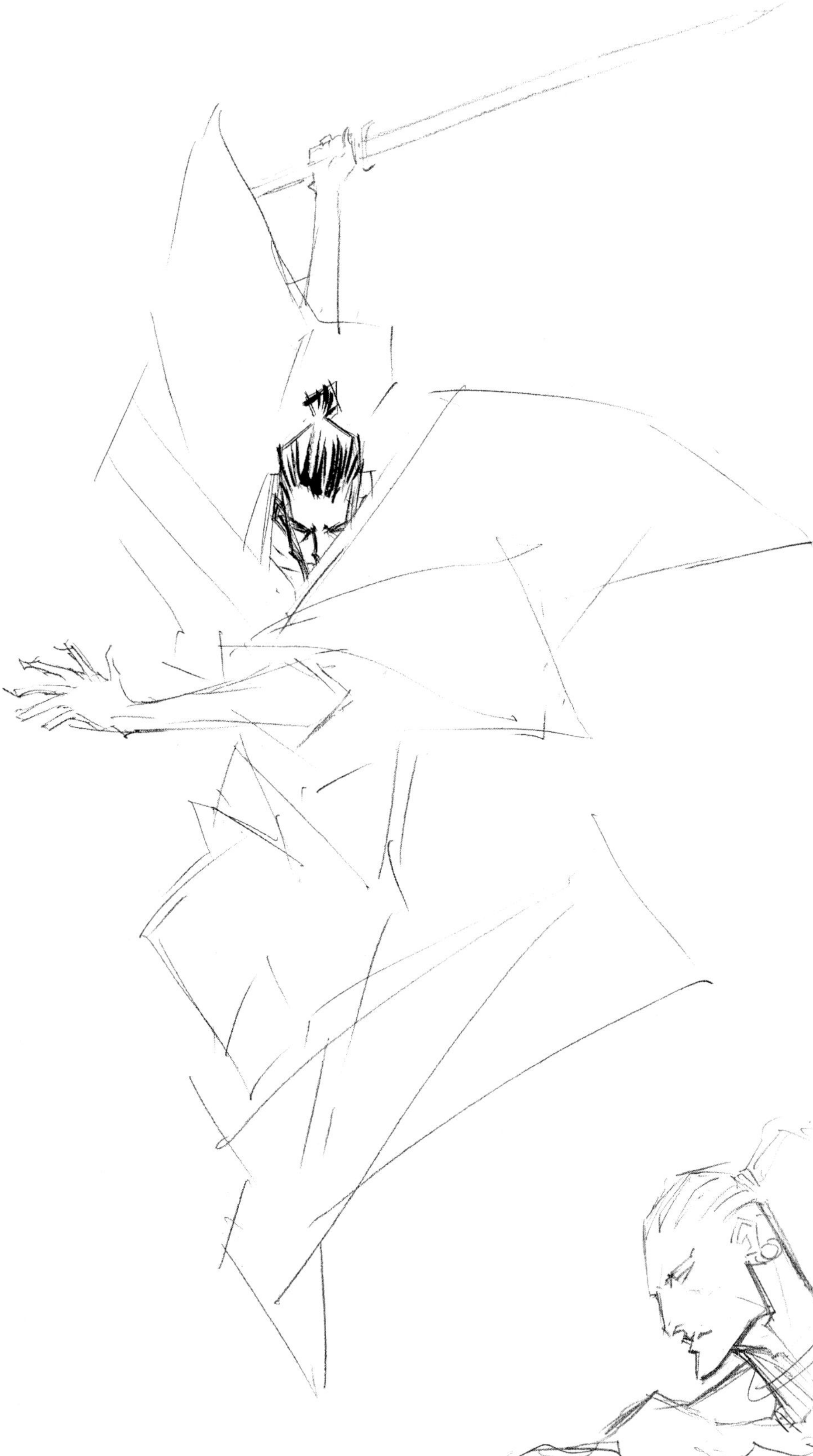
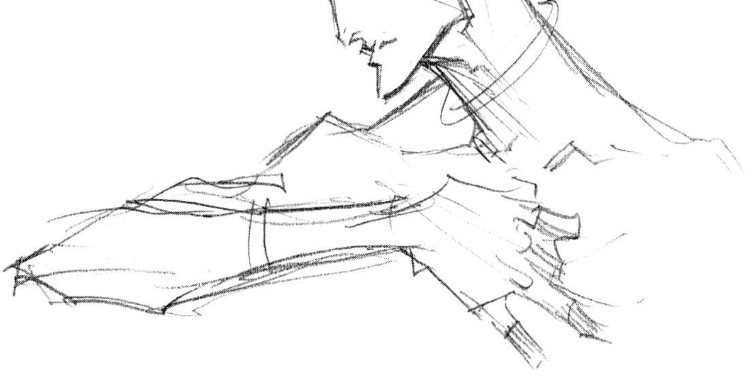

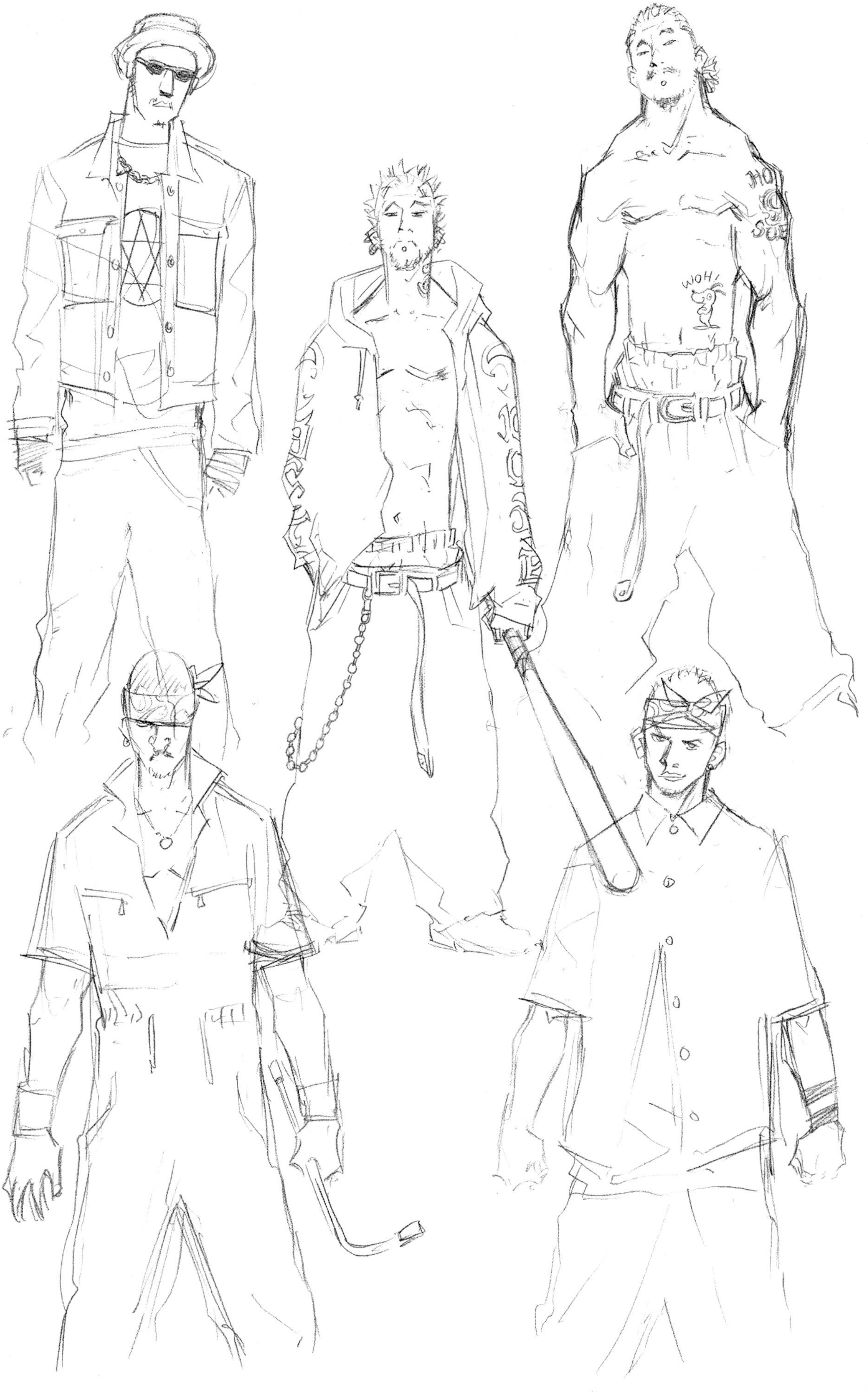
WOH!

>>> chapter 5

第5章

>>> 5. Kapitel

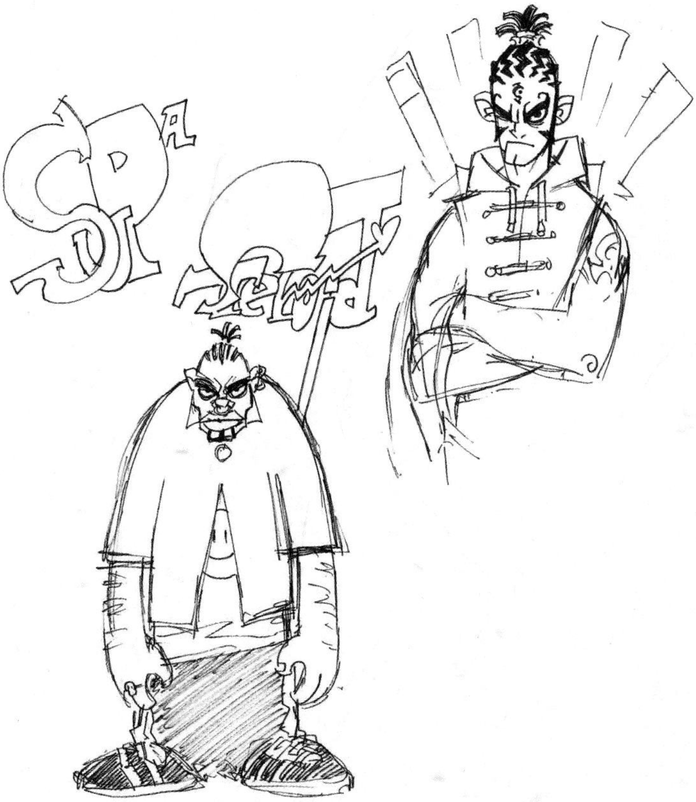

»Mercenary
»傭兵
»Söldner

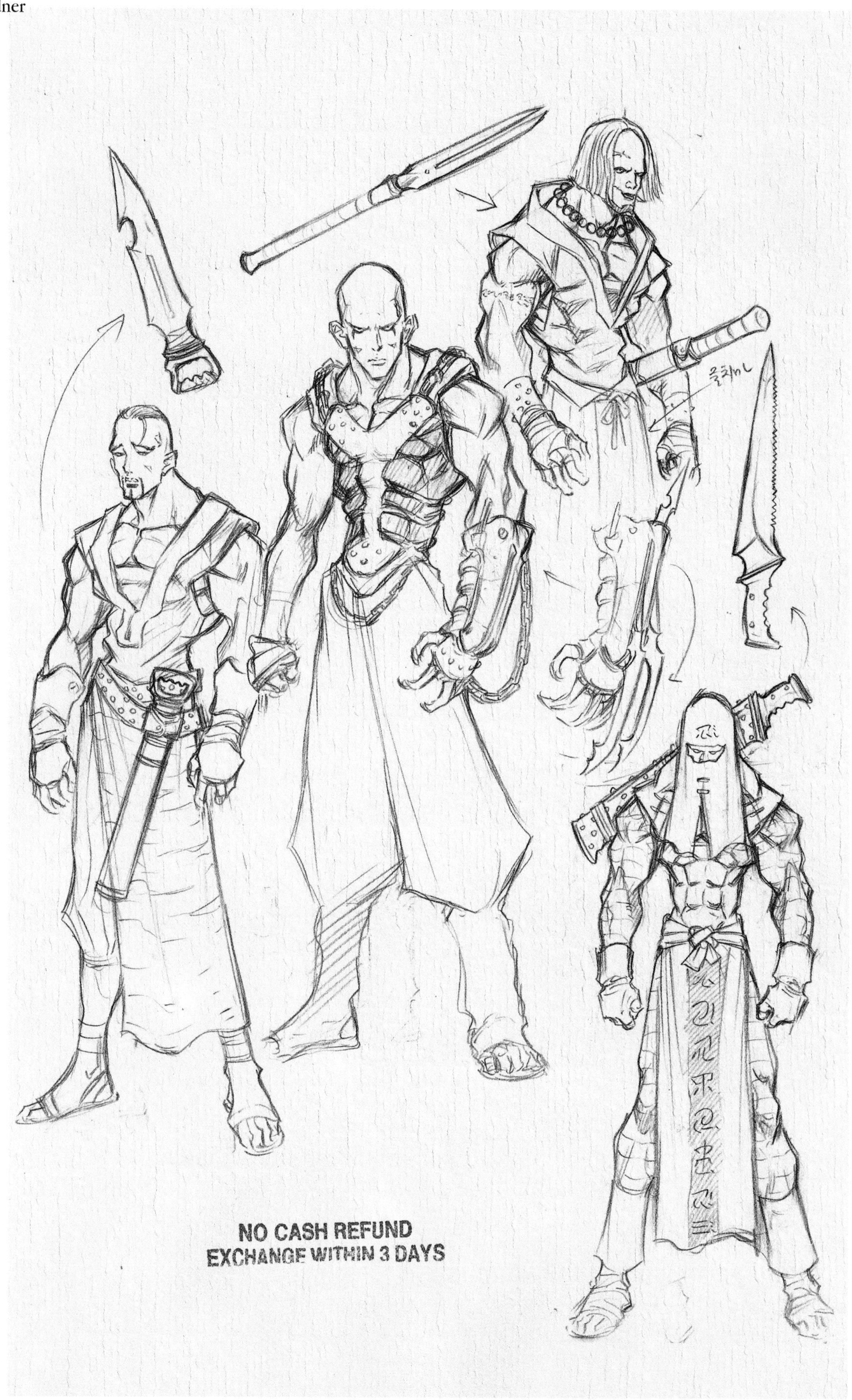
NO CASH REFUND
EXCHANGE WITHIN 3 DAYS

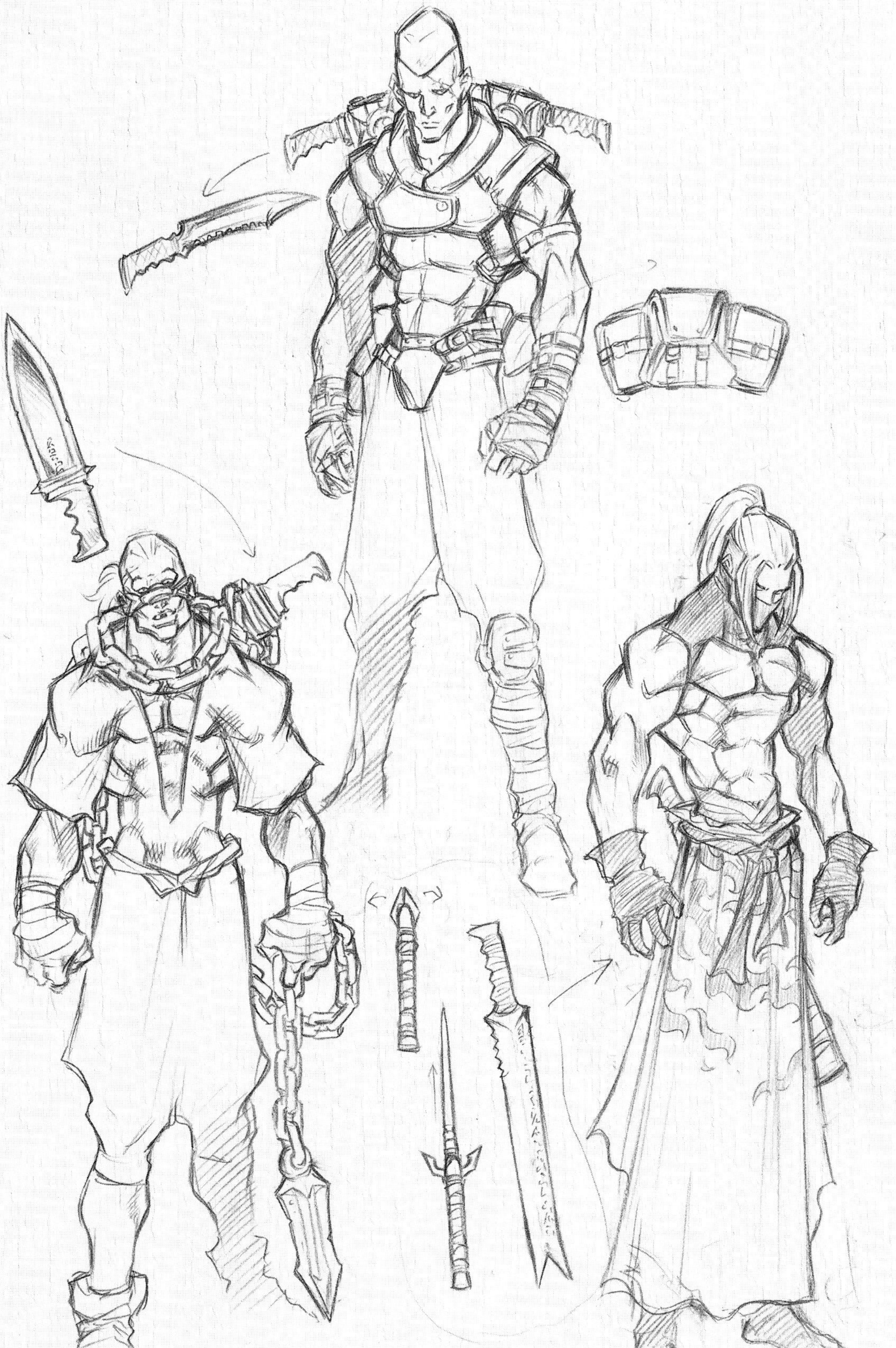

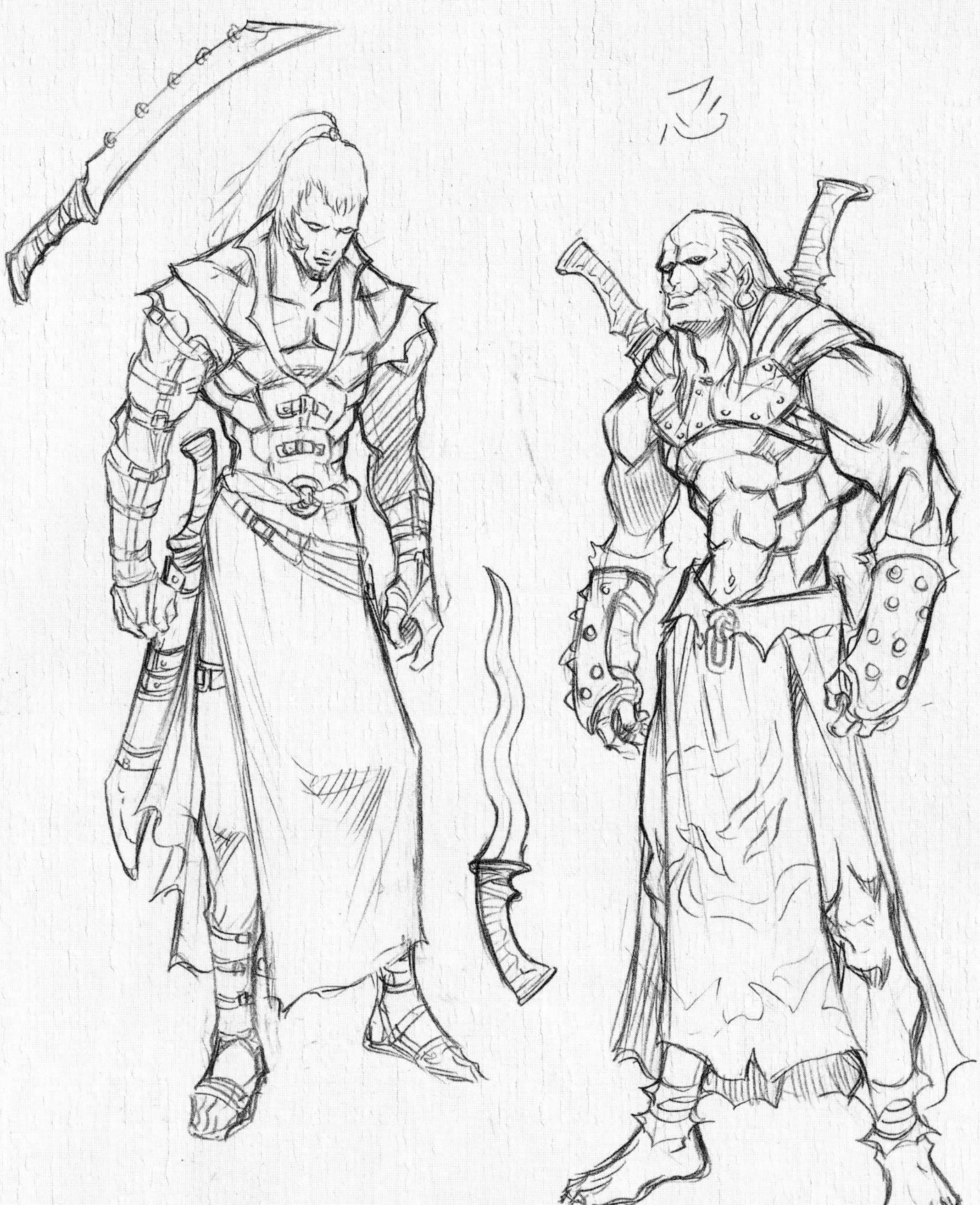
忍

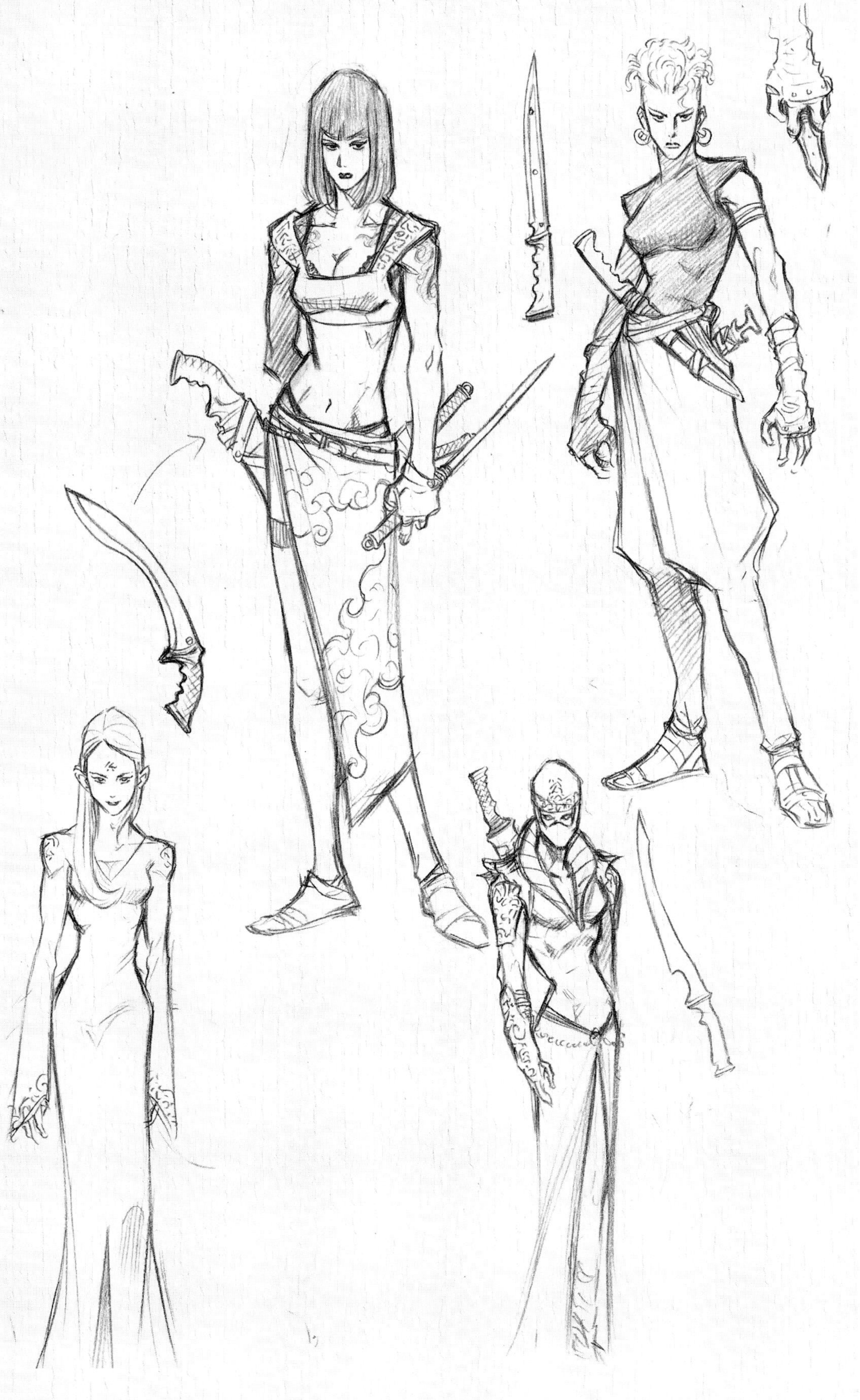

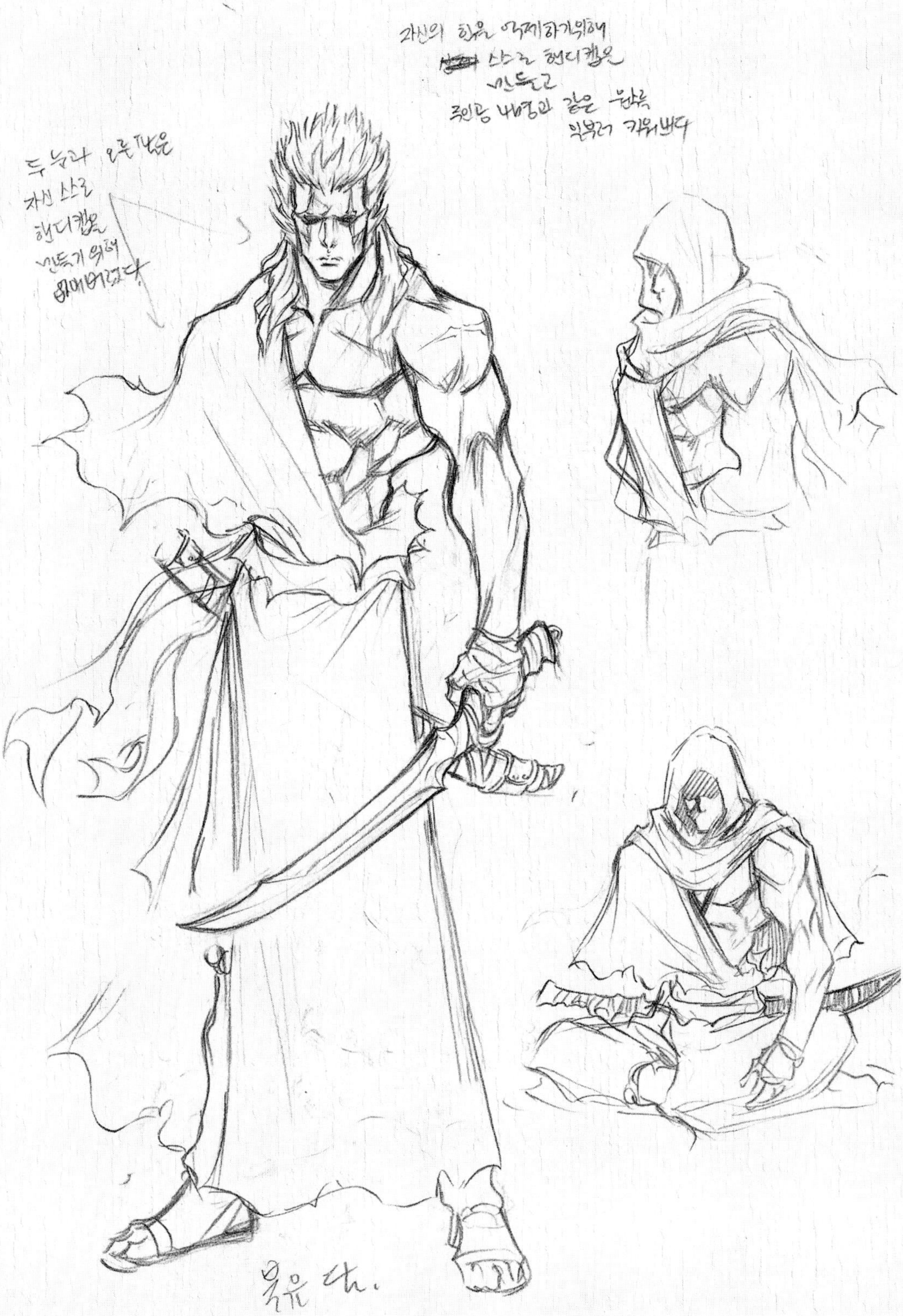
자신의 힘을 억제하기위해
스스로 핸디캡을
만들고
주인공 네명과 같은 원수를
일부러 키워냈다
두 눈과 오른팔은
자신 스스로
핸디캡을
만들기 위해
없애버렸다.
묵유단.

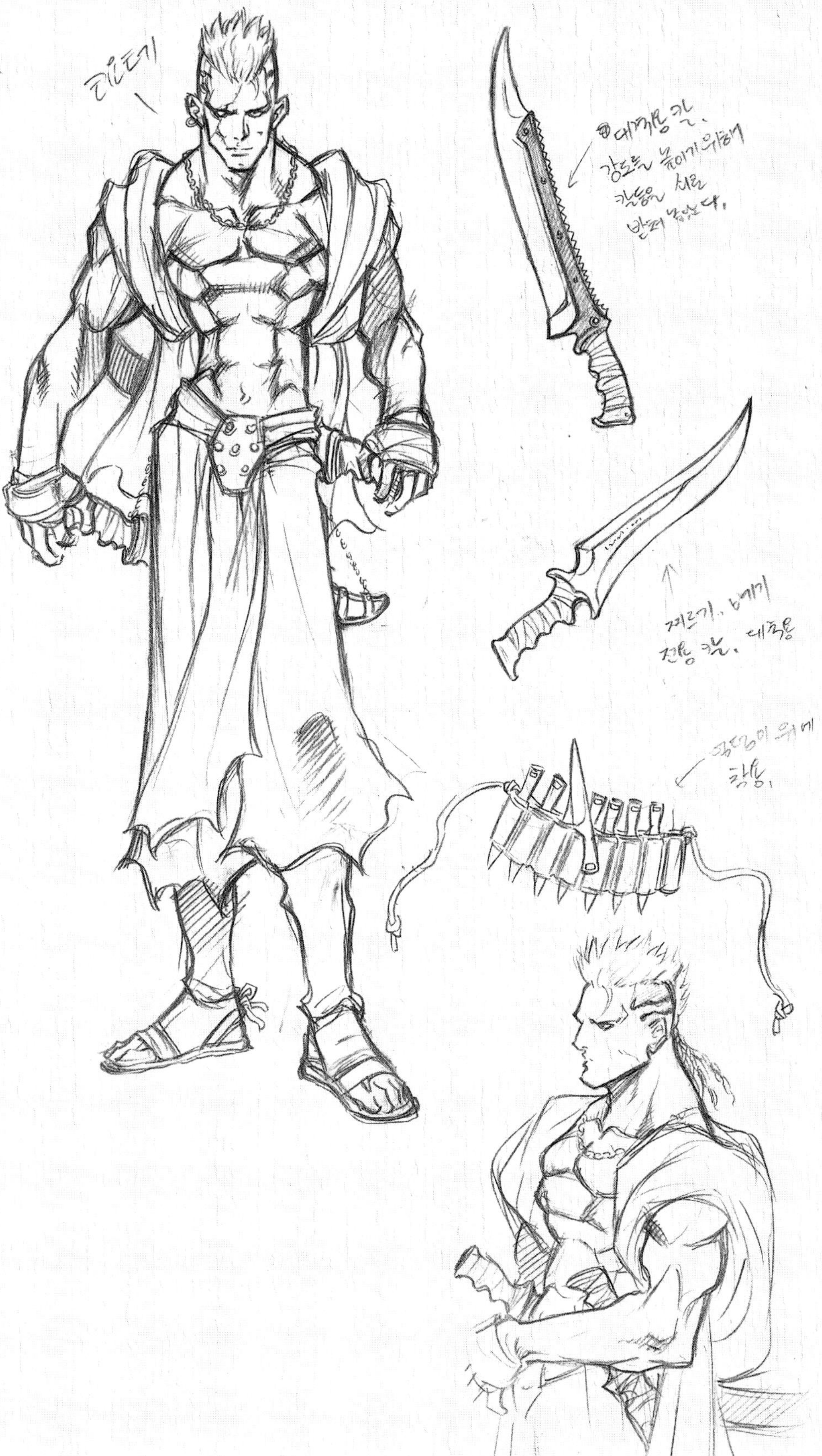
대검용 칼, 강도를 높이기 위해 칼등을 서로 받쳐 놓았다.
찌르기, 베기 전용 칼. 대검용
망토의 위에 착용.

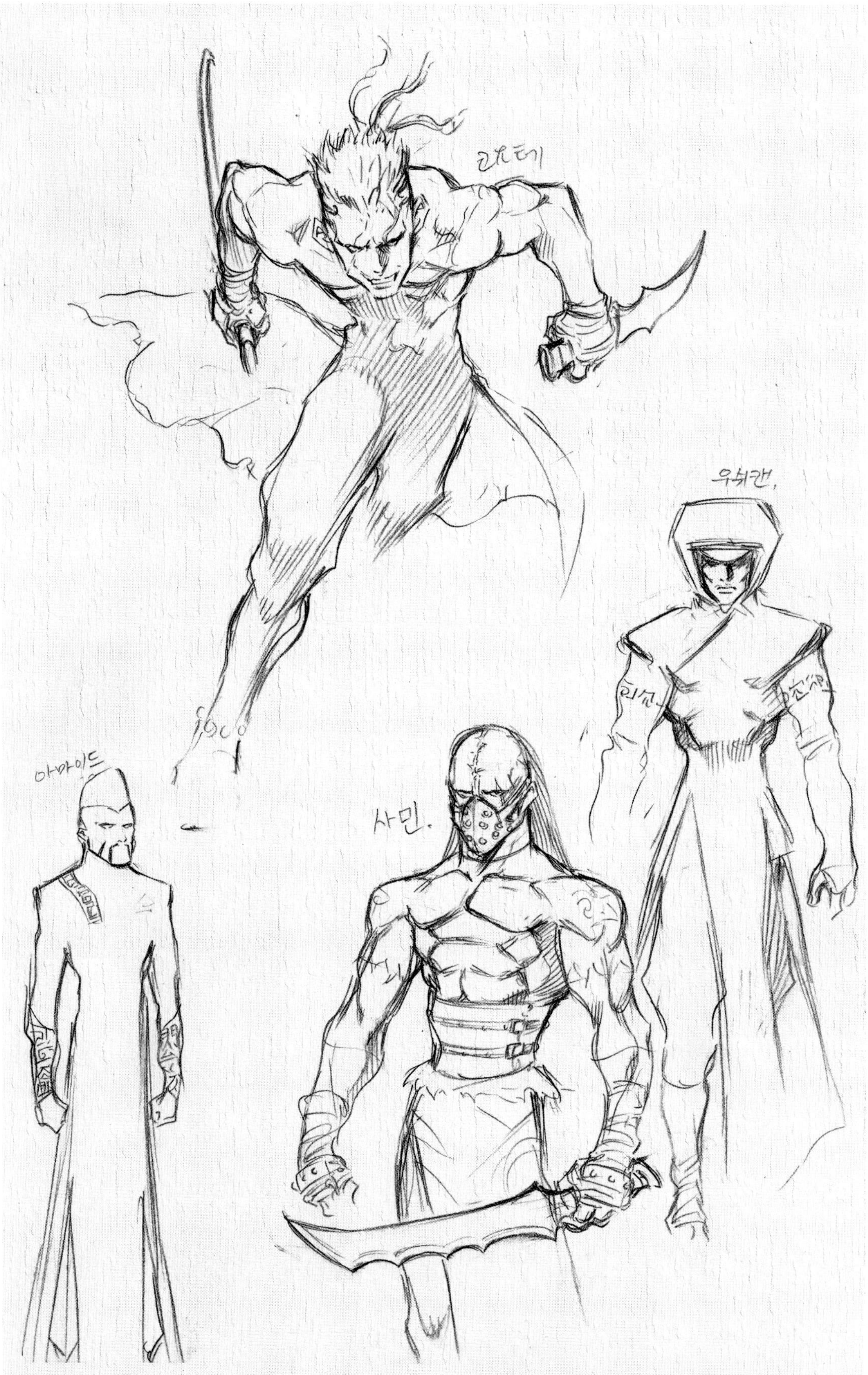
우쉬칸,
아마이드
사민.

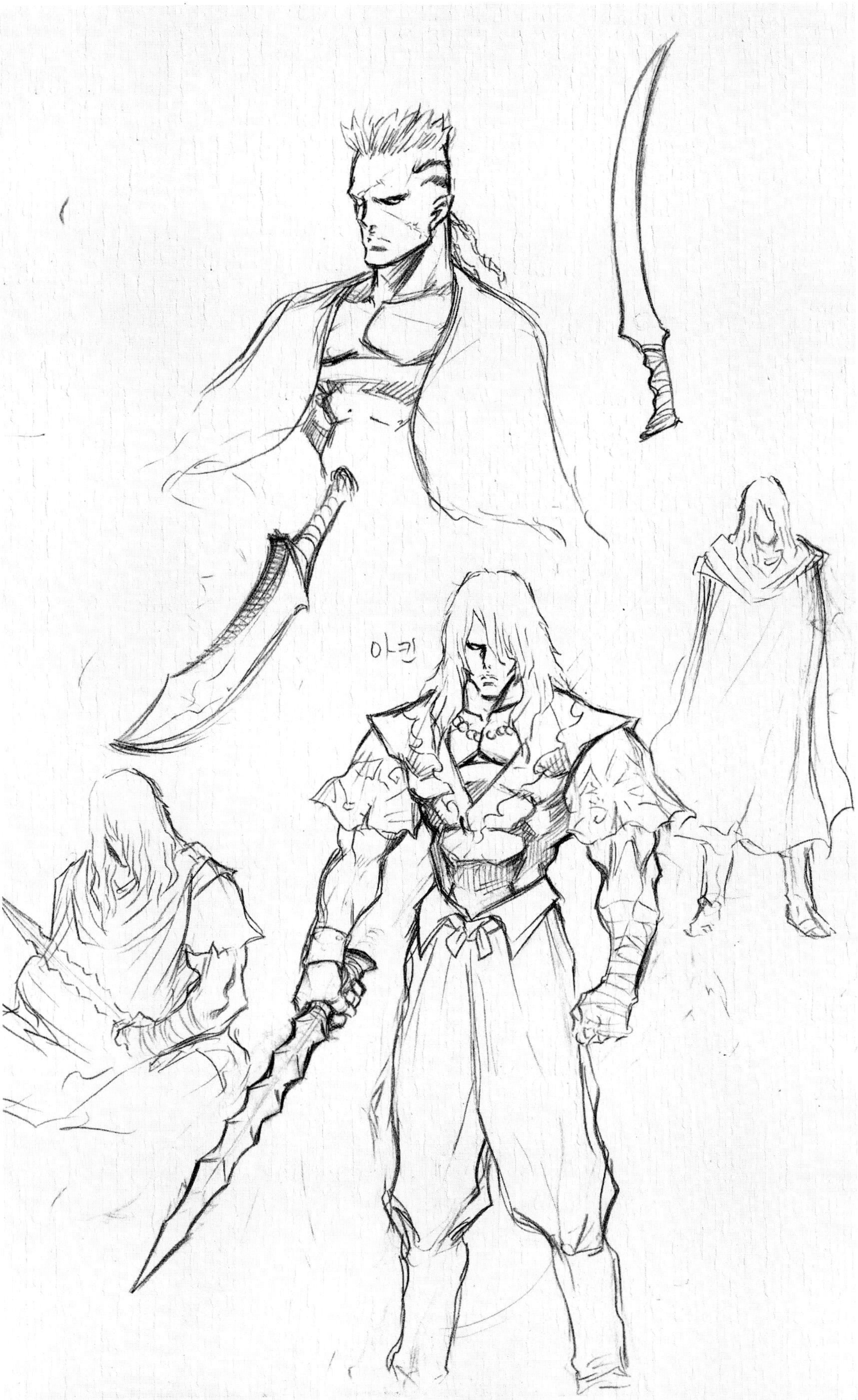
아킨

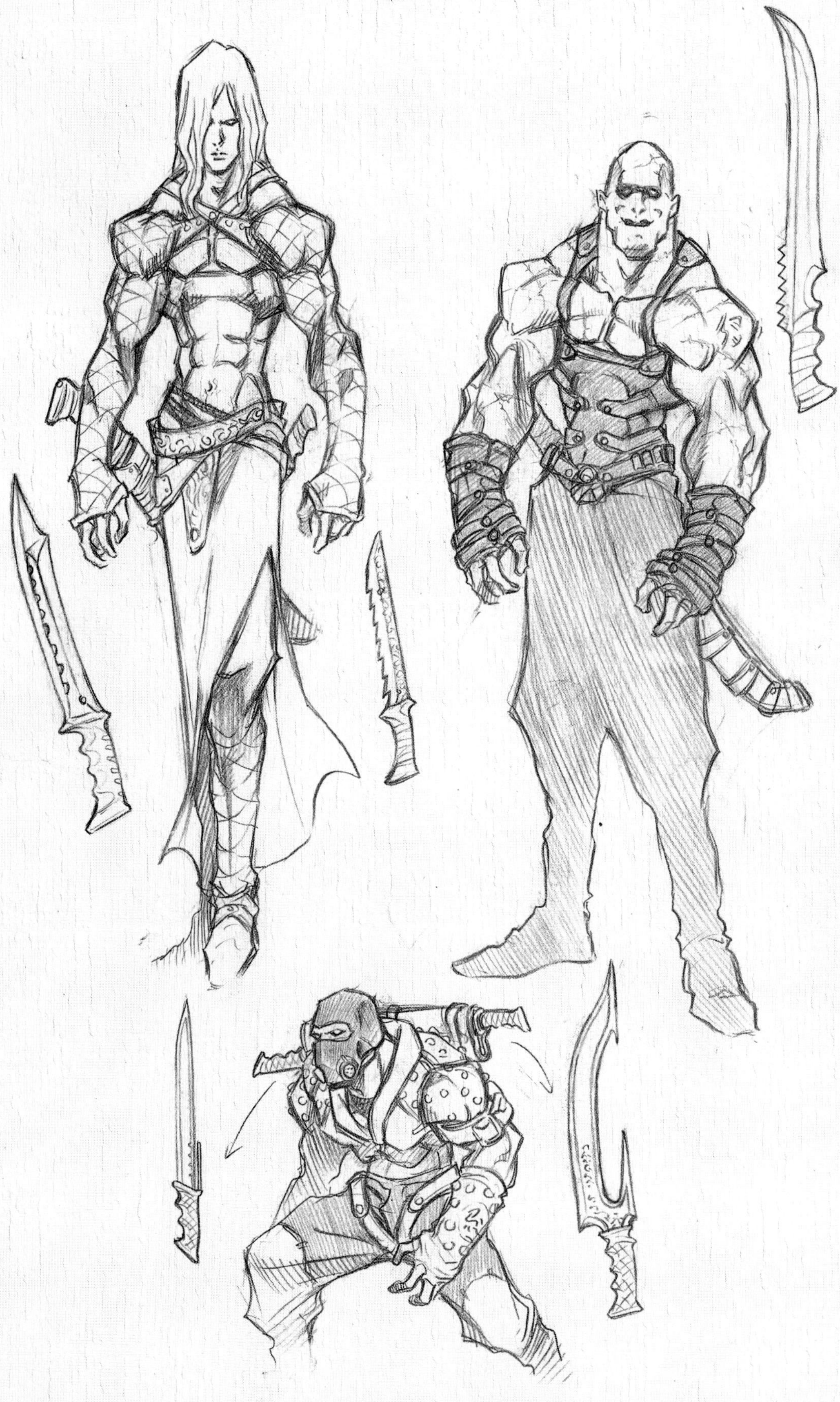

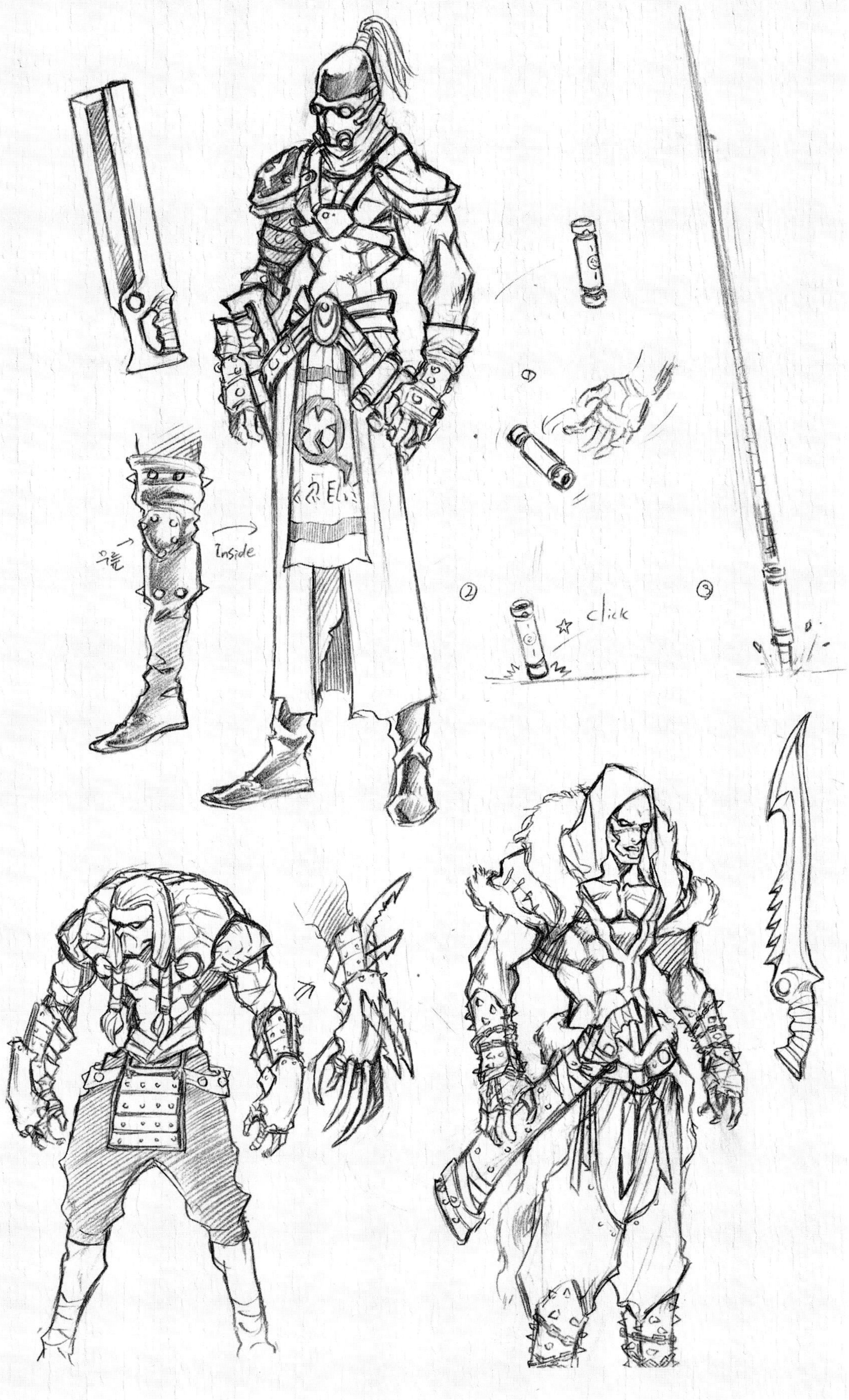
Inside
click

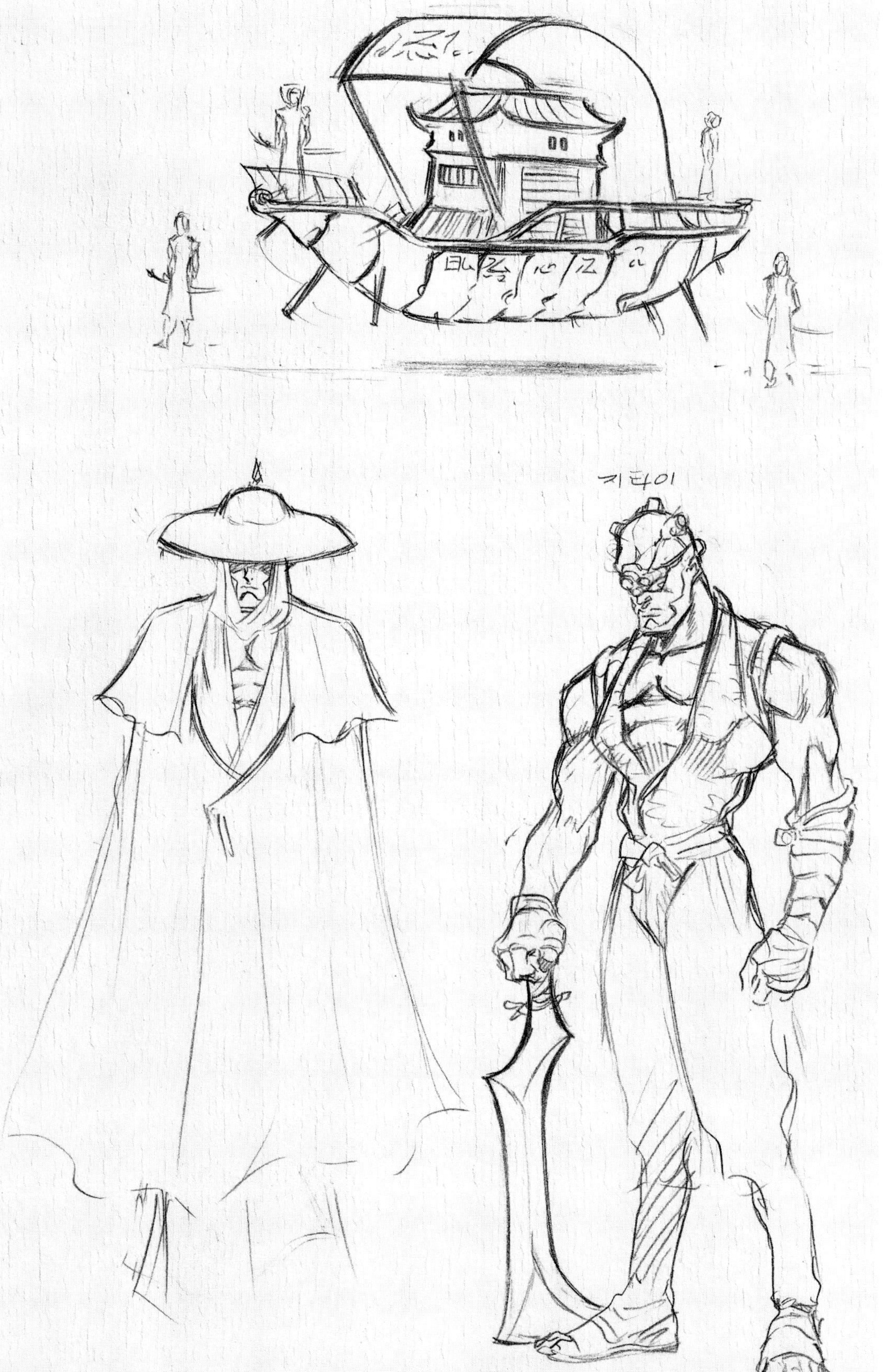

지타이

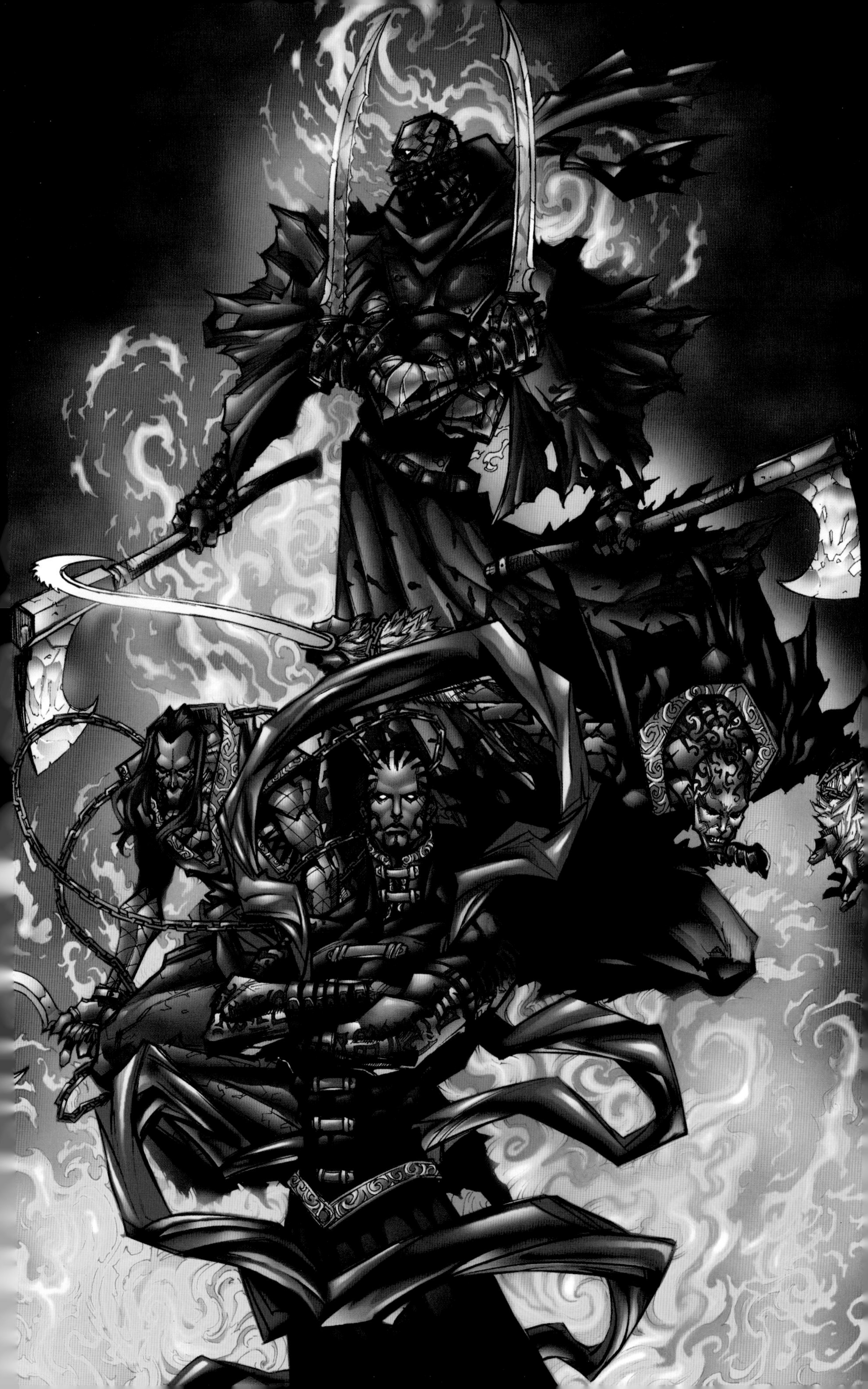

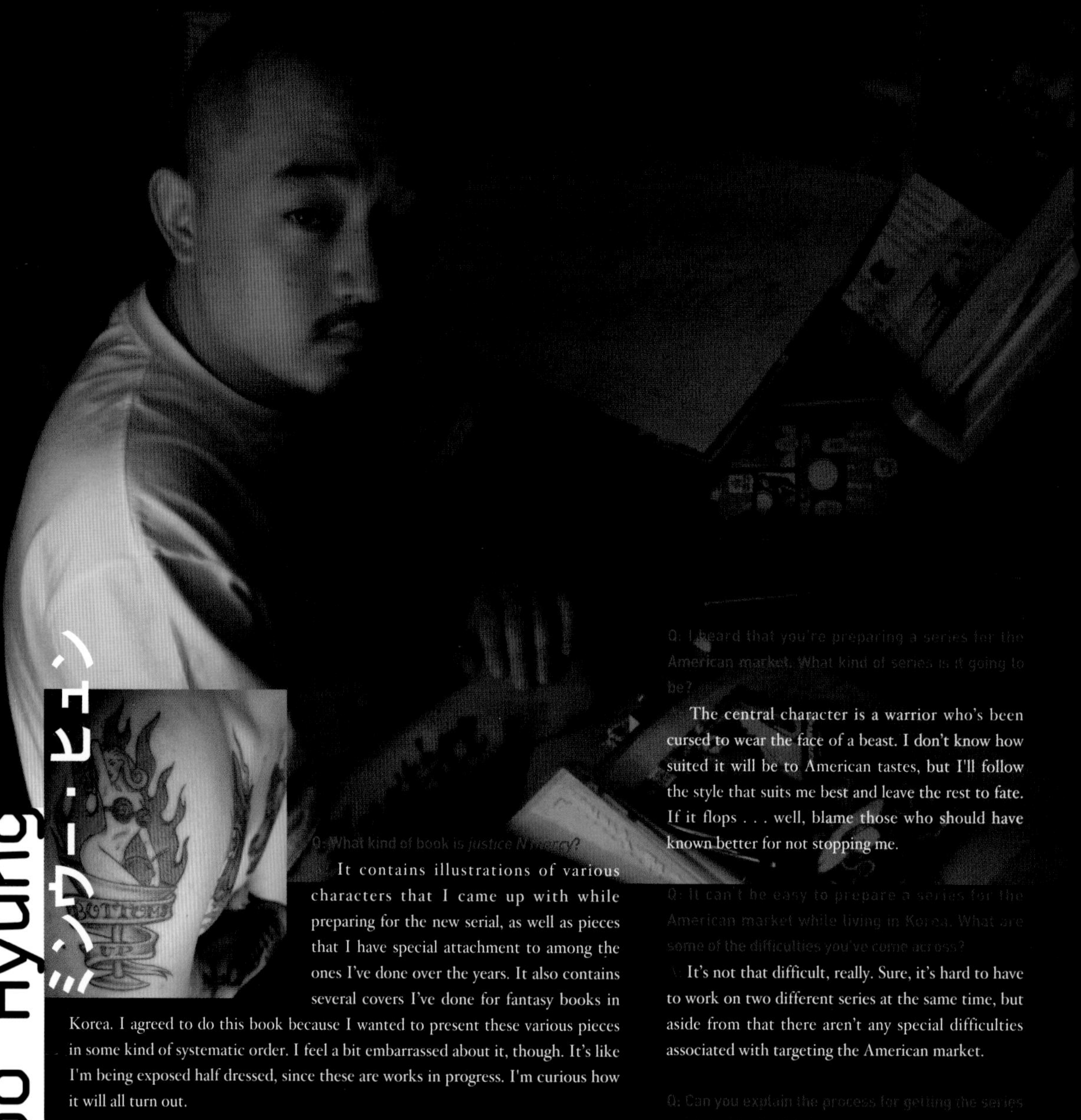

interview インタビュー

Min-Woo Hyung ミンウー・ヒョン

Q: What kind of book is *justice N mercy*?

A: It contains illustrations of various characters that I came up with while preparing for the new serial, as well as pieces that I have special attachment to among the ones I've done over the years. It also contains several covers I've done for fantasy books in Korea. I agreed to do this book because I wanted to present these various pieces in some kind of systematic order. I feel a bit embarrassed about it, though. It's like I'm being exposed half dressed, since these are works in progress. I'm curious how it will all turn out.

Q: What does "justice N mercy" mean?

A: You mean beyond the literal meaning? It doesn't have some deep meaning. It's just what I have tattooed on my arms. I guess it's a kind of self-expression.

Q: You are sometimes considered a cult artist and an artist with a distinctive personal style. What do you think about these labels? And is there a vision to your work that you can share with us?

A: I've heard that my work has a cult following, but I've never been able to give a satisfactory answer as to why. All I can say now is that I don't know why. It is nice to hear that I'm an artist with a distinctive personal style, no matter what the reason for that may be. My vision depends a lot on external factors—it changes according to what I happen to find interesting at the moment. External factors may include movies, paintings, characters, action figures, and books.

Q: Have you ever thought about what kind of impact the comics genre might have on popular culture?

A: To be honest, no. I don't know enough about each to have opinions on their relationship.

Q: Who would you describe as a "good artist"?

A: I'll be as honest as I can—I think *I'm* a good artist.

Q: Where do you get the inspiration for your work?

A: Mostly from movies, comics, novels and art books, but there are a hundred other images as well that suddenly come upon me during the course of the day, giving me ideas about different characters. They're too many to mention.

Q: I heard that you're preparing a series for the American market. What kind of series is it going to be?

A: The central character is a warrior who's been cursed to wear the face of a beast. I don't know how suited it will be to American tastes, but I'll follow the style that suits me best and leave the rest to fate. If it flops . . . well, blame those who should have known better for not stopping me.

Q: It can't be easy to prepare a series for the American market while living in Korea. What are some of the difficulties you've come across?

A: It's not that difficult, really. Sure, it's hard to have to work on two different series at the same time, but aside from that there aren't any special difficulties associated with targeting the American market.

Q: Can you explain the process for getting the series published in the U.S.?

A: It's the same as in Korea, mostly. You come up with the content, then prepare sketches . . . One difference is that in Korea, you do hundred percent of the ink sketches by hand, but in the States, you often use a computer. (Even when you use a computer, the main goal is to make the drawings have a hand-crafted feel.)

Q: What do you think are the main trends in the American comics market?

A: Well . . . Living in Korea as I do, I can't say that I know the American market very well, but I think the American market is in the midst of what one might call the Warring States* period. In addition to the kinds of American comics that have been traditionally popular, there has been an influx of a large number of manga-style works that bring in a lot of diversity and energy. The market seems to be evolving, moving in a new direction. Still, I don't know how much of a boost this new trend will give to the depressed American market.

*A colloquial phrase in Korea that means there are many trends in a certain area. Literally, the phrase refers to a period of wars during the fifth Century B.C. in ancient China.

Q: What do you focus on most in your work?

A: The basic theme that runs through my work is masculinity, power, and strength.

Q: What are some of your favorite American comics?

A: I like Ashley Wood's *Hellspawn* and many others. I tend to be an omnivore where comics are concerned.

Q And your favorite artists?

A: Ashley Wood, Simon Beasley, Kent Williams, and John Van Fleet.

Q: I heard you went to the August 2003 Toy Con in Hong Kong. What was the reason for the trip?

A: I'm extremely interested in dolls and action figures that depict Hong Kong's street culture. I'm making some of my own action figures, too. I just wanted to know what was new in the field.

Q: What kind of figures do you like?

A: My taste changes every day . . . but one thing that's been consistent is that I like a kind of belligerent look in my action figures. I also like Michael Lau's Urban Vinyl street culture-style works.

Q: Do you have special plans regarding these figures?

A: At the moment, a Hong Kong company is in the process of producing action figures from the *Priest* series. I also have a lot of personal interest in figure making. If I get a chance, I would like to market the figures I've made personally. But if this plan flops . . . you can blame those who should have known better for not stopping me.

Q: You have tattoos on your arms. What do they mean?

A: Nothing in particular. I just wanted to get tattoos one day, so I did.

Q: What kinds of music and films do you like?

A: It's all about style for me as far as films are concerned. I don't care about the content. As for music, I like anything that has a groovy beat. (Sometimes I enjoy listening to film soundtracks as well.)

Q: What do you when you're not working?

A: Hang out with my buddies or go different places with my family.

Q: What are your friends like?

A: Actually, they're quite diverse. Musicians, a tattoo artist, a screenwriter, etc. I guess most of them don't have nine-to-five jobs. (I don't hang out with other comics artists much.) And most of the friends I spend time with are . . . simply crazy.

Min-Woo

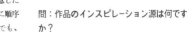

問：「正義と慈悲」とは、どんな本ですか？

答：新しいシリーズの準備をしている際に作った様々なキャラクターのイラストや、長年描いてきた中で特に気に入った作品などを集めたものです。韓国のファンタジー小説の表紙用に描いた作品もいくつか含まれています。この画集を出す事に同意したのは、これら様々な作品を一つの場所に順序良く収めておきたいと思ったからです。でも、ちょっと恥ずかしいような気もします。というのは、ここに集められている作品の多くはまだ制作中の未完成のもので、羊分裸を見せているような気分だからです。どんな出来になるか興味津々です。

Korean Comics
KOCCA
grimy
.net
용비불패
Yong Bi Bul Pae

PRIEST

問：「正義と慈悲」にはどんな意味がありますか？

答：言葉どおりの意味の他に？ 特にありません。私の腕の入れ墨です。自己表現と言ったところでしょうか。

問：カルトアーティストとか、独特のスタイルを持つアーティストと話題になりますが、こういうレッテルについてどう思いますか。あなたの作品のビジョンについて説明していただけますか？

答：確かにカルト的なファンが多いと聞きますが、なぜそうなるのか満足な答えが出来た試しがありません。なぜか分からない、というのが正直な答えです。理由がどのようなものであるにせよ、獨特のスタイルを持ったアーティスト、と言われるのはうれしい事です。私のビジョンは、いろんな外部の要素によって、またそのとき何に興味を持っているかによって変化します。外部の要素とは、映画、絵画、キャラクター、アクションフィギュアや本などです。

問：漫画が、ポップカルチャーに与える影響について考える事はありますか。

答：正直なところ、どちらにもあまり明るくないので、その関係について考える事はありません。

問：上手いアーチストとは？

答：正直に答えようとすると、自分が上手いアーチストだと思います。

問：作品のインスピレーション源は何ですか？

答：主に映画や漫画、小説、アート・ブックなどですが、どこからとも無くキャラクターのアイディアにつながるような画像が頭に浮かぶ事が一日100回以上もあります。多す

問：あなたの作品において、最も重点を置くものは？
答：常に私の作品が対象とするのは、男らしさ、力、強さです。

ぎて全部話しきれません。

問：アメリカ市場用にシリーズを準備中と聞きましたが、どんなシリーズですか？
答：主人公は、野獣の顔をつけるよう呪いをかけられた戦士です。アメリカ人の趣味に合っているかどうか分かりませんが、自分のスタイルにあったように作っていくしか無いと思っています。後は運命に任せるだけ。もしも、失敗した場合は、私を止めなかった周りの人たちを恨むしかないですね。

問：韓国に住んでいながらアメリカ市場用のシリーズの準備をするのは大変な事ではありませんか。何か特に難しいと感じた事は？
答：そうでもありませんよ。二つのシリーズを同時に進行させるのは確かに難しい事ですが、特にアメリカ市場に関して難しいと感じた事はありません。

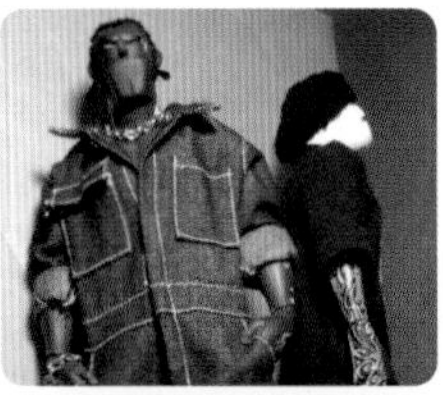
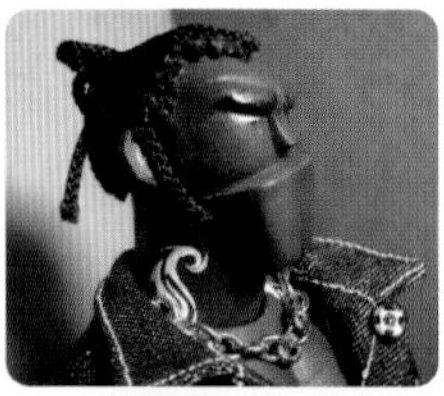
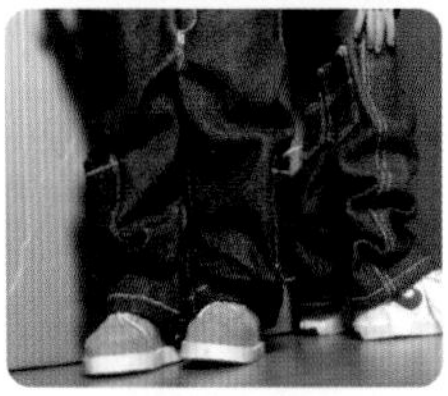
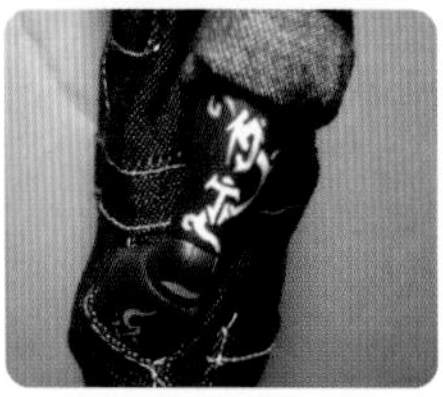
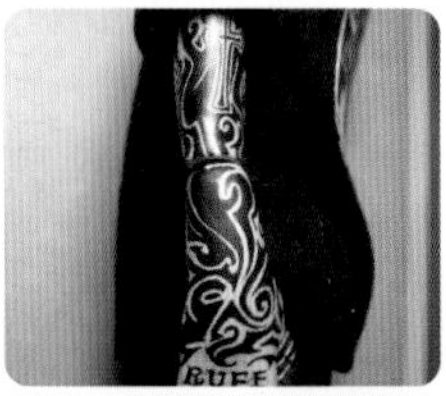
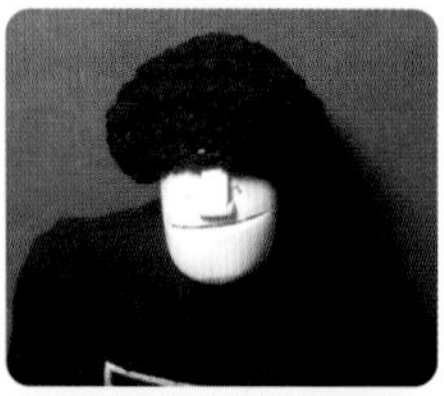
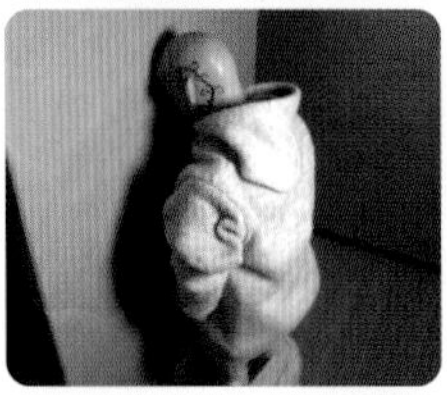
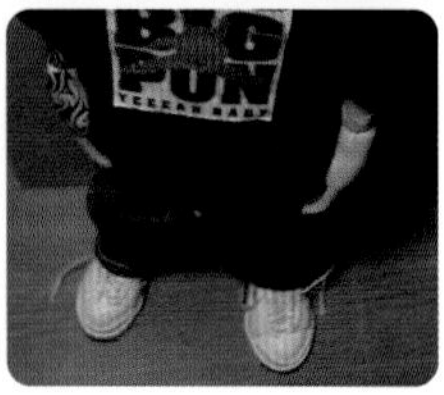
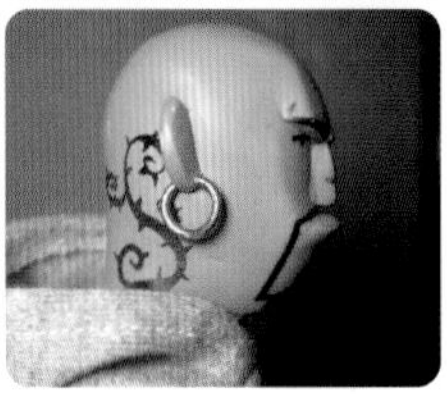

問：アメリカでのシリーズ出版に関するプロセスを説明していただけませんか。
答：ほとんど韓国と同じです。まず内容を決めて、スケッチをする。韓国と一つだけ違う点は、韓国ではほぼ100パーセント手作業でペン入れをしますが、アメリカではコンピュータを使う場合が多いという事。（コンピュータを使う場合でも、絵を手書きのように見せることを目標とする。）

問：アメリカの漫画市場における主な傾向とは？
答：韓国に住む者としてアメリカの市場を良く知っているとは言えませんが、アメリカ市場は、現在「戦国時代」ではないかと思います。今まで人気があったアメリカの伝統的なコミックの他に、多様性とエネルギーの元となる漫画タイプの多くの作品が流れ込んでいるようです。市場は新しい方向に進んでいるようですが、この動きがどれだけ景気の悪いアメリカ市場に影響を及ぼすかは分かりませんね。

問：一番好きなアメリカのコミックは？
答：アシュレー・ウッド（Ashley Wood）のHellspawnやその他多くの作品ですね。漫画に関しては、雑食主義なので。

問：一番好きなアーチストは？
答：アシュレー・ウッド(Ashley Wood)、サイモン・ビーズレー(Simon Beasley)、ケント・ウイリアムズ(Kent Williams)、とジョン・バンフリート(John Van Fleet)。

問：2003年 8月 に香港のToy Con に行かれたと聞きましたが、理由は？
答：香港のストリートカルチャーの象徴である人形やアクションフィギュアにとても興味があるんです。自分のアクションフィギュアも製作中です。新製品をチェックしたかっただけです。

問：どんなものが好きなのですか。
答：毎日変わるんですが、そうですね、常に好きなのは好戦的な感じのアクションフィギュアです。マイケル・ラウ（Michael Lau）のア・バン・ヴァイナルから出ているストリート・カルチャー色の強い作品も大好きです。

問：なんか特別な計画があるのですか。
答：今、香港のある会社がPriestのキャラクターのアクションフィギュアを製作中です。私も個人的に人形作りには興味を持っています。機会があれば、自分で作った人形を売りたいと思っています。もしも、失敗したら私を止めなかった周りの人たちを恨んでください。

問：腕に入れ墨があるようですが、意味は？
答：特にありません。ある日入れ墨がしたくなったのでやっただけです.

問：好きな音楽や映画は？
答：映画に関してはスタイルを最も重要視します。中身は何でも良い。音楽は、とにかくグルービーなビートであれば何でも良いです。（時には映画のサウンドトラックも聞きます。）

問：仕事をしていない時は何をしますか。
答：友達とぶらつくか家族とどこかへ行くとか。

問：友達ってどんな人たちですか。
答：はっきり言って、いろんな奴がいます。音楽家とか入れ墨師とか脚本家とか。大体みんな9時5時の仕事していませんね。（他の漫画家とはあまり付き合いがありません。）よく遊ぶのはとんどは、かなり常軌を逸した連中です。

ミンウー

F: Was für ein Buch ist justice N mercy
A: Es umfasst Illustrationen verschiedener Charaktere, die ich schuf, während ich die neue Serie vorbereitete, und Arbeiten, an denen ich von allem, was ich über die Jahre hinweg geschaffen habe, besonders hänge. Außerdem enthält es mehrere Cover, die ich für Fantasybücher in Korea gemacht habe. Ich habe zugestimmt, dieses Buch zu machen, weil ich wollte, dass diese verschiedenen Arbeiten in einer Art Systematik präsentiert werden. Dennoch bin ich ein bisschen verlegen. Es ist ein bisschen so, als würde man mich halbnackt ausstellen, denn es sind Arbeiten in verschiedenen Entwicklungsstufen. Ich bin neugierig, wie das alles sich entwickeln wird.

F: Was bedeutet »justice N mercy«?
A: Du meinst, außer der wörtlichen Bedeutung? Es hat keinen tieferen Sinn. Es ist eben nur das, was ich auf meinen Armen tätowiert habe. Ich nehme an, es ist eine Art Selbstausdruck.

F: Du wirst manchmal als ein Künstler mit Kultstatus und unverwechselbarem persönlichem Stil bezeichnet. Wie denkst du über diese Etikettierung? Und gibt es eine Vision bei deinen Arbeiten, die du mit uns teilen kannst?
A: Ich habe gehört, dass meinen Arbeiten eine Kultbewegung folgt, aber ich war noch nie in der Lage, eine zufriedenstellende Antwort darauf zu geben, warum das so ist. Alles, was ich sagen kann, ist, dass ich es nicht weiß. Es ist nett zu hören, dass ich ein Künstler mit einem unverwechselbaren persönlichen Stil sei, egal, was der Grund dafür sein mag. Meine Vision hängt viel mit äußeren Einflüssen zusammen–sie ändert sich entsprechend zu dem, was ich zufällig in dem Moment interessant finde. Äußere Einflüsse können Filme, Bilder, Charaktere, Actionfiguren oder Bücher sein.

F: Hast du je darüber nachgedacht, welche Einflüsse dieses Comicgenre auf die Populärkultur haben könnte?
A: Um ehrlich zu sein, nein. Ich weiß über beide zu wenig, um eine Meinung bezüglich ihrer Beziehung zueinander haben zu können.

F: Wen würdest du als einen »guten Künstler« bezeichnen?
A: Ich werde so ehrlich sein, wie ich kann

F: Was fokussierst du am meisten bei deinen Arbeiten?
A: Das elementare Thema, das sich durch all meine Arbeiten zieht, ist Männlichkeit, Leistung und Kraft.

–Ich denke, ich bin ein guter Künstler.

F: Woher nimmst du die Inspiration für deine Arbeiten?

A: Überwiegend aus Filmen, Comics, Romanen und Art Books, aber es gibt hundert weitere Eindrücke, die plötzlich im Verlauf des Tages auf mich einwirken, aus denen ich Ideen für verschiedene Charaktere entwickle. Es sind zu viele, um sie alle aufzuzählen.

F: Ich habe gehört, dass du eine Serie für den amerikanischen Markt vorbereitest. Was für eine Art von Serie wird das werden?

A: Die zentrale Figur ist ein Krieger, der dazu verdammt ist, das Gesicht eines Biests zu tragen. Ich weiß nicht, wie sehr sich das für den amerikanischen Geschmack eignet, aber ich werde dem Stil folgen, der mir am besten liegt und den Rest dem Schicksal überlassen. Wenn es floppt . . . na ja, dann kann man die Schuld auf die schieben, die mich nicht gestoppt haben, obwohl sie es hätten besser wissen müssen.

F: Es muss schwer sein, eine Serie für den amerikanischen Markt vorzubereiten und in Korea zu leben. Auf welche Schwierigkeiten bist du dabei gestoßen?

A: Ach, es ist eigentlich gar nicht so schwer. Sicher, es ist hart, an zwei verschiedenen Serien gleichzeitig zu arbeiten, aber abgesehen davon gibt es keine besonderen Schwierigkeiten im Zusammenhang mit dem amerikanischen Markt.

F: Kannst du den Prozess bis zur Veröffentlichung der Serie in den Staaten erklären?

A: Es ist fast genauso wie in Korea. Am Anfang steht der Inhalt, dann die Vorbereitung der Skizzen . . . Ein Unterschied ist, dass man in Korea das gesamte Inking mit der Hand macht, während in den Staaten oft ein Computer benutzt wird (aber auch wenn man einen Computer zur Hilfe nimmt, ist es das wichtigste Ziel, den Zeichnungen einen handgemachten Touch zu verleihen).

F: Was hältst du für die wesentlichen Trends im amerikanischen Comicmarkt?

A: Nun... Da ich in Korea lebe, kann ich nicht behaupten, wirklich gut über den amerikanischen Markt Bescheid zu wissen.

Aber ich denke, dass sich der amerikanische Markt inmitten der so genannten »Warring States Period*« befindet.

Zusätzlich zu den verschiedenen traditionell beliebten, amerikanischen Comics strömt eine Vielzahl an Arbeiten im Mangastil auf den Markt und bringt große Vielfalt und Energie mit sich. Der Markt scheint sich zu entwickeln und in eine neue Richtung zu bewegen. Dennoch weiß ich nicht, in welchem Ausmaß dieser neue Trend dem geschwächten amerikanischen Markt Auftrieb ver-schaffen wird.

F: Was sind deine amerikanischen Lieblingscomics?

A: Ich mag Ashley Wood's *Hellspawn* und viele andere. Ich neige dazu, bei Comics ein Allesfresser zu sein.

F: Und deine Lieblingskünstler?

A: Ashley Wood, Simon Beasley, Kent Williams und John Van Fleet.

F: Im August 2003 warst du bei der Toy Con in Hong Kong. Was war der Grund für diesen Trip?

A: Ich interessiere mich sehr für Puppen und Actionfiguren, die Hong Kongs Straßenkultur darstellen. Ich entwerfe sogar einige eigene Actionfiguren. Ich wollte einfach nur wissen, was es Neues auf dem Markt gibt.

F: Welche Art von Figuren magst du?

A: Mein Geschmack ändert sich jeden Tag . . . Aber immer gleich geblieben ist meine Vorliebe für ein kriegerisches Aussehen meiner Actionfiguren. Außerdem mag ich Michael Lau's Urban Vinyl Street Culture-Style-Arbeiten.

*Eine umgangssprachliche Redewendung in Korea, die für viele, gleichzeitig existierende Trendbewegungen in einem bestimmten Bereich steht. Wörtlich bezieht sich der Ausdruck auf eine blutige Kriegsperiode im alten China, die im 5. Jahrhundert vor Christus statt fand.

F: Hast du besondere Pläne mit diesen Figuren?

A: Im Moment sitzt gerade eine Firma aus Hong Kong daran, die Personen aus Priest als Actionfiguren zu produzieren. Außerdem habe ich selbst großes persönliches Interesse am Herstellen von Figuren. Wenn ich die Chance hätte, würde ich gern meine eigenen Figuren vermarkten. Aber wenn dieser Plan schief geht . . . dann kann man die Schuld auf die schieben, die mich nicht gestoppt haben, obwohl sie es hätten besser wissen müssen.

F: Du hast Tattoos auf den Armen. Was bedeuten sie?

A: Nichts Spezielles. Ich wollte eines Tages Tattoos haben und so ließ ich sie machen.

F: Welche Art von Musik und Filmen magst du?

A: Bei Filmen geht es mir ausschließlich um die Machart. Der Inhalt ist mir egal. Bei Musik mag ich alles, das einen coolen Beat hat (Manchmal höre ich auch ganz gerne Soundtracks zu Filmen).

F: Was machst du, wenn du nicht arbeitest?

A: Mit meinen Kumpels rumhängen oder etwas mit meiner Familie unternehmen.

F: Wie sind deine Freunde so?

A: Eigentlich sind sie ziemlich unterschiedlich. Musiker, ein Tattoo-Künstler, ein Drehbuchautor usw. Ich tippe, die meisten von ihnen haben keinen Nine-to-Five-Job (mit anderen Comickünstlern hänge ich nicht viel rum). Und die meisten Freunde, mit denen ich Zeit verbringe, sind . . . einfach verrückt.

Min-Woo

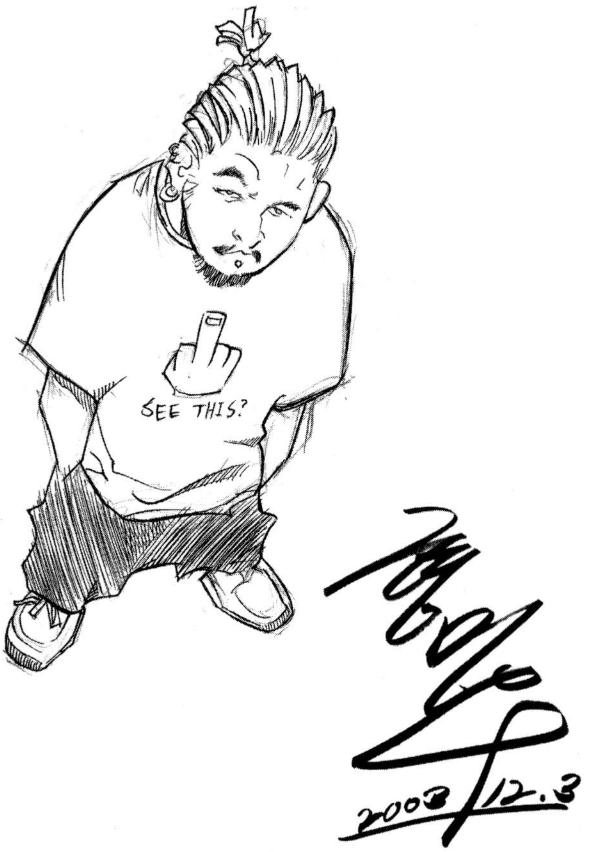
SEE THIS?
2003 12.3